Dara Shukuh
Captive Visionary of His Times

Dara Shukuh
Captive Visionary of His Times

Rakesh Gupta

KALPAZ

ISBN: 978-93-5128-220-4

Price: ₹ 790

First Published, 2016

Published by

Kalpaz Publications
C-30, Satyawati Nagar,
Delhi – 110052
E-mail: kalpaz@hotmail.com
Ph.: 9212142040

Printed at: G. Print Process, Delhi

Cataloging in Publication Data—DK
Courtesy: D.K. Agencies (P) Ltd. <docinfo@dkagencies.com>

Gupta, Rakesh, 1946- author.
Dara Shukuh : captive visionary of his times / Rakesh Gupta.
pages cm
Includes bibliographical references.
ISBN 9789351282204

1. Dārā Shikūh, Prince, son of Shahjahan, Emperor of India, 1615-1659. 2. Sufis—India—Biography. 3. Princes—India—Biography. I. Title.

BP80.D288G87 2016 DDC 297.65 23

Contents

Preface 11

Chapter - 1

Dara's Times – Rapture and Rupture 17

• Introduction • Asiatic Mode of Production (?) • Patrimonial State (?) • Genealogy (?) • Micro-politics • Holistic State (?) • Simultaneity • Organic Whole • Absolute Sovereignty: External Limitations • Patronage of Caliph • Turko-Persian Influence: Sunni vs. Shii, Qandahar • European Rivalry-Sea Trade and Visits to Mecca • Establishment of the Core of Sovereignty • Nomad-like Movement • Personality • Courtly Culture • Societal and Economic Dynamics • Mughal Transition • Inequality among Urban Muslims • Indian Muslims and Administration • Racial Prejudice • Jahangir and Politico-religious Fault lines • Urban Life: ordinary conflicts and the lay out • Patron-client relationships • Merchants and Markets • Atrophy • Monarchy and Rural exploitation • Temporary Assignments • Crisis.

Chapter - 2

Birth, Family and Personality of Dara 67

• Birth • Sagittarius • Born to Baba Khurram • Mothers and Daughters • Eternity • Dara on Eternity • Dara- What is in a name! • Letters of Dara Shukuh/Shikoh as signifiers • Chroniclers' Assessments of Dara • Akbar, Dara, Shah Jahan and Aurangzeb • Celebrations • Fathers • Miracles, Myths, Magic • Circumbulation, Intervention of Magic or Blind Faith in Mystics • Kinship-Kingship • Gratis, Popular and the Populist Culture • Example of transference practiced by Hindus and Muslims • Education • Nasiriya College, 13th century • Akhlalq • Schooling • Curriculum (13th century) • Mental Culture • Education under Akbar • Science and Religion • Dara-Mind • Development of his Mental Make up • Rationalism • Allegory/Simile/Mysticism • Classicists • Romanticists • Communication • 16th and 17th century • Allegory in Islam • Persian Poetry and Dara • Rationalism • Loyalty • Loyalty to Factions • Dara's sense of loyalty and fair play • Marriage and Family • Ranadil and Udepuri • Love for Nadira Banu • Children.

Chapter - 3

Qadiri Scholar **105**

• Sect • Sunni and Shia • Sufis • Etymology and Concept • Sufism as Freemasonry • In Central Asia • Special quality • Elements • Soofee doctrine-Burke, 1815 • Sufis in the Mughal Period in India • Different persuasions of Sufism • Sufi Orders • Chisti –Silsila • Naqshbandi Order • Naqshbandi Sayings: Negation of Being • Qadariyya Order • Impact of Sufis • Dara's Sufi Identity • Rising Graph of an Intellectual • 'Sweet Fruits' 'Born Of Clay' • Mystics in his poetry and borrowed Symbol • Qadiri Ghazals • Dara as Hagiographer (Tazkiras Writer) • Possible Motives of Dara • Safinat-ul-A'lwiya • Sakinat-ul-l' Alwiya • Selective Biographer • Shaykh Abd Shaykh Adl-al-Haqq and Shaykh Abd ar-Rehman • Dara's Letters • Contact with Sarmad • Rebuffing the Orthodox • Sufi Scholar • Tradition of Syncretic Scholarship • Translations for Common Perspective • Fore Cry of Compositeness • Multi-Cultural Society • Public Domain: Scholar of Co-mingling • With Baba lal and Chandrabhan.

Chapter - 4

Trajectory of Heir Apparent **141**

• No Civil War or Class Struggle • Politics and War: Implosion • Scholar-Soldier • Shah Buland Iqbal • Earlier Appointments • Early Signs of Hostility sans Religion • Incidents Relating to Aurangzeb's early Hostility • Shah Jahan's Tactical Postings of his Sons • Dara's Administrative Skills • Indiscrete utterances and Shah Jahan's Sex forays • Negatives of the Administration • Administration and Marriages • Lobbies, Factions and Parties • Junta during Jahangir's Reign • Political Parties in Shah Jahan's Court • Succession Issue • Religious Frill • Composition • Sadullah Khan and Dara Shukuh • Mir Jumla: astute turn coat • Dara Before and During Shah Jahan's illness in 1657 • Steps during and after Shah Jahan's brief illness • Dakhyn politics at this juncture (1665-1657) • Sex and War • Little Entente • Motivations causing the Little Entente • Absence of vision and mental incapability • Acumen • Shah Shuja versus Sulaiman Shukuh • Raja Jai Singh's Treachery • Raja Jai Singh's rationale • Victory Undone • Dress rehearsal of Treachery • Cobra and Snakes • Before the Battle of Dharmat • Communication Network • Blocking information and winning over the Nobles • Aurangzeb and Mir Jumla • Aurangzeb's Consolidation of Forces • Shah Jahan's Advice and Khalilullah's Counterpoint • Dharmat Battle • Rajputs slaughtered and Jaswant Singh's flight • Shah Jahan conceded to Dara Taking the field as fait accompli • Dara's Departure for Dholpur • Forces • Dara's Dholpur plans and weaknesses • Reasons for Precipitate Action • Failed to understand the Lull • Dara dithered on Advice • Battlefield Formations at Samugarh • Formations and Mughal Soldiery • Defensive-Offensive (?) • Shah Jahan's sin visited Dara • Hard and Soft Soldier (?) • Other Features of War • Jump in Chronology • Deorai Clincher • Betrayals as Game Plan • Deorai Exchange • Raja Rup Singh's Betrayal • Features of Battles.

Chapter - 5

Hare and the Hound 191

• Emotion and Refusal • Advice • Betrayed • Sultan Muhammad takes the keys • Shah Jahan's Ineffectual Retaliation and slump • Confinement and new plan of Shah Jahan • Aurangzeb's Justification • Strategic issues (I and 2) • Aurangzeb's possible reasons • Operation Murad Baksh near Mathura • Dara at Lahor (now Lahore) • Hamlet's dilemma-Dara's style • Half-hearted Measures at Beas and Satlej (Satluj) Rivers • Multan or Kabul? • Bhakkar onwards • Aurangzeb left to deal with Shah Shuja • Dara with Rao of Cutch • Dara the Gambler • Flight from Deorai • Jiwan Khan • Journey in Disgrace • Common people support • Dara and Raziya • Khawasapura • Alarmed • Malik Jiwan and popular Revolt • Evening of life • Dara and Aurangzeb exchange • Ascertain • Captive (Local) and Martyr (Universal) • Split of an Acorn • Visionary Mystic.

Bibliography 213

Index 219

For

Jayant and Shikha

Love songs turn into dances of mimes,
Folklore exit from tradition's faultline.
Rise to smile and sparkle in dark alleys
Communion is love of human divinity.

Preface

This work has been written with a view to assert equality and not a priority of any religion as an ideal in the Indian State during medieval times and the need of the hour today. In order to get to the terrain of the theme of accommodation of diversity in a land mass called *BharatVarsha* in ancient times ('India, that is Bharat, under the present Constitution) during medieval period I have chosen to write on Dara Shukuh. The second reason for doing so is my concern for composite culture under siege in the present times. I have not read the present day concerns and theorisations into the medieval period though dealt with it on the basis of positions of scholarship on the period as well as chroniclers' accounts.

I came to the dramatis persona of this text owing to two factors. One, in 2011, during a discussion on my novella on Raziya Sultan in the library of India Habitat Centre I was asked about Dara Shukuh. 'I knew very little about him' was my cryptic answer. Even though I was defending Raziya almost on the same grounds that I look at Dara now. That year I collected the chronicles of his time and updated my readings of these texts from the 13th to the 17th century. For reasons beyond my comprehension (perhaps timidity) after reading Gopal Gandhi's drama in poetry form on Dara Shukuh, I postponed the idea of writing on Dara. I started to revisit this theme in 2014 and the result is this text. My notes then and now do not differ substantially. I looked at them after finishing this text.

The whole enterprise is an individual effort for want of any institutional support that I always found to be difficult to handle. I have also very little connections with historians to seek support from, for most of the ones I knew are either no more or I have gone out of that orbit. Individuals have been of immense help. Ms. Aqsa Agha,

Centre for Historical Studies, has been of invaluable help. My indefinable dependence on Raj Kumar of the Centre of Social Systems for his sound opinions about the text and looking after its technical aspects till its completion made him indispensable.Urvija Gautam, research assistant in 2011 for a few months, Centre for Historical Studies and Anushree of the Centre for Political Studies, Jawaharlal Nehru University. They gave very warm and cooperative support. I am extremely thankful to Madhura Damle, former student of the Centre for Political Studies and currently a faculty member at the Presidency University, Kolkata and Dr. Mayuri Sengupta, University of South Wales, Australia who was in Kolkata during that time. Both helped me in collecting rare books on and by Dara Shukuh from the National Library, Kolkata. Both of them overcame the deterring heat of Kolkata, travelled long distances and overcame the archaic rules of the library to procure these texts.

I am grateful to all of them. The special reason for this is that we as a people have entered a phase of politics where it has become increasingly difficult to maintain diversity and a freedom of dialogue in the name of straight jacketed conservatism with a violent core amounting to fear, paranoia for some and schizophrenia for others.

All of them gave a recluse an opportunity to speak without any interruptions, name shouting, ridicule, and, accusations that occupy the public space in the different fora in current period. Locke had warned against a brute majority despite giving priority to it. He was pleading for a Constitutional oligarchy. We have to work now a democracy under the Constitution at the least for an oligarchy today, if not a way of life of the ordinary people.

The text is also a sad realization of the difficulty of Being and Becoming, that Dara faced as a Sunni and becoming a gnostic and Free Thinker / Free Mason. Some European chroniclers called it a tactic to ultimately prepare for war of succession when he offered a hand of friendship to the Jesuits. He was on good terms with the Sikh Guru during his time. He remained a part of that transition at the cost of annoying the orthodox whom he made fun of in his earlier writings detailing lives of Sufi saints. His later writings show his fear since he said that he was saying things about the Upanishads and the Quran for his own understanding and not for anyone else in the society. His dialogues and translations work was in the spirit of understanding and friendship.

Not long after he paid with his life at the altar of the old order that had begun to change from the times of the Dihli Sultanate when the concept of Jahan-dari (public / people-based) was appearing to contest that of Din-Dari (religion-based).

Such contestation of orthodox and heterodox or secularists and religionists/ gnostic believers and agnostics and the believers and atheists occur in miniscule formats faced by individuals on different occasions on personal fronts and public space. The dangers to the liberal mind grow as a result of the traditional values that in any cases hide outlived truths. Criticism leads to new emotional change and the old ones reassert. Criticality is meant to demolish the old and create new emotions and values in continuity and not engage in contestations. Coexistence is the norm.

Given the inflexibility of the mind they become contestations that cost human lives till infinity for the process never ends. The progressions and regressions sub late. The movement towards the values of a new awakening is a complex web of new contestation and accommodation rather than a dialectical rejection as an alternative on the basis of emerging social forces. The function of criticality is to negotiate the transition with accommodation of differentiation that begin to shoot the existing hierarchy and in turn that criticality gets shot in the next stage. The paradigm of criticism changes from religion versus religion to contestation within a religion and its transformation between religion and modern secular. Then it changes to religion versus secularism. The further advance of the process tried out in existing socialist societies is now a discredited project though not an exhausted one.

Chapter 1 deals with Dara Shukuh's times conditioning his being through crisscross of rapture and rupture. Chapter 2 deals with the operation of his times in formation of his being in relation to events of his birth, early life, family and the family related events during his formative years, his mental makeup within the Royalty in terms of the then ideology involving astronomy, astrology, myth, miracles, magic, science of Ptolemy and Avicenna. Chapter 3 delineates his mental growth as a Qadiri within the framework of Akhlalq (man of letters and man of the sword) and Sufism beyond the Sunni birth mark, if birth marks can ever be categorized in such ethnic/religious terms. It deals with his writings in a chronological order; his poetry the use of allegory and simile. This is discussed in the context of Arabic and Persian poetry's techniques like allegory in his rubais. We discuss his writings of mature period. Chapter 4 looks at his political trajectory of being Shah Buland Iqbal (Heir Apparent) and losing in battles his rightful claim to the crown and cause that he stood for. Chapter 5 deals with his flight and martyrdom. Put together a captive of power politics he was a visionary to follow the path of accommodation of diversities which was part of the state ideology since the later part of Akbar's State. We compare him with other greats of his times and Raziya Sultan. This ideology kept reasserting notwithstanding Aurangzeb's partial though unsuccessful restoration causing considerable damage.

We have avoided discussion on other individuals except where necessary and this includes Aurangzeb, Shah Shuja, Murad Baksh or the various Rajput Rajas though their essential details find a place. Only their links with Dara's story have been followed. We have not done a discussion on his concept of beauty as a poet, calligraphist and shaping of an album and architecture. That could form another theme to be explored.

The spellings of Dara Shukuh in this book have followed the spellings as found in the English translation of Jahangir-Nama or TUZUK-I-JAHANGIRI translated by Annette S. Beveridge. Other spellings of the same name have been retained as used by authors and commentators in quotations and citation of titles of their works. Similarly the spellings of the second part of his eldest son's name Suleiman have been followed. As far as possible earlier diacritical marks have been eliminated for the simplified versions of these names. Technical words in Turkish or Persian have similarly been eliminated in favour of the English ones. Dihli and Agra have been spelled as Dihli and Agrah as per the manner of its writing and pronunciation then, so also the names of other places and cities. Some words of the time have been used with their meanings in modern day terminology in the brackets. Similarly names of places and persons have been given as used then with modern names in the brackets. Photographs of places, palaces, forts, mausoleums and persons have been avoided.

The bibliography includes Dara Shukuh's own writings in book forms in the secondary sources since I found them in edited and annotated forms in the works of other historians. This is also true of the translations by other historians.

I am thankful to Mr Amit Garg for publishing this work in rocord time.

In no way can my benefactors be held responsible for the product's many inadequacies. I alone must carry that cross of an author.

Gurgaon, 2016

Chapter - 1

Dara's Times – Rapture and Rupture

Introduction

Different analytical categories, like Asiatic Mode of Production (hereafter AMP) propounded by Marx, Patrimonial State propounded by Weber and the Genealogical theorisation of Michael Foucault make significant contribution to our understanding. They are not sufficient to analyse the dynamic of development within the feudal economy of the Mughal State in terms of its orientation and bringing the people of heterogeneous Indian society together. The first two talk of its structure. The third focuses on its macro-micro power politics.

Asiatic Mode of Production (?)

The AMP, as a concept, elaborated the features of state ownership of land, public water works, ground rent and changelessness. These features were not there in case of the Indian State-Social formation. They were definitely not there as an ideal type condition since there was enough to show contrary features with regard to irrigation, landholdings and possibility of change. The early Marxist writings on AMP have been challenged by Marxist scholars here and abroad. The Patrimonial State theorisation, based on Weber's writings, reduced the high-noon of feudal State as an enlarged Household. This approach pointed to the lack of bureaucracy and kinship rule and neglected how politics shaped the kinship. They had also been challenged by other observers of the State during the colonial period. The Foucauldian approach, not yet fully worked out, helped to explain the replication of power relations obtained in the Centre at the micro level and the difficulties of possible escape route from them. This was partially borne out by the analysis of class revolts and their failure in the Mughal Rule. The courtly Culture was linked with the popular culture through the macro-micro politics.

Hauz Shamsi water work during Iyaltimish's time was balanced by wells being bored by private individuals during that period. These were dug with the private enterprise of merchants. There was evidence of Hindu merchants getting these wells bored in the area now known as Raisina Road and **Palam Baoli.** The inscription in Palam village mentioned Dihli's name as Yogini Pura when it was famous. The existence of this city was corroborated by the Jain texts of the time. Its construction of the step well was mentioned to be in the land of Hariyanaka in the thirteenth century. A fourteenth century inscription in a village Called Saravla (currently in the Raisina road area), mention the name of two merchants who got it built. They were Khaitala and Paitala. In the Naraina area (Dihli) another well was constructed by a person named Sridharan.[1]

The one canal that was built during the time of Firoz Shah to draw water from the Jamuna River went into disuse till Akbar's time. Subsequently Shah Jahan renewed and extended it to what is known as western Jamuna Canal. Sultan Firoz Shah got two streams made into the city of Firozah which was deficient in water. He got two streams into the city from two rivers: one from the river Jumna, the other from the river Sutlej. Both were conducted through the vicinity of Karnal, and after a length of about eighty Kos (more than a mile), discharged their water by one channel into the town. As a result spring harvests, which used to fail earlier, started to succeed.[2]

The same canal had got into disuse. It was subsequently desilted and extended during Akbar's time to incorporate new areas and named as Shaikhuni.[3] During Shah Jahan's time the same canal was taken off at Safedon to supply water to Shahjahanabad. This came to be known as Nahar - i Bihisht.[4] Further, considerable private efforts went into water works for irrigation. In order to gain legitimacy local rulers in the fouteenth century tried to get canals and step wells constructed, as is evident from the information from Nagaur. In any case canal irrigation was not an established system in most part of the country. Mukhia stated:

> "...for all practical purposes canal irrigation appears to be more of a recent phenomenon."[5]

The Indian State was interested in revenue and not in managing Water works for irrigation purposes. So, it introduced land system but not help in the **process of agricultural production**. That process was a private endeavour and the producer was the master over the means and process of the produce.

It was also evident from various subsequent and former chroniclers that temporary bridges were constructed for crossing flooded rivers in wars/for war and fun related activities. Gardens were laid out by the members of the royalty and the nobility for horticulture or cooling the living conditions. The State was *not a hydraulic* one (Witfoegel) providing for irrigation facilities since it had no facilities nor ownership therein. One of the characteristics described for the Asiatic Mode of Production was provision of water works. The powers over village communities were called 'Oriental despotisms' used for seventeenth century Eastern societies. The hypothesis was that they drew their legitimacy from the function of increasing productivity through provisions that individuals could not undertake.

The observations of Babur about irrigation in Hindustan belie the argument that the State was providing for irrigation. He said:

> 'The greater part of the country is flat. Many though its towns and cultivated lands are, it nowhere has running waters. Rivers, and in some places, stagnant water are its irrigation channels. Even where, as for some towns, it is practicable to convey water by digging channels this is not done. For not doing it there may be several reasons, one being that water is not at all a necessity in cultivating crop and orchard. Autumn crops grow in downpour of the rain themselves; and strange it is that spring crops grow even when no rain falls. To young trees water is made to flow by means of buckets or a wheel used to lift water from a well.'[6]

At Agrah buckets for the purpose were used. **People themselves** built water tanks to collect water from tanks and build houses in a locality which were small and unattractive or just set up walls of Khas-grass. In no time a village came up.[7] There was no reference to the State providing for a wheel, or a pulley or a well for irrigation purposes. Instead there was mention of nature of hamlets, people's knowledge of rain crops and technology of wheels though not the Persian wheel.

The route from Asiatic production to class societies had been different-European (slave) or non-European (feudal).[8] The feudal State in India was despotic but not in the sense of being hydraulic or typical European feudal. This State was based on revenue. The *Iqta* was turned into transferable *Mansab* but managed individually with the mixed practices of hereditary and non-hereditary rights. The point was that both the State and societal labour-urban and rural were involved in the process of providing for irrigation at least since the thirteenth century. Even if we refer to the State we find private enterprise therein. Jahangir noted that his mother Marayam - Zamani in the parganas of Jusat had got a garden and a well built.[9] This was an individual effort keeping in view paucity of water for travellers. It was a Sarai, i.e. a resting place, as per a subsequent historian.

Given the structure of power the surplus went in the form of tax to the ruling monarchy, slowly changing after 1526, but completed after 1556. The Monarchy began to emerge after Babur, despite the Sher Shah Suri's interlude of half a decade, and consolidated with Humayun and Akbar till at least 1757, i.e. the Battle of Plassey when The East India Company took over the collection of Revenue in Bengal and the transfer of power after 1857. It was a long period from the comparative perspective of the short rules from the Mauryan Empire onwards inclusive of the period of Dihli Sultanate. The ancient monarchy had glorious times but pale in duration and stature of the Mughal State.

Secondly, the duration of the Mughal Empire was not shorter in comparative terms from the then British Monarchy. The period of Humayun seemed to be more like that of Queen Mary-a short one. The period of Akbar (1556-1604) favourably compared with that of Queen Elizabeth (1555 to 1603). The Mughal period compared favourably with the Romanovs and the Manchu's in Russia and China, respectively. The Romanovs controlled power from (1613-1762) and then a cadet branch of theirs the Holstein-Gottorp-Romanov (1762-1917). The first phase was for one hundred and fifty one years and the second was for again one hundred and fifty five years. The Mughal State did not compare unfavourably with any of these States in terms of longevity, majesty and territoriality.

The point is that medieval India did not witness quick succession of rulers during the Mughal period during 1556-1707. The subsequent period was marred by the social contradictions emerging and finally overtaken by the British colonial conquests by 1857. The quick succession of rulers is a post -Iyaltimish phase. The fight was among the Shamsi (Iyaltimish) nobility on account of racial jealousies between Slave, Turkish, Mongol, Habshi and free Khalji nobles.

The system was based on personal loyalty and hierarchy on the basis of Iqtas, i.e. transferable land assignment for revenue purposes and providing stability to the rule. The Tughluqs and the Lodis tried making these permanent. This was in contrast to the rule of the Ghor's of Ghazni since they had, owing to clan/family properties, no cementing factor in their region. The subsequent period showed that the Iqta system and the Mongol menace on the outskirts of the kingdom unified the ruling class/nobility into a cohesive section. The Turk, Ghorian and Khalji dispensation kept the Sultanate going till the second decade of the 14th century.

Post Qutub din Aibak's death in 1210 to 1316 when Allaudin died was a good hundred years of the Sultanate with three charismatic rulers, viz, Iyaltimish, Balban and Allaudin. Raziya was mentioned not for the purpose of longevity either of her life or her rule. She was the first Queen in her own right and that people of Dihli supported her cause.[10]

India did not then follow an ideal type of ASIATIC MODE OF PRODUCTION or any European model. The Despotism in England moved towards money economy under their Monarchy, in Russia it moved towards second serfdom while in India it had the kernel of transition to money economy made evident by internal-external trade with-in the feudal structure of shifting Mansabdari system though it got atrophied. The Russian experience showed a second serfdom in 1861 land reforms.[11] In India there were peasant revolts.[12] The Mughal system atrophied by the 17-18th century. In the 16-17th centuries the State did not either curtail the merchant or the revenue collector so as to kill the kernel of transition. It had imposed restrictions on the revenue collectors to prevent them from over collection of calculated ratio of the revenue. The ruling structure was benevolent in India and England but backward looking in the third. In the Indian case the window of opportunity existed but atrophied of its own, especially with the colonial onslaught.

In the later part of the sixteenth century and the seventeenth century unlike the Tudor monarchy, Monarchy here did not indulge in sea loot and plunder. It did not open into a gate crash for silver and gold as Elizabeth's Navy, captained by Admiral Drake, who looted the Spanish ships of their wealth and reached England through the Pacific inviting the dreaded Spanish Armada's doomed and defeated attack[13]during the 1580's. As far as sea trade on its western coast was concerned the Mughals entered into treaty relations with the Portuguese and allowed the British and the Portuguese to fight it out since the Portuguese had harmed the Mughal Royalty and looted Indian merchant ships. It was a case of sea diplomacy and not robbery under Akbar, Jahangir and Shah Jahan.

In India sea trade was much older. For instance in Ahmedabad in 1410 the *bazaars (*markets*)* were abuzz with commercial activity, on account of foreign traders attracted to the mart.[14] At the time of Akbar's accession in 1556, the Portuguese were established on India's Western coast with a few settlements in the East. The firangi (foreigner), as the Portuguese were known then, had imposed a regime of passes for ships going in and out of docks towards the Red Sea for trade or visit to Mecca. Usually both sea trade and religious travel by royal and other ships needed this certification, which had to be purchased. Otherwise the Portuguese used to confiscate the cargo. Akbar had agreed to the pass system. But he had to deal with the violations by the Portuguese who had Goa in their control. The system had operated since 1502. His men occupied the port cities of Surat, Broach, and Cambay. The Portuguese asked for exemption of the duty for their merchandise in Cambay. The Emperor granted this. He issued a Farman in 1573 saying that the Portuguese should not be disturbed in Daman by the officials working in Surat, Broach, Nausari and Velodra (Vadodara) and instructed that pirates in the region should not be helped. So the royal ships were free to move without passes. As a result in reality the

Portuguese bore a loss of 18,000 pardaos by way of customs duty. The beneficiaries were Indian merchants and the nobility. There was a further decrease of 5,000 cruzados per year to the Portuguese. The Indian merchants started to load at ports like Mocha which the Portuguese could not check. At Diu they used to get information about the practice of Indians. The Indians loaded their ships with gold, silver, brocade, coral and other commodities. This was not in the interest of the Portuguese who were not in Mocha but in Diu.

Noticing the harm in this practice owing to the free passes given to the Emperor, the Portuguese started to engage in piracy. In 1577 they captured five ships as also the Emperor's ship. This annoyed him immensely for it was an attack on his sovereignty. RAO, an Indian official in Goa pleaded for the release of Akbar's ship and despatched their own ships to Surat to help Akbar's ship. After negotiations, the ship was returned. This ship had carried 600,000 crusades, besides coral, brocade and other items. The tensions were resolved through diplomacy but not by the threat of a contingent raid.

The Portuguese acts of confiscation of ships were alarming news that spread to other parts of the country spoiling relations with Akbar temporarily. Angry, Akbar cautiously tried to oust them with the help of Qutub-ud-din Khan and enlisting the support of officers in Malwa, Gujarat and the rulers in the Dakhyn. He wanted to drive the Firangis out of the Indian Ocean. Yet there was no expedition against them during his reign. The system of passes continued.[15]

During Jahangir's reign the Portuguese robbery came up majorly. It challenged the Majesty of the Emperor and the Queen Mother by capturing her ship RAHIMI (1613-14), [16] full with 700 people and merchandise worth one hundred pounds in 1617. The importance of sea trade was noted by Jahangir, who had got two coins (of gold and silver) heavier than the earlier ones struck at Cambay.[17] Jahangir also noted the incidence of Franks looting of four cargo ships that frequented the port of Surat in violation of a treaty. He despatched an officer to seek compensation.[18]

The scandal involving Rahimi was unbearable involving Indo-Portuguese, Indo-English and Portuguese-English in a triangular conflict. Even here the Indian Emperor did not resort to cheating on the interests and wealth of either of them. The Portuguese were made to pay compensation of three lakhs of rupees. The English found a presence in the person of Mr. Doe at the Imperial court but felt thwarted by the Court's tactics. He was critical especially of Nur Jahan's role and that of what he called a *junta* composed of her brother, step son, Khurram and father Mahabat Khan. The Indian side was interested in playing the Portuguese off by the increasing sea power of the British as a check, and, decrease the waning Portuguese sea power in the region and its interest. This happened but without any economic gain to the English. They found a presence at the Court but not influence. The Portuguese proselytising activities and funds to their priests stopped in Agrah. The English, who were the ascendant naval star, and the Portuguese fought in 1615.This conflict was marked by the burning of the Portuguese ships, so ended their influence and trade.[19]

This politics of sea trade brought out the civilised Mughal diplomacy in contrast to the naval plundering of the Spanish ships by the English in Americas and the sea robbery of the Portuguese against the Indians, respectively. They were involved in collection of bullion but styles were different in congruence with their power and character. If one was looking at the Peacock Throne, one needed to look at this mercantilist kernel of the Empire: diamond Wealth. May be this was out of the Royal realisation that the Mughal sea power was not of the comparable strength and restricted despite earlier friendship and Treaty relations.

Patrimonial State (?)

Secondly, the Mughal State was not a patrimonial State as propounded by Weber in his description of Sultanism. He believed these to be personal rule of the absolutist centre of personal power of the monarch with his security forces paid from official purse, i.e. a mercenary army and a personalised **bureaucracy** without striking any roots in the local population. These were its features. The praetorian forces were more for keeping the dissenting people suppressed. Stephen P. Blake extended the patrimonial model to the Mughal State as an enlarged image of the Emperor's Court and *haram* (household) and personalised army with a nobility tied in loyalty to his divinely derived sovereign power replicated all along the society in economy, polity and city scape. The regalia of the personalised household was transferred to the country on a mega stage through **peripatetic movement**[20] of the court and the haram that imbued in the population grandiose message of the Great Mughals. The State controlled the markets, banks, allowed sea trade with the Europeans, depended on the land tax, and the merchants had no impact on the State. The bureaucracy was centralised around the person and the courtly culture was only replicated down the line determining popular culture, the guild and banking systems were not market oriented and commodities had only use values for the royal household and the ruling nobility. So it fit the patrimonial state of Weber.[21]

This was a distortion of the evolution of the State, the buildings that were constructed, especially of Dihli and its further course. Under Iyaltimish Dihli, as was then known, was known as Hazrat Dihli-a world Centre of civilisation in the 13th century. Under Firoz Shah Tughluq Dihli had at Firozabad a population of 5,12,000, the wall fort of Firoz Shah had 22 gates and 17 reservoirs since Dihli was a water scarce region owing to soil erosion, shifting course of the river and increasing population to the point of congestion. Three canals were built during the period of Firoz Shahi. As per a contemporary chronicler, Isami, Futus -I -Salatin, merchants of Dihli, irrespective of geographical provenance, ethnic grouping, or traditional taboos of his business associates, they **associated freely** with the traders flocking in this veritable Eldorado of Dihli from all parts of Asia and India.[22] Those from India were *saudagars* (traders) operating between China and East Africa, Seth's, *Sahans*, *Multanis*, *banias (caste)*, i.e. *Baqqals* and the *Banjaras*. Grain, sugar and salt was traded. The Dihli traders were Multanis. The State facilitated roads and their protection for this trade provided for by way of resting places, availability of water and food and security from the robbers.[23] Usury was practised and for this Sarafs (jewellers) were there. The State thus did not show any sign of discouraging trade and merchants across the land routes during the period of Dihli Sultanate. *Mandis (wholesale markets)* were provided for essential commodities.

The Mughal policies were not suffocated by the designs of a personalised rule of unthinking and unintelligent self-satisfying autocrats. The Monarchs were not opposed to the further development of the economy in terms of merchant capital, market and land rights. For listening to complaints apart from *jharokas* and officers there were special bells in front of the forts so that the ordinary people could come with complaints. Two European authorities uphold the openness of the state - G. B. Malleson and John F. Richards. Habib said of Richards's position, arguing, on the basis of "qualitative evidence", that the Mughal Empire stimulated economic growth.[24] And he said

> "I am not willing to concede that this stimulation might have stemmed from a parasitic relationship with agriculture."[25]

G. B. Malleson, writing in the nineteenth century, on the basis of his wide education and experience in India, compared Akbar favourably with Queen Elizabeth and Charles VI of France. Disputing Elphinstone, he praised him for efforts to create a composite society and reform the revenue system. To quote him,

> 'I have tried to show what he was as an administrator, as an organiser, as a promulgate of a system which we English inherited, as a conciliator of differences, which has lasted through five hundred years of prejudices which have locked for all times.'[26]

On Akbar's land system he showed how the rearrangement of land and revenue administration had caused popular happiness.

> 'Akbar admitted the progressive happiness to the generation amongst whom he lived.'[27]

As for investing in agriculture, he noted that during natural crises Akbar provided for grains to be sown, store houses to be made under local officers. This was the preparation of the ground for the continuation of the Empire till 1707, when it started to break up owing to its own internal contradictions.

There existed in this State a *Haram*-not a scene of pleasure or house hold alone. It was an arena of politics of wars, successions, conspiracies, expeditions, alliances, use of family members against each other in conflict situation, marriages in the interest of power, feasts of succession and accession, deference to authority of elder men and elder ladies and calculated matrimonial alliances linked to impending or future successions. These alliances cut across different religious sects among the royal blue blood and royalties of Rajputs and other Muslims and Hindus of the nobility. It was as good a place for celebration and pomp and show as the royal assembly halls were, or public appearances were. Briefly, it was not a miniature household expanded into a State, it was the State penetrating into the household. So it was a reverse of what Blake delineated in his model of the Patrimonial State. For evidence in this regard the writing of Gul-Badan, Humayun Nama, a rare text, is a proof. Written during Akbar's reign, Humayun' wife lists both aesthetics and real-politik of the State in the Household.[28] Like the State had patron-client relationship, so did the Household.

If the household suffered from polygamy and succession wars it did not mark the State an extended household. After all these, issues of the household led to conflicts of personal ambition in the absence of a law of Primogeniture. It was found in all medieval monarchies. The problem remained very much with the Tudors as with the Mughals, in the latter case since Babur himself. As during Henry's case the laws of the land were circumvented by the Monarch interested in marrying and disinheriting the women so married. Two aspects of the society came in conflict-law and religion. Lady Grey, Elizabeth, Mary of England and Mary Queen of Scots fought after their brother's death. Similarly Humayun faced problems with Kamran and Danial.

The more tantalising issue was of the result of this conflict in the State. Since Henry the VII's time, but especially since the time of Henry the VIII, the issues of nationhood emerged symbolised by both the Royal Navy and the Reformation. In India a cohesive culture and individual mercantile entrepreneurs emerged with a reformist composite ideology. It did not fit into the doctrines of Ghazali. So our argument did not become polemical/rhetorical, it assumed a substantive content.

The evidence of Akbar's rule after 1558 indicated that the State was seeking to achieve an inclusive community and an impersonal bureaucracy that could serve future needs. The colonial period attempted, after 1857, to foster community differences by ostracising the Muslims, and built a bureaucracy that was unfriendly to the people. In a certain sense, the Rule of the Company followed by the Crown was more of a continuation of the Monarchy's model of ethics and politics of the Victorian England. The Indian India remained a Suzerainty of the Crown with British India being directly under the Crown. From 1757 to 1857 loot and plunder took place under Lord Clive (as it did: Admiral Drake with regard to the Spanish in the Americas). The subsequent trial in the British Parliament of

Warren Hastings, revealed the extent of corruption under the company and loot and plunder since the days of Robert Clive.

The Mughal State, like benevolent despotism of its times, was striking roots among the people and prepared grounds for the expression of *inclusive politics* despite difficult and in some cases insurmountable divides. Akbar's State in its reach was as large in geographical area as Ashoka's empire or the subsequent British Empire. It was as concerned with the governed as the Tudor State was. The latter had problems with Scotland. The Mughal Empire continued to have problems in the *Qandahar* and the Dakhyn. In the Dakhyn, Aurangzeb passed away without fixing the problem of annexing it. Both, the Tudors and Mughals had problems of succession. Akbar resolved this rather early. Elizabeth continued to be intrigued. While she had lesser problems with Edward VI and Mary of England, she had major experience of conspiracies, truce, killings, captivity and execution with Mary Queen of Scots.[29] Both of them had the same father but different mothers. The Mughal State for its entire duration faced it. The intrigue was civil war in case of Dara Shukuh, or a revolt against the English Monarchy and establishment of the first failed Republican government by Oliver Cromwell. Both promoted merchant capital with different agrarian relations. One was caught in the specific circumstance of his times and the other pushing merchant capital, but both belonging to mystical thought. One A Sufi and the other was a Puritan.

In substantive terms the State showed signs of a market, monetisation, labour relations in agriculture, horticulture, cash crops, usurious capital, urbanisation, *karkhans* (small scale factories), skilled labour, artisans, a merchant class, sizable capital as in Surat equal or more to the trade of East India Company, banking that prevailed then, the credit system showed the prevalence of the market but manufactory was not yet part of the economy. So it was the merchant capital that existed. This atrophied under the contradictions of the Mughal Empire subsequent to the 18th century.[30]

Genealogy (?)

The State in India was like a palimpsest of history. Its character at different layers and at different times was packaged in disputations among historians of many persuasions- liberals, Marxists, foreign/

Indian. They conveyed the complexity of Sovereignty's evolution, structure and processes linked with the State. We noted above only two versions of its interpretation. More work needs to be done on the State in India, during the medieval period/ feudal stages, in terms of Michael Foucault's concept of Genealogy. It amounted to examining the power relations in terms of objective and subjective genealogy. Genealogy dealt with power relations that existed at all levels. It further emphasised impossibility of escape from them. Foucault mentioned three aspects of the concept with regard to the individual. To quote him

> 'Three domains of genealogy are possible. First, a historical ontology of ourselves as subjects of knowledge; second, a historical ontology of ourselves in relation to a field of power through which we constitute ourselves as subjects acting on others; third, a historical ontology in relation to ethics through which we constitute ourselves as moral agents.'[31]

It is difficult to come across the texts of history dealing with the Medieval Indian State in terms of Genealogy though it is not difficult to find its elements in structural analysis of power with regard to revenue collection, temporary land assignments, growth of money economy, ruling elites/class and magnificence of the state, operative grid of power relations and popular culture and their appearance at all levels. Even if we considered the local level population from times immemorial class and caste domination buttressed new social stratification. If the menials performed scavenging in ancient times, they became hired labour in the agrarian society by the seventeenth century. Feudal power relations were visible along with earlier forms of domination. Chattel slavery and kinship and caste bonds with earlier social contradictions underwent sublation in the new social dynamics. If the hierarchy of caste, and the hierarchy of ruling class was taken into consideration power relations came into play at all levels and they constituted the individual into an organic whole. The escape from it was as difficult as it was at other times following it.

Micro-politics

The concept of micro politics becames relevant here allowing State intervention at the decentralised or local level as it operated to control people's behaviour. The interventions aimed to control the behaviour of a large scale of people. Foucault urges that it shaped preferences, attitudes, and perceptions of individual subjects in theory. It amounted to an ideological intervention through schools, *Farman's* (Edicts) relating to celebrations, calendar, land, land rights and tenure system, religious activity, *fatwas*, administration and coercion (prisons), aesthetics, popular and court culture. The latter involved dresses of clothes according to rank with coarse cloth starting from the bottom going up to forms of *zardozi* and gem studied garments and shoes, brocade decoration as per status and other symbols of power and punishments.

Holistic State (?)

The State was not holistic in the totalitarian sense implied in Popper's phrase.[32] It was not rooted in a party or an ideology, historicism and / or teleology. It was rooted in situations and the people inhabiting therein. In this case an individual had to discover himself governed by the grid of religion cum caste and community relations and way of life. There was hardly any possibility of an individual episteme. This had to be discovered in feudal mind-set. Any individual consciousness at the political level operated at the level of patron-client relations within the class or caste system among the nobility, the peasantry or the administrative class that came from the same source of feudal families owning either individual or assigned land with or without the salary from the treasury. A rebellion was unthinkable for most of the community was either tied to the land or the *karkhanas*. The absence of popular or individual revolts were the sign of the State-society coexistence or a strong Mughal state and a weaker society and vice-a-versa at different episodic points of its history.

It was a State based on State-society simultaneity.[33] John Meanie observed that 'Sovereign Power' was as indispensable condition of the democratisation of 'civil society'. He concluded that a democratic order cannot be built through State power and it cannot be built without State power. If we paid attention to the historical antecedents of the Indian State, the interaction of the State with social formations in terms of ideology, social solidarities, social fragmentation, family lineages, and religious propensities of the rulers and ruled determined the reach of the State in terms of the dharma and danda (i.e. Ideological and

Coercive State apparatus). They were tied in a mutually binding relationship- of social and production relations. The system may atrophy or move forward depending on the rupture in the social relations. In places society asserted itself at certain period and at other places the situation led to an assertion of the State. If the temples asserted themselves during the Chola period (Burton Stein, Segmentary State) in the Mughal period the State asserted itself and guided the religious ideology of Islam out of the confines of Sharia to a state primacy ideology of Suhl-I Kul. The State became central to the development of economic and societal processes. The relations between the King and the temples were fluid and both had depended on each other for existence.

Simultaneity

The salient features of simultaneity were: (1) the simultaneous development of State and Society interests; (2) increase the territoriality of the State-Society from the nuclear regions to the periphery through ideological legitimation (Hindu, Islam, Colonial, Liberal, Marxist in that historical linear order for the sake of argument). The reality of this development may follow a more nuanced and complex trajectory. For example the Dihli Sultanate expanded into newer regions but never very far. The Mughal Empire spread with force, Sunni religion in contra distinction to Shiism and Hinduism, which helped the State to expand as did Buddhism and Hinduism in the earlier phase.

The societal conflicts revealed themselves in politics and vice-versa. Babur had noted that in the Fargana valley his concession to Shiism was responsible for a revolt by the Sunnis. The Dakhyn, especially, posed a problem both because of Hinduism (Marathas during Aurangzeb's times) and Shiism (*Bahamani* kingdom), or, even Sikhism in the Punjab (Aurangzeb's time). Jahangir noted in his memoirs the hostility that he had towards the then Sikh Guru Arjun Singh, whom he got killed. At the same time during Shah Jahan's times the State-Sikh relations were good.

The State-Society simultaneity expressed itself in territorial expansion through administrative hierarchy, and social rankings. The state officials, the *Mansab* system under Akbar, the preceding phase of the Iqtas under the Ghorian institutionalisation and the Rajput polity determined the social and state hierarchies in the Dihli Sultanate defining the property relations administered by evolving mechanism - beginning with loot, plunder and destruction of property and harvests through movement of armies to the system of taxation under Akbar after assessment of crops, land, revenue, prices, management of bazaars, maintenance of *karkhans*, roads and infrastructure for movement of merchandise for internal trade and dealing with multiple foreign traders and their relations with a friendly approach beginning with Akbar's rule, if not earlier. Contradictions developed, mediated and assumed new shapes but with the ground reality, state policies and intervention. To illustrate this quote from Ain-I-Akbari was interesting. It said, that Akbar

> '...showed, besides, no partiality to the Mohammadans: and when in straights of money, would even plunder the mosque to equip his cavalry.'[34] Further he pointed out to the abolition of *Jizyah* (religious tax), fair play in fixing revenue, punishment to stressful imposition of ground rent by local officers, the mismanagement of *jagirdars (land holders)*, the creation of conditions for not complying on was his.[35]

Organic Whole

It was a whole in an organic sense of state acting as revenue collectors, Ulamas, Sufi mystics or muftis, determining the state ideology and managing political conflicts among and within the provinces as far flung as Qandahar, Bengal and the Dakhyn, in its penetration in the lives of the urban and rural people at all levels. It was organic in the location of the Muslim community, plural nobility, composite cultural practices and administrative control to establish its hegemony. It made some rich, some pauperised and/or the royal treasury now full then empty. This was a case of the State dominating the society with getting a popular response at the level of comingling and Bhakti. Everyone was affected by it. It must however be noted that it was not an entrepreneur like the independent State of India engaging in huge water works for power and agriculture.[36]

It started to further this wholesomeness by employing Indian Musalmans and Hindus in administration. It was a process that began as tenuous experimentation with Tughluq's and Khaljis. (Firoz Shah, Allaudin Khalji). The 15th-16th centuries witnessed a sea change in these policies in accordance with the change in the nature of the State under the Mughals. An orthodox Sunni emperor like Aurangzeb employed Hindus in his administration, though he re-imposed the decision of extra religious tax to be paid by the Hindus.

The State counot be considered as outside of society as a parade of political dynastic changes and the ruled being indifferent passive spectators, as many scholars hold, especially belonging to the theory of Asiatic Mode of Production and the Patrimonial State. They became part and parcel of the wholeness of a state that focused on its magnificence of appearance and essence. The appearance was magnanimous and the essence was feudal exploitation. The State's glamour with its riches, pastimes of hunting and partying, its celebration of religious festivities, its panoramic parade from the announcer's voice to the public courts were part of the ideological apparatus that sub-served the coercive apparatus. This was no theatre of the street. It could be the theatre of the absurd where the apparent scene of glory hid poverty at the base. The Sufi dervishes sang and danced along to bridge the gap between the rulers and the population by articulating the poor's miseries its own raptures and ruptures.

The Statecraft was in terms of autonomy that it achieved by balancing economic interests, social contradictions, revenue collectors and peasantry, *zamindars* and *mansabdars*, agricultural poor and the differentiated peasant class and merchant capital. This autonomy was exercised through the ideological and oppressive state apparatus among sects and communities on the one hand and the rebellious cases of local satraps along with dealing with robbers and criminals, on the other hand. At times both the olive branch and the stick combined.

For example the focus on hunting from the thirteenth century down to the seventeenth (not referring to the subsequent period since we are not concerned with it) was significant in the absence of any training in military strategy, tactics and its craft- matchlock to guns, horses to elephants, and men and machine linkage. It was serious enough to the point that if somebody spoilt the game he was maltreated, as was recorded by Jahangir in his biography. The educational institutions that talked about religion, mysticism, astronomy, astrology and the Persian wheel replacing the Indian pulley in India that Babur had noted was part of the wars of succession where different interpretations of religion and military prowess were involved. The aesthetics of the monuments and the gardens symbolised romantically by the Taj Mahal, the necessity of water and its fountains, the water ways around them, the orchards and fruits that were praised and new varieties introduced by Kings down the line from Babar to the seventeenth century and later are as much a part of the economy of horticulture and market in the urban centres as of the economy. The architectural marvels of masonry workers and their imagination through Persian-Turkish-Indian sensibilities were part of the other of the military prowess of the State in terms of sovereignty represented by forts and fortifications. To take one example the fort at **Bhakkar** on an island in the Satlej River was important from the thirteenth century downwards and with passing of decades and couriers it kept on becoming stronger. Both Humayun and Dara Shukuh, among many others used it on their escape routes. Qanungo suggested that at Bhakkar.

> 'The fate of Humayun seemed to dog the footsteps of unhappy Dara'.[37]

European artillery, with four thousand troops, part of Dara's treasury and military equipment were to guard Dara's family and fortunes under the charge of faithful Eunuch Sayyid Abdur Razzaq. The Fort enjoyed the majesty of being the military stronghold, like the fort of Fatehpur Sikri, Red Forts of Agrah till the end of the reign of Jahangir and Agrah and Dihli, under Shah Jahan, of the power of the Medieval State. These were the symbols of actual power of Sovereignty. The battles, especially the succession battles involving field tactics, river crossing and military hardware were related to positioning in the open ground, river banks as well as sieges of the forts. They came to represent sovereignty. The revolts by Tribals(described as robbers, like Khokars, Jats, Gujjar's) and the peasants (Irfan Habib noted) and sectarian conflicts beginning with the thirteenth century between Shiism and Sunnis (at the beginning of Raziya's rule) the unique case of Humayun being influenced by Shiism, were dealt with sternly involving brutality in many cases.

Absolute Sovereignty: External Limitations

Was the State strong and absolute? The answer to this question is a big NO. A State stood always at the cross-point of internal and external linkages of its times. The constraints on its sovereignty and reach externally and internally were ever changing but compulsively present as a complex web. The Mongol presence on the borders was linked to the attitude towards the New Musalmans (Mongols married to musdims in India) at home. The politics of Sunni Empires had directly affected the Indian internal aspects of sectarian profiles in politics. In latter periods the attitude of the European powers and their sea superiority mattered for the Mughal Monarchy and its policies of trade or visits to holy Mecca and seatrade.

Patronage of Caliph

The texts of Kautilya showed that the Mauryan State was constrained to adopt foreign policy diplomacy to deal with its neighbours. The wave of Alexander into the Punjab and the Huns much later showed the external impact on internal developments. The Medieval State in India at the beginning was confronted with external threats and influences since the incursion of the Muslims in the eleventh century. The presence of the Muslims in the society was evidence of the social scape. The desire and elation of Kings of Dihli Sultanate to get recognition from foreign powers, like the Caliphs, or the Iranian Monarchy was celebrated with pomp and show in the courts of the changing dynasties from Iyaltimish[38] through the reign of Firoz Shah[39] to the reign of Mughal Emperors, though in the last case it was not so much a question of following similar foreign policies. In case of Iyaltimish he allowed the Mongols' predatory activities on his borders in order to keep them at bay and not enter his Sultanate. Relevant to this then was the value Dihli Sultans attached to Persian and Caliph Recognition. The attitude to prevent the Mongols from troubling India by letting Mongols free depredations outside the north-western border reflected this limitation.

Turko-Persian Influence: Sunni vs. Shii, Qandahar

The Mughal Emperors carried with them into India the Islamic sectarian conflict. Babur carried in his DNA the links of Timur/Turkish royalty and Chagatai blood traced to the Mongol lineage from Chinghiz Khan's dynasty. Babur established an empire here that was called Mughal- an expression that would have shocked him in his own times. The word was used for the Mongols.[40] So the Mughal Emperors-Babur and Humayun carried with them the Sunni Shia syndrome as well. These were Arabic –Persian divides.

To add to this external limitation we noticed that the Iranian factor came to have a strong bearing on the internal policies. Humayun, the next Emperor, had strong links with Persian Monarchy (Safavis) and was a SHIA Monarch in a dynasty that swore by Sunni Hanafi identity. During Jahangir's reign, despite the interlude of Akbar's concord based on Suhl-i-kul (world peace) he was forced to assert his Sunni identity owing to the external pressure. Apart from initial years of his rule Akbar rose above this schism. Jahangir only to an extent did so, and, Shah Jahan specially insisted on his Sunni identity from time to time. The reputation of the two remained within the veneer of Akbar's policy of rising above the sectarian schism .

During Jahangir's time in 1622 he received a letter from the King of Persia to the effect that Qandahar (also spelled as Kandahar) belonged to the Persians now in the hands of the brothers (Mughals). That it had to be returned to them as promised by Humayun and Akbar. Jahangir did not dispute this claim. It went to Persia in the same year.[41]

During the reign of Shah Jahan the issue kept cropping up and Murad, Dara Shukuh and Aurangzeb were involved in unsuccessful expeditions except for taking over Bust, against Qandahar, as per Inayat Khan's Shah Jahan- Nama.[42] Shah Jahan's foreign policy was to go against Persia to isolate her along with other two Islamic powers, namely Transoxiana and Turkey. It was in line with Shah Jahan's foreign policy of aligning with Turkey and Transoxiana, as part of the Sunni identity in foreign policy.[43]Qandahar was a contentious issue between Persia and India since 1522. Like the play of musical chairs, it kept shifting from Persian to Mughal hands and back. The Mughals gained it during Akbar's time, lost it during Jahangir's rule and the contest was on during Shah Jahan's reign. The latter had assimilated the dependencies of Bust and Zamin Dawar, investing eight lakhs of rupees in its fortifications and calling it the *'subah'* of Qandahar.

European Rivalry-Sea Trade and Visits to Mecca

The issue of Sovereignty came up during Akbar's period and continued to invite the attention of the Mughal State thereafter with regard to sea-power and maritime trade. Apart from defending interests of **sea-trade** the State had to assert its power on the **ideological issue** of visits of the Royal inmates of the ships visiting Holy Mecca. The State had to deal with the predominant Portuguese, emerging English and small Dutch presence on India's shores from Hugli in the East to Goa and Surat in the West. Under treaty agreements with Akbar, Indian ships had to acquire Portuguese certificates to enjoy the Right of Passage for the ships to pass to the Red Sea. On the Portuguese pass was the religious insignia of Christianity. This was intolerable under Islam. Yet it challenged the Mughal consciousness of their own grandeur, power and identity. It was tolerated though.

Secondly, the Portuguese looted Indian ships during Akbar's reign, who also issued Farman (edict) for reducing the number of trips to Mecca to once per year and to take the land route to Mecca for holy visits by the members of the Royal Family.[44] During Jahangir's time this problem remerged.[45] The factor of the entry of the English sea power helped the State to play them against the Portuguese.[46]

The fifth year (1631) of the reign of Shah Jahan experienced the breach of State sovereignty in Hugli. Abdul Hamid Lahori noted

> 'á party of Frank merchants, who are inhabitants of sundip, came trading to Satganw….occupied some grounds on the bank of the estuary…in course of time, these Europeans increased in number, and erected large number of substantial buildings…fortifying them with cannons, muskets, and other implements of war…known by the name of Port of Hugli…. European ships used to go up to the port, and a trade was established there.'

They exported men and material and cheated the locals by paying cheap rents for their buildings. The Emperor took note and an attack against the 'Firangis' was launched. Lahori narrated the ultimate capture of many Firangis. 4,400 Christians were arrested and nearly 10,000 local inhabitants were set at liberty. These foreigners, out of fear of capture of their ship carrying 2000 men, blew their own ship so that it did not fall into the hands of the royal forces.[47]

In the wake of the British sea power emerging on Indian coasts the Mughal State adopted a policy of friendliness for economic reason of sea trade and counter balancing the Portuguese in the western sea board. The architecture of control of Indian Ocean had not yet reached a completed paradigm. Alfred Thayer Mahan's[48] strategy of controlling the Indian Ocean from the Strait of Hormuz to the Straits of Malacca had not yet been put in place by the English. It implied a triangular control of Strait of Hormuz, control of the Port of Triconnamalee in Sri Lanka and the Strait of Malacca. Successive European powers had followed this strategy. The key in this strategy was the control of the Port in Sri Lanka. Any defeat here meant loss of control over the sea route.

In order to deal with the Portuguese challenge, the Mughal policy was not to confront them. It aimed to achieve a balance between an established Sea Power here and an emerging one, the British. It gave tenuous British influence in the Court and check mated the Portuguese without annoying any one. There was however no doubt that as per Indian diplomacy the English at the Mughal Court had no easy access. Findlay noted the defeat of the Portuguese at the hands of the English as well as their travails at the Court of Jahangir. The influence at the Court was the possibility of access through a maze of patron-client relationship to get to the then ruling "junta" headed by Nur Jahan.[49] Indians had their own ships, merchants and merchandise. Perhaps their ships were not as large as those of the Europeans nor were there any companies for trading in foreign lands. In matters of sea trade and relations with the Europeans, the Indian State had eschewed recourse to the assertion of military power. Instead went in for diplomacy of making the Europeans fight out, amongst themselves for their presence under Indian patronage.

Establishment of the Core of Sovereignty

The core of Sovereign power lay in its military prowess within and without. The setting up of the Mughal Empire and its history proved this fact, at the Battles of Panipat (1526, 1557). Babur described in his journal how on the battlefield Ibrahim Lodhi was out-manoeuvred in military tactics. He was so encircled that he could hardly escape. The description of his head being brought was thus given

> 'By God's mercy and kindness, this difficult battle was made easy for us! In a single half-day that armed mass was laid flat upon the earth….Ibrahim was thought to have fled. Therefore while pursuing the enemy, we ordered two of our warriors to lead swift pursuit to

> Agra and catch him. It was the Afternoon Prayer when...Tahir Tibri had found Ibrahim Lodi's body in a heap of the dead, brought in his head'.[50]

Immediately, Humayun was sent to Agrah to take control of the place and the treasuries, the head of the Sovereign King, the Agrah fort and the treasuries and then to control Dihli in a similar fashion. These were the symbols of sovereignty that passed into the hands of Babur. All this came as a result of war. Similar pattern of post-war gain of predominant power can be traced back to the ancient times beginning with Persian Wars between Athens and Sparta.[51]

Sher Shah Suri snatched it from Humayun. In alliance with Persia, Humayun, by now a Shia, again moved to Hindustan.[52] The death of Babur raised fears among the Amir's (Nobles). Araish Khan, an Amir, referred to a custom in Hindustan that the common people rob and steal on such an occasion. The Humayun Nama noted:

> 'His Majesty Humayun had ordered that it would be best to dress someone in red, and to set him on an elephant, and to let him proclaim that Babur has become a dervish and has given his throne to the Emperor Humayun. People were at once reassured by the proclamation, and all offered prayers for his welfare.'[53]

Humayun's adaptation with Shia sect and support from Persia to get back Hindustan and other territories in Kabul was commented upon by Annette S. Beveridge in her introduction to Humayun Nama thus:

> 'Humayun's coquetry with Shiism in Persia is one of the most entertaining of the episodes of his sojourn there, and it had consequences in arousing distrust in him, which cropped up from time to time.'[54]

The following factors played a role in establishing the Mughal Sovereignty. These were the military prowess in war (including Coercive Apparatus), the charisma of the Emperor (charismatic personality of the Emperors acquired from different religious, social factors and war-heroism), alliance with the Safavi Empire and the ideological factor of Sunni-Shi'(Persian in origin) criss-crossing sectarian politics (Ideological Factor) and the acceptance of the Emperor by the local population (Public Opinion). No single factor was responsible for the acquisition, establishment, consolidation and extension of the Empire in a country like India. These factors at times pulled in different directions to be pulled back in the state balance.

India did not suffer from war-lordism that challenged the Chinese Empire under the Manchu's. This had meant fragmentation of sovereignty among provinces.[55] The tendencies of centralisation had begun with the Iqta system. In the Mughal period the system that evolved was far ahead and more complex than that available hitherto. In periods of crisis and at the time of Humayun's brief rule and Akbar's accession of *subahs*, *sarkars* and *mahals showed the existence* in India of centrifugal tendencies that had to be controlled to re-establish central control.

Humayun did not have enough time to firmly establish his administration. The establishment of power required then the control of forts, army, *bazaars*, routes, trade, treasury and territory to establish an economy for bringing prosperity through tranquillity. This fell on Akbar's sixteen years old shoulders under Bahram Khan and later when he came into his own after relieving his Regent. When Humayun tumbled out of life, India was again beset with fissiparous tendencies. Akbar had to face the task of winning over the centre of power in 1557 and establish the Mughal Empire anew.

To Babur belonged the vision of development of war hero's perspective of All-India conquest. In the period of Akbar's rule India was integrated from Punjab and Sindh to Bengal and down south short of the Dakhyn with a power centre. The policy combination that achieved territorial integration was expeditions, quelling of rebellions, diplomacy, and implosion of court politics, inter community marriages, alliances with Rajputs and a policy of concord. The affected parties were the local principalities, called Zamindars who were more with trouble makers than in open rebellion. The troublemakers had their roots among Court leaders, potentates of provinces, Afghans, Rajputs and local zamindars some supported by hills people and/or Afghans.

The annexation polices were followed in Punjab and Sindh, among the hill peoples, and the Rajputs. In the region of Dihli, Agrah, Allahabad, Awadh, Bihar, Rajasthan and Gujarate alliance politics continued throughout Akbar's times.

For example, in Punjab, after the 1557 battle of Panipat, and preoccupation with Hemu, his forces faced the problem from the inaugural year and went on till 11th year (1566) of his accession and then in 1578 in the 23rd year, then in 35th, 37th, 41st and 47th regnal years.[56] The incorporation of territories of Dihli, Agrah, Awadh and Allahabad beginning with fifth regnal year of his reign was a continual process from 1560 to 1581. Similar was the process in Bihar beginning in 1574 and touching 1590. Mughals were in constant military move against recalcitrant power wielders. This was true of the Kings in Ajmer, more owing to the fall out of the events in Gujarate. These chiefs were local but got embroiled owing to the court politics and Afghan revolts.[57] Putting down the revolts or expeditions were constant signs of a process of assertion and reassertion of the sovereign power at Agrah / Dihli during the Mughal period.

The core of this was the military might of the Army which was dependent on cavalry and artillery traced to Turkey through Persia. The country's *rayaya* or *raiyats* (ordinary rural population) and the rural and urban ruling elite were joined both horizontally and vertically with a system of hierarchical army and land systems under *Mansabdari Administration*. Both wings went hand in hand. Since the land assignments were of an all India character to both Muslim and Rajput nobility the core of sovereign power was eco-military-administrative. It was difficult to determine the motor of policies that drove them. Was it military priority or economic priority? There is some difficulty in finding an answer for it. The wellbeing of the community was as important as the riches of the ruling class. So without being a military-bureaucratic complex it helped to keep the sovereignty afloat and winning except in cases of Qandahar, Dakhyn and the English Sea Power.

Nomad-like Movement

For asserting State Sovereignty the Emperor and his Court had to be on the move. The Emperor's entourage included the military commanders either with or without the Emperor's person. The movement of the Emperor was continual for expeditions, for hunting, for tourism, for expeditions or discovering the land. It meant the royal court and haram moving in a hierarchical fashion involving the royal family, nobility, support staff and the military. It gave a feeling of the

Sovereignty being nomadic, reminiscent of the Central Asian nomadic movements of the period of Babur. The tours of the Emperor not only implied the Jalal of the Emperor through his grandeur but also the might of his power and the effect on unity. He had to be seen to be believed. We noticed that each of the Emperors was more out of fort than a resident at any of the Forts. He was mostly out as a visible symbol of grandeur and might of the Mughal power.

Stephen P. Blake calculated the movement for each of the Emperors in relation to the years of his reign. During the period of 1556-1739 Mughal Emperors spent nearly 40 per cent of their time in camp, on tours of one year or more. The imperial camp was known as exalted or sublime camp, camp of good fortune and victorious camp.[58] At the centre of this was the camp of his majesty, followed by his haram, then by the highest of the nobility and so on. Gul-Badan Begam described the play of pomp, power and politics during such camp movements.[59]

Personality

The Emperor represented the Glory of God shining from that centre and in the forts. Both in theory and practice this glory or charisma was given a solid foundation. Skirting the issue of the ruler's position in Islam we noticed that a secular concept of Kingship developed. The idea of 'Jahandari' was enunciated earlier. The writings of Ghazali and Tusi were adopted here to provide for an administrative concept. Barni had suggested that State laws were the key to the welfare of the people in his work **Fatwa-I Jahandari** and that this need not be referred to or based on either the Sharia or the view of the **Ulema.**[60]

The concept of necessity determining law involved the State Sovereignty and gave the freedom to the Emperor to be the sole determinant of the need of the hour. In the seals of the Emperors this glory was stamped. The seals were in Akbar's Farman of 1558. It thus read 'he is without need'. This was an invocation. The seal itself mention names of two of his preceding ancestors followed by names of all the Predecessors back to Amir Timur' (etymology of Timur is iron). He himself was described as 'Jalaluddin Muhammad Akbar Padshah Gazi'.[61]

The country had undergone changes by the fifteenth and sixteenth century. The Mughal Empire therefore was not the same as in the

13th and the 14 centuries.[62] The despotism of the Dihli Sultanate was necessitated by the closed and narrow circle of the ethnically heterogeneous ruling elite composed of Arabs, Turks, Khaljis, elements of the Mongols and Habshis (Berbers) and Indian Muslims. The ethnic fission was severe in predominantly Turkish nobility. The reign of Iyaltimish forced him to create Shamsi nobility. Raziya lost out since she showed her inclination for a *Habshi*. No Indian Muslim could be appointed in high office till Allauddin. Even then this was not acceptable.

Chandra noted that the writings of Fakhr-i-Muddabir and Barani were rigid and unchanging one. But social relations were changing and putting a strain on the Sultanate. A new contradiction was emerging which was unmanageable by the State. The Mughal State and the ideas of Abul Fazl replaced those of the earlier period. The Mughal State brought the desirable change.[63] The ideas of equality were conceptually a difficult terrain to tread. Since ancient times, the theories of equality had not been able to delink themselves from inequality of society. Here again the shift from inequality to equality had to be welcomed as a qualified change that generated the forces of progress in economy and society that the Mughal State attempted to do.

Athar Ali, like Chandra, **rejected the continuation theory about the relationship of the Mughal State with the Dihli Sultanate**. He talked about a new theory of sovereignty, among new administration and enlarged ruling class. Almost summing up the Mughal sovereignty he pointed to the ideas of *blueblood*, *social* contract and of **Mahzar** propounded in 1579 that gave to Akbar the position of an *interpreter* of Islamic law, and, in matters where the existing law was silent the Emperor assumed the role of the *legislator*. All this was derived directly from God. He posited a primitive version of the modern State in the Mughal State.[64] It was difficult to understand how primitive the version was. As far as Sovereignty was concerned, he pointed out multiple sources of it during Akbar's period on the authority of Abul Fazl. Fazl's idea of **social contract** implied secular character and its foundation in alleged social needs. The idea was originally mentioned by Blockmann in his introduction to the Ain I Akbari.[65]

> 'A man may resist his king and judge when he acts contrary to law and may even help to make war on him.'[66]

Much later in the seventeenth century Locke denied sovereignty. The Hobbesian rationalism was based on laws of mechanical motion in physics provided the basis for absolute sovereignty.[67] His absolute sovereignty was unalloyed absolutism of the modern state. It would be better not to call the Indian State's sovereignty as primitive or contemporary version of Hobbesian State. It would only be limited sovereignty resting on Indian conditions of high noon of feudalism.

If we go by feudal ideology and the way Qanungo looked at Akbar, he came close to ideas rejected by traditional Islam: Neo-Platonism and Avicenna's rationalism.[68] These were not linked to any version of mechanical materialism. Akbar remained within the medieval paradigm despite his significant shift away from the then prevalent religious dogma.

The writings of Abul Fazl need to be examined in this case. The idea of Social contract had to be closely examined in the circumstances of India since it was different in the seventeenth century England. Fazl's preface suggested the ideas of Divine royalty, define the word 'Padshah' meaning stability and possession and origin, lord, i.e. he was the origin of stability and possession. Royalty was described by him as light emanating from God or *farr i izzidi* (the divine light) and the tongue of antiquity called it kiyan khwarah (the sublime halo). These provided to the king attributes of paternal love to the ruled, large heartedness, courage, power of requital, claims of people of different status settled impartially, increase in faith, prayer and devotion and who used reason to temper with desires that lead to restlessness or used reason to temper ambition, and did not please people without reason. He ruled to achieve equilibrium in body or biological terms as he looked after the political constitution through hierarchy of ranks by establishing a proper relation among different constituents. Finally, used his knowledge on men and matters to regulate business accordingly.

The argument of consent as a way out of anarchy or contingent anarchy involved in the theory of social contract did not exist in Fazl. At the beginning of modern times in England people of the city entered into contract to avoid violence and anarchy and achieve peace. The earliest constitutions made at the city-level were for peace to avoid anarchy that Men of cities created by pursuit of self-interest – commodious living.

Here the ideas of divinity and its halo constituting the Emperor and entrusting him with knowledge and reason to establish the rule of a hierarchically organised society with the help of a ruling Oligarchy were underlined. There was a faint echo of Plato's ruler-ship of Philosopher-Kings in the idea of haloed pre-eminence of the Monarch's person ruling for equilibrium of immobile hierarchy with a just hand. We do not have even in this comparison the idea of reason in Fazl's descriptions that are explicit in Plato's argument. There was no idea of contract among the people to create a Sovereign. On the contrary there was a throwback to haloed tribal history.

Fazl refered to the Divine lineage in mythology and history of the Mughal Emperors. That idea was traced back to Alanqoa who combined the Timuride and Genghis Khan's Ancestry. She was described thus:

> '...was the daughter of Juyina Bahadur of the Qiyat tribe and the lineage of Barulas....The lights of piety shone from her countenance, and divine mysteries could be read on her forehead...she was given in marriage...to Dobun Bayan, the ruler Mongolia and her cousin, and thus this unique holy pearl was joined to the ruler ship of humanity...she became leader and monarch of her nation.'
>
> Fazl got into mythology or religious mysticism. He said 'one night she, who had been nourished by divine light, was resting in bed, when suddenly a magnificent light shed its rays into her tent. The light entered her mouth, and she became pregnant by the light, just like Mary the daughter of Amram. God be praised! From Adam until her, holy human souls had been nurtured stage and stage through all contradictory degrees....'

The Mughal rulers descended from Yulduz Khan. His sacred line reached Alanqoa. So many great ones were the products of the Divine light without human intermediary. Now on Akbar, he said:

> '...The beginning of the appearance of H.I.M. (Akbar) on that day so that after travelling through the various stages he would appear in world through the pure vessel of H.H. Maryam Makani.'[69]

Jahangir's Memoirs afford to us the divine royalty of Akbar in his personal traits of the latter. Beveridge praised Jahangir's Memoirs since they offered a bigger plum on Akbar than any other.[70] Jahangir noted, Akbar's middle height, inclining to be tall, his complexion hue of wheat, his eyes and eyebrows black, lion bodied, broad chest with long hands and arms, fleshy mole, very agreeable in appearance, of the size of half a pea. His august voice was very loud, and in speaking and explaining had a peculiar richness. In his actions and movements he was not like the people of the world, and the glory of God manifested itself in him. Then he followed this description in praise of his lineage thus,

> "Greatness in his manner, kingship in his lineage,
> As if Solomon would have put the ring on his finger."[71]

Therefore lineage mingled with myth and religious thought. These were the bed rock of his charisma and prudent use of reason for Suhl-i-Kul his plummet of sovereignty. It is here that in historical terms his sovereignty rested on the lineage. Further his strategy of co-optation of the Rajputs, cultivation of the loyalty of his Hindu subjects by practising mysticism rather than Islamic Sunni Hanafi Code, militarily defeating the Afghan rebels and the tribal hills kings and winning over smaller sarkars and jagirdar established his charisma. The issue of sovereignty was asserted by Jahangir in relation to treating Persian King Abass' I ambassador on the issue of Qandahar.[72]

Courtly Culture

The high culture that developed had mixed elements. Thackston mentioned models of **Iranian kingship** and the perfect man in Sufism influencing him,[73] **marriage alliances** with the Rajputs, his **administrative capabilities**, his ideological aspects of discussions **challenging** the **Ulamas** in his newly constructed 'Ibadatkhana' and promotion of **translations**[74] of Sanskrit texts into Persian, not Turkish. The latter language had seized to be the court language in the third year of Akbar's reign. So to say, he was a son of the soil. Born here and moving to mysticism within Islam and Hinduism through a process of dialogue to develop a world view of peace and concord made him a proto-nationalist.

The political culture of sovereignty was based on principles of accepting the *segmentary society* and moving it in the direction of evolution towards harmony and equilibrium among sects within and among religions. Blake said of his political culture,

> 'It was not in accordance with the Sharia, the state system included the non-Muslim elite which was not unknown within Islamic tradition'.[75]

Blake went on to state the Indo-Persian character of the culture and its **Syncretic** characteristics. Since the household was a reflection of the State and not vice versa, it was marked by observation of many religious festivals and many Hindu begams' and Shia ladies' betrothal with the royal sons. Kings were born to Rajput and Shia ladies along with the Sunni wives.

Finally, it must be concluded as did Henry Maine that Oriental despotisms survived owing to their sensitivity to the people and did not pursue absolutism in the Austin's legal sense. It may further be asserted that the European idea of social compact was different from the Mughal Emperor's composite culture since the former was based on bourgeois (burgers or men engaging in money economy and exchange value). In this case the compact was among sects, among and within religious groupings through mysticism, through common living on day-to day basis and cohabiting the same locales and on their margins i.e. villages, qasbas and cities and mohallas within cities. It was not the bourgeois economic rationality in which man became the measure of all things. In Akbar's reign the nobility tied to the system of 'Jagirs and Mansabdari' was the grid of concord. Common living styles, quarters, mansions, spoken language (Persian) and ways of living and wielding power, position and patronage became the basis. It was like the Court determining social behaviour and life style. This was the socially embedded Sovereignty with the structure of ruling power and the ideological roots in mysticism, rationalism and astronomy and astrology.[76] All the Emperors engaged in solar and lunar weighing of themselves and the equivalent wealth being distributed among all and sundry in and outside the court and the haram.[77]

Societal and Economic Dynamics

At the time of the Ghaznavi invasion, political anarchy was registered. There were fifty nine principalities; society was not bound by Buddhism for it was in decline. The rise of Brahmanism was not yet the dominant unifying strand. The Rajput lineages of Suryavanshi and Chandravanshis had not jelled into a central monarchy. The existence of fiefs, forced labour, caste system, rigidity and untouchability were practised post Harshvardhan's rule, comparable to Greece before the rise of Macedonian power, i.e. artistically alive to its heritage but politically fragmented.[78]

About fifty years before the Muslim invasion, Muslim mystics and saints had penetrated the country and settled in a number of important places, living outside fortified towns with lower sections of society owing to the caste system. They were thus able to mix with these people. In Benares, Bahraich, Muinud-din-Chisti in Ajmer (hereafter Chisti), and Maulana Razi-ud- Din Hasan Saghani, famous for his work titled Mashariq-ul-Anwar, was born in Badaun. There was a Muslim colony in Kannauj. In UP and Bihar people attribute Muslim shrines to the time or before the Ghuride invasion.[79] There were no conversions in villages, no riots. In *qasbas* and cities those converted were outcastes like weavers, elephant drivers, butchers, fishermen and the like. Colin Davis observed the Musalmans here,

> '...were responsible for organising internal social life of their own, quiet different from that of their Hindu neighbours with whom they have otherwise mixed freely in all the common affairs of life.'[80]

Even in Ghur the people were non-Muslims till the twelfth century when Ghyasuddin and Shihabuddin appear in the state of Ghur. The latter one created the dynasty of slaves (could rise on the basis of their loyalty, acumen and become Amir's through Manumission), which led to the establishment of the Dihli Sultanate despite Rajput and Jats recurrent resistances.[81]

Under the rulers of Dihli Sultanate, Nizami held that the State respected artisans and merchants composed of Muslims and Hindus. It did not follow the proselytising policy. On the authority of Irfan Habib, Nizami suggested that conversions took place on the basis of mundane considerations. Similarly mystics converted Punjab tribes. Here the Khokars living between Tibet and Lucknow were converted. Suhrawardi, leading a conservative *silsila (Orders)*, was influential in Multan. Chisti, more liberal and well known, was influential in other regions with Ajmer as the Centre. The Hindus (merchants and zamindars) acted as intermediaries between the State and the peasantry. The Hindu elite was prosperous in comparison to the masses. Ibn Battuta noted how the Hindus followed their customs in relation to cremation and suttee. The dresses were similar, the purdah existed with difference in the manner of covering the head and face. Travel arrangements for individuals of both communities were provided for. Ibn Battuta described how commonality and differences were followed among these two communities vis a vis the travellers. No one objected to the supply of water to any traveller even when they did not visit each other's houses. In the **khanaqs (resting places on roads usually maintained by the State/Sufis)** evidence was found of their mutual contacts. Some titles of the nobility at the court had Hindu names to them: Malik Chaju, Rashid Pundit or Haran Mar. The Iqta system did not yet have any impact in the countryside.[82] The religious tax on Hindus (Jizyah) was imposed. Isami maintained that during the reign of Raziya heretics (mulhidan) attacked the Jami Masjid. They were mercilessly put out of existence. They were perhaps of the Shia sect. There was no denying the facted Husain comment on this

> 'The historical value of this was great. It shows that the State in those days granted no amenities and no religious toleration to dissenters in Islam.'[83]

Despite Islam being the common language of discourse in the Dihli Sultanate in terms of organisation of Muslim society, heritage of literature traced to the Arabs, providing a way of life and inheriting from the Prophet a vision of an equal society yet created unequal society. There were sects among Muslims. The orthodox Islam of Sharia had its other in meditation by the mendicant for the ecstasy of the One. The society of Muslims was equally segmented among Turks, Arabs, Mongols, Khaljis and *Habshis*, Indian Muslims and New Musalmans (originally Mongols but married locally and settled in Multan).

There were differences in dress etiquette, style of living and their pro-state and petitioning roles Vis-a-Vis the State. The State was directly supported by the Ulema for the nobility and the dynasty and the Sufi dervishes petitioned for the poor, respectively. Their roles were defined more by their being close either to the King or those who kept their distance. These differences were magnified by Suhrawardi and Chisti, respectively.

There were class differences among the city Muslim dwellers and the ones who lived on the outskirts performing menial functions merchants, artisans and Traders. There were conflicts in the urban centres owing to this division.[84]

The Hindus were also class divided and had their own religious differences. There was a large peasantry counter balanced by landlords with their patrons among kings. There were the rural class divisions since caste system had created outcastes living on the land outside the boundary of the village as well as the operation of the notion of rigid inequality in all its manifestations. The Buddhists, Jains, Shaivites, Vaishnavite, popular mythologies among them the Gods, language and cultures of the North and the South were different even if commonalities were evolving with regard to political and administrative structures in contiguous territories.

The differences between the Hindus and Muslims were many-followers of polytheism and believers of a revealed book by Abraham, The former were considered non-believers.[85] Caliphs had imposed Jizyah but the practice was pre-Islamic followed by the Prophet. In other countries such taxes were known. It was Host tax in France, common penny in Germany, scutage in England and Turkish danda in India.[86] The meaning of this tax underwent a changed under Caliph III and further change under the Ummayyids. Those who converted were also to pay to keep up the revenues. Further on the tax was imposed not on communities but on villages. It affected the entire population composed of Hindus and Muslims. After the 14th century, we noted above there were changes in the society, state and statecraft.

Mughal Transition

The society was in the process of change from a traditional to a semi modern one. Durkheim gives a distinct division between a traditional and a modern one. The former was segmentary glued by customs, culture and group consciousness. The modern was based on individuation. The glue was interdependence of work and production of agriculture for city and complimentary work in the modern society. The former was altruistic and fatalist while the modern was based on work complementarities. The transition was marked by the development of a *class* which was described as an *organ*. The traditional society had commonality through religion, similar work, educational and religious training and life style.[87]

The Mughal society had feudal (traditional) with many stages overlapping – (a palimpsest) and money economy(potentially modern), feudal ground rent (traditional) yet market in land, merchants in the cities, internal and external trade (potentially modern) religious divides and education among two communities (traditional) and an attempt to bridge these (common good) and karkhanas in the cities (not manufactory), hired labour in cities and the countryside, differentiated peasantry and revolts (common). In pre-modern society, peasant revolts were restorative, messianic, revolutionary or just issue based.

K. M. Ashraf mentioned about the commonalities of the two communities, way of life and class divides. Islam did not uproot the institutions. The class divide was in social and not religious terms. There were common practices among Hindus and Muslims during the Mughal period.[88] The elites were composed of feudal nobility, and, Muslim and Hindu Merchants. As noted by Babur villages were small, simple and people did not have much by ownership of utilities, and inhabited by the Hindu peasantry. We witnesed commonalities of living among the two communities.

There was the common system of 'purdah' (veil) but styles were different. During the Sultanate period noted by Isami, we noticed the act of giving up purdah by Sultan Raziya.[89] The Hindu Marriages were based on caste system,[90] or gotra, while the Muslim marriages were divided between Na-Haram and Haram. If among the Hindus there was Suttee (sati) system, it was Jauhar among the Muslims. In the villages Hindus and Muslims had separate quarters. Castes and traders lived in their own quarters. Hindus were bareheaded and barefooted wearing only a dhoti on the lower limbs below the waist. Muslims were non vegetarians and in contrast Hindus were vegetarians. The Muslims did not eat pork. For the Hindus the cow was sacred. During the mutiny of 1857 the rumour of the gun grease being of pig and cow pulled all stops and led to the mutiny, described by Marx as a nationalist struggle.

Inequality among Urban Muslims

Muslim masses were converts from the masses of Hindus. Conversion to Islam did not bring to the new convert any material advantage or way of living. The converts were influenced by their earlier social practices in matters of living and rituals. Nizami talked about the revolution brought about by Islam into India by way of *urban* society. Ashraf mentioned lack of impact of Islam on the basic living condition of Indian Life. The change was among the classes and not the masses. So, it was Islam that succumbed to the spirit of class division and forgot all about the message of equality of the Quran.[91]

Indian Muslims and Administration

Rizvi took the position that the Indian Muslims were the largest group during the Turkish rule. Hindus selectively rose to administration under Allaudin with opposition from the nobility. This was an exception. By the end of the sixteenth century class divisions among Muslims became very pronounced. Fazl mention Afghans as a separate class but considered Sayyids, Shaykhs and Shaykhzadas as castes like the Rajputs and Brahmans.[92]

Racial Prejudice

Racial prejudice continued in varying degrees of severity and being muted at different points of time. Babur himself would have been shocked to hear about the nomenclature of his dynasty as Mughal. The Dihli Sultanate was known as Turks, Afghans, Tughluks, Lodi's and Khaljis. They were not the same race. Even among the same race, tribes were mentioned. In case of Iyaltimish the *Ibaric* tribe was mentioned. Turkish of different versions Chaghatai Turkish was Babur's language. Turkish was spoken before third year of Akbar's reign. The Emperors never called themselves as "Mughals". They called their dynasty as *silsila-igurniyya*, the *Gurkanid* dynasty, from the word of Mongolian origin *gurkan meaning son-in law*.[93] The adjective was used in Jahangir's Memoirs as well. Then Humayun had Turanis and Iranis on the south of the Oxus who became an obstacle in allowing him centralise the empire.

Jahangir and Politico-religious Fault lines

The interaction among Hindus, Muslims, Jains and Sikhs had their own fault lines of politics not determining racial prejudices. Jahangir noted that Guru Arjan Singh was killed under his orders since he had given hospitality to his son Parvez's friendship, who had revolted against him, in line with Khusrau's (eldest son of Jahangir) actions. Jahangir noted Arjun Singh in addition was gathering large motley of supporters and provided hospitality to Khusrau.[94] In a different context he considered the Serwas (Jains in Gujarat) as infidels and seditious. They were regarded as peers by 'Banyas' who built temples for them. They had two sects and were loyal to Akbar. They were ordered to be put out of the empire as per Jahangir's 'fatwa'.[95] During Akbar's time, like the Jains, Sikhs were also friendly.

Urban Life: ordinary conflicts and the way out

The non-religious ordinary day disputes in cities like Shahjahanabad, a microcosm as well as macrocosm of the Empire, were dealt with by the committees of caste-craft based *mohallas* (quarters). These mohallas were of elites and the poor. The chiefs of mohallas decided on inter-mohalla disputes, judged disputes over land and other issues of property, took decisions on rituals, negotiated taxes with city authorities, arranged security against internal and external disturbances, and in concert with other chiefs, decided on common interests.[96]

Patron-client relationships

The elite mansions were determined according to rank in the court, patron client relationships and the patriarchal system. Mutual respect was counter balanced by values of loyalty[97], praise and support. The elites supported the peasantry and the merchants established relations with the Court through a network of patrons and clients. The backbone was the Mughal royalty, imperial personage and the temporary *mansabdars*, *jagirdars* and the merchants like the layout of Shahjahanabad was like the head being the Red Fort and the spine being the bazaars and the quarters of the city led by the Jama Masjid[98] and the elite quarters. The existence of these linkages went right upto the Emperor.

Merchants and Markets

Markets for a variety of goods and animals exited since the thirteenth century. There were two of the three separate *bazaars* for two of the three essential commodities. There were *mandavis* near Mandavi Darwaza during Allauddin's times for purposes of revenue. There were buildings for storage of grains to supply during seasons of drought. There was no central market like in Shahjahanabad.

Cloth markets were well dispersed in the city and its numerous mohallas. The principal bazaar was adjacent to madrash-i-muizzi according to Barni.

The essential commodities were grains, cloth and horses, slaves and others were fuel, meat, salt, wheat, corn, varieties of sugar, butter and, rice.[99]

The crafts that flourished during these centuries in Dihli were for varieties of cotton, silk, carpets and woollens, and iron ware. In addition there was stone cutting, cap making, oil making, soap making, gold making or *zagari,* spinning, dye making and sugar making.[100]

During the period of sixteenth century Ashraf noted other features of the market. There were banking practices for giving loans and keeping *hundis*. There were bonds for lending money on interest (never mind Islam) and there were in both the communities' money lenders. The system of usurious loans and compound rates of interest led to heavy indebtedness of the poorer people who borrowed small sums but could not repay while the greater resources of a noble and in the last resort his power and influence came to his rescue.[101] Guilds did not exist nor did the banks invest in business.

Atrophy

Habib noted that the Indian economy, owing to collection of large share of surplus in the ruling class and considerable Surplus in the urban sector during the Mughal period there was a high percentage of population employed in industrial crafts. In terms of volume of output per head it was comparable to the early twentieth century. On the issue of production for use or exchange value, he held that in various fields of production like calicoes at Lucknow or precious metals, or the independent craftsmen, did not show the possibility of this being a general tendency. The artisans generally produced on orders at fixed rates. There was regular labour system, e.g. production of ship building, manufactories did not exist, and karkhanas did not involve themselves in commodity production, except only as a putting out system. If the system of agrarian exploitation was added with the emergence of land rights and a market for the land even then it was difficult to say that the cusp of feudalism was bursting into capitalist development. Merchant capital atrophied.[102]

Monarchy and Rural exploitation

The backbone of Mughal polity was the economy administered through the Mansabdari system. The Mansabs were the dominant apex form of administration. They went up from 65 per cent (during Akbar's time) to 90 per cent in (Jahangir's time).The peasantry was pauperised, menials starving, and the elites were the beneficiaries through the system of mixed land system of temporary landholdings and ones with permanent hereditary rights. The land tax went to the State (treasury) and the household of the monarchy. Partly the salaries of the Mansabs which varied were paid from the royal treasury, after the payment to the labourers. Some share the peasants kept and a certain portion went to the priest. Stephen P. Blake mentions the existence of Patron-client relationship at all levels of the rural population which was composed of *zamindars*, money lenders and grain merchants, peasants with large land holdings and small holdings. There were the service providers like the artisans e.g. weavers, potters, dyers, gold smiths and black smiths, landless labourers and servants.[103]

The lower rung of the social ladder was populated by the Hindus. The possessors of land were called the *zamindars*. They were recipients of the peasant's revenue. They were a heterogenous class. There were zamindars who were *khudkasht* in addition to those who tilled *Khairaj* lands which helped the entry of[104] the Rajputs, *Ghakkars*, without endangering the basic foundations of the Mughal system because it was a tax that could be distributed among rural classes.

Temporary Assignments

The system of land holdings under the Mughals underwent a change with the introduction of the Mansabdari system in 1575.

During 1556 -1575 it was in the process of change from the Tughluq and Lodhi system of permanent landholdings, after about 400 hundred cases had been examined in the early years of Akbar's time.[105] In the latter case the landholders with fixed hereditary territory was in the hands of Afghans. Under the Mughals a noble's income from assignment approximated to his salary fixed according to his rank in the hierarchy and the expected and actual strength of his armed contingent. The holding was not a jagir in the sense that it did not have any fixed territorial unit. The change in the holding took place every three or four years. It also had no connection with the administrative units of *sarkars* and *parganas*. Jagir could be assigned throughout India. This enabled an all India perspective and diluted local lineages. A Rajput could have it in the Dakhyn or in Gujarat. The tripolar system that was central to the Mughal Empire, was thus described by Chandra,

> '...a gradual development of a triangular or tripolar relationship between the central government, the *zamindar*, and the cultivators in which the *khudkash*t predominated. This apparently was the basis of the so-called 'Mughal Stability'.[106]

The administrative system and the police functions helped maintain this stability. The faujdar performed a dual role of an aid to the zamindar for revenue collection as well as a check if he transgressed the stipulated role and revenue amount. There was a *waqianavis* above him and the zamindar. This system of checks and balances worked from top to bottom.

Crisis

The crisis emerged in the system about a hundred years later. A contradiction emerged between the agrarian relations and the administrative structure reared upon these relations.[107] The empire was beset with recurrent crises. First, the problems related to the existence of caste bonding of zamindars and producers across villages were difficult to handle by the Mansabdars if the former resisted revenue collection. The caste linkages were not spread in contiguous villages. Second, the peasants also revolted owing to the agrarian crisis. Land market in the countryside, money lenders, and usurious capital made the peasantry pauperised. Third, the merchant capital of the cities was not necessarily entrepreneurial even when there was extensive internal and external trade in which the entire ruling class and members of the Royalty participated. Fourth, the religious concord worked upon during the reign of three Emperors did not prove to be the sufficient basis to resist the orthodoxy of Islam that was subterranean during Akbar, Jahangir and Shahjahan's rule despite episodic flashes. During their time destruction of temples was noted, as also mosques, but became a major problem during the second half of the seventeenth century under Aurangzeb's reign. This happened despite a few signs of the continuation of Hindu administrators and conservative Sufi links with the Suhrawardi *Silsilas*. Fifth, the empire was peripatetic for the court was constantly on the move in camps to quell rebellions (apart from engaging in tourism), reintegrate the territories and recurrently recapture territories like Qandahar, and the Dakhyn, and manage smaller rajas' revolts and the ones of people who lived in far flung hills i. e. hill tribes called robbers.

Sixthly, the great Mughal Army, centralised hierarchical was also weakened by the administrative system of the provinces, if in revolt since Zamindars onwards it was concentrated in fragmented pockets of client administrators, sons, grandsons or loyal nobles who also commanded their own forces. The last were homogenous marked by rebellious elements. Different factions and individuals took sides, shifted sides, made secret alliances on the basis of shared secret hatreds and family alliances. The ruling class itself suffered from elite conflicts. The role of feudal lords and their links with merchants existed. The changing profile of Mir Jumla during the reigns of Shah Jahan and Aurangzeb in the context of conflict in the Dakhyn and the conflict between the four sons of Shah Jahan was graphically a reminder.

Seventhly, the monarchy **did not** have a law of primogeniture. Following the example of the Prophet successors were not supposed to be named. Following problems within his family and the succession issues, Islamic states faced similar problems. In his own life time Babur faced it, Humayun suffered it to the extent of one of his brothers put before the firing siege his baby son, Akbar. Akbar faced the revolt of Prince Salim. Jahangir faced the issue with his sons but especially with Prince Khurram, who was called **Bi-daulat** by Jahangir and Nur Jahan. Prince Khurram was as loved and patronised by his father as Muhammad Dara Shukuh was by Shah Jahan. Both were patronised by the reigning fathers. Dara had become a victim of the times he lived in. All of them were believers in astrology. All of them believed in lunar and solar weighing of themselves. The politics of the times and its ideological matrix was part of their fate and the mental makeup of the feudal order.

Eighthly, the Mughal Empire had merchants, markets, commodities produced and traded. It did not produce a capitalist revolution, like one saw in England by the middle of the 17th century symbolised by a mystic like Oliver Cromwell. Both the ruin of rich landlords through usury and the impoverishment of the small producers led to large amount of concentration of capital. It did not necessarily lead to capitalist revolution as it caused a change in England[108]

End Notes

1. Upinder Singh, *Ancient Dihli*, Oxford University Press, 1999, p. 90.
2. Shams-I-Shiraj Afif, *Tarikh—Firoz-Shahi*, pp. 299-300.
3. Abha Singh, *'Irrigating Haryana: the Pre-Modern History of the Western Jamuna Canal,'* in Irfan Habib, edited by, *Medieval* India *1*, Researches in the History of India, 1200-1750, Oxford India Papers, New Dihli, 2015. pp. 52-55.
4. *Ibid*, pp.57-61.
5. Harbans Mukhia, *'Was Their Feudalism in Indian History?'* In Hermann Kulke, edited by, *The State in India, 1000-1700,* Oxford India Papers, Dihli, Chennai, Mumbai,1997, p. 121.
6. Dilip Hiro, *Babur Nama*, Penguin Classics, 2006, pp. 265-266.
7. *Ibid*.
8. Maurice Godelier, *'The Asiatic Mode of Production'*, Anne M. Bailey and Joseph R. Olo era, edited, The Asiatic Mode of Production, Science and Politics, *Routledge and Keegan Paul, London, Boston, Henley,* pp. 264-277.
9. Henry S. Beveridge, Edited, *The Tuzuk-I- Jahangiri*, Low Price publications, ND, 2015, p. 64.
10. On ruling class of the Sultanate see Irfan Habib, *'Formation of The Sultanate Ruling Class of the Thirteenth Century,'* Irfan Habib, edited by, *Medieval India1*, op. cit. Oxford India Papers, 2015, pp. 1-22.
11. Perry Anderson, *Lineages of the Absolutist State*, Verso, Ebooks, 2013.
12. Irfan Habib, *Agrarian system of Mughal India* (1556-1707), Asia Publishing House, 1963.
13. Jacob Abbot, *Queen Elizabeth*, Ebooks, kindle.

14. Mahmoud Bukhari, *Tarik-I Salatin- I Gujarat*, Ed. A. Tirmizi, Medieval India Quarterly, Aligarh, Vol. 5, 1963.
15. K. S. Mathew, *Akbar and Portuguese Maritime Dominance*, Irfan Habib, edited by, Akbar and His India, Oxford India Papers, New Dihli, 2014, pp. 256-265.
16. Ellison Banks Findlay, *Nur Jahan, The Empress of Mughal India,* Oxford University Press, New York, pp. 131-33
17. Henry S, Beveridge, op.cit. 2006, p. 418.
18. *Ibid.* p. 255.
19. Ellison Banks Findlay, op cit, pp. 129-131.
20. Marc Bloch noted that in the first phase of feudalism in England travel by Emperors and noblemen, for example, in 1033, religious beings, and even ordinary peasants was prevalent in England to establish an interlocking system. Marc Bloch, *Feudal Society*, Routledge Classic, www.Routledge.Com/ classic, London, New York, 2014. Kindle loc. 1702.
21. Stephen P. Blake, *Shahjahanabad, The Sovereign City of Mughal India, 1639-1739*, Cambridge South Asian Studies, paperback, April, 20012, p. 121.
22. Hamida Khatoon Naqvi, *Agricultural, Industrial and Urban Dynamism under the Sultans of Dihli, 1206-1555,* Munshiram Manoharlal Publishers Pvt. LTD. 1986, pp. 143-144.
23. *Ibid*.
24. Habib, p. 285.
25. Irfan Habib, 'Review', John F. Richards, *The Mughal Empire*, being Vol. 1, part 5, of the new Cambridge History of India, Cambridge University Press, 1993; Indian Edition, Foundation Books, New Dihli, 1993, Xavier+320 pp., index, 6 maps, in Irfan Habib, edited By, *Akbar And His India*, Oxford India Papers, ND, 2012, p. 304.
26. Colonel G. B. Malleson, Edited By, *Rulers of India*, Akbar CSI, Oxford, Clarendron Press, 1896, pp. 3 per cent of 2963. In Kindle EBooks.
27. *Ibid.* p. 76.
28. Princess Gul-Badan Begum (Princes Rose Body), *The History of Humayun, (Humayun Nama),* transl. Introduction, edited by Annette S. Beveridge, IDARAH-ADABIYAT- I DELLI, QASIMJAN STREET, DELHI, 2009.
29. John Young, *Life and Times of Mary Stuart, Queen of Scots,* A Mariner Book, Houghton Mifflin Company. Boston, 2004.
30. Irfan Habib, *Potentialities of Capitalistic Development in the Economy of Mughal India*, in Irfan Habib, edited, *Essays in Indian History, Towards a Marxist Perception*, ND, Tulika Publishers, 1995. pp. 228-230.
31. Paul Rabinow, *The Foucault Reader*, Edited By, An Introduction to Foucault's thought, with major new Published material, Penguin Books, 1984. p. 351.

32. Karl Popper, *Open Society and its Enemies*, The University of Kagenfurt, 1994.
33. Brajadulal Chattopadhyay, *'Political Process and Structure of Polity in Early Medieval India'* in Herman Kulke, edited by, op. cit., Dihli, Calcutta Chennai and Mumbai, Oxford, 1997.
34. Abu L -Fazl Allami, *The Ain-I-Akbari*, translated Blochman, M. A. third Edition, Oriental Book, New Dihli, Reprint Corporation, 1977, part1, p. 174.
35. *Ibid.* pp. 232, 239.
36. Pranab Bardhan, *The Political Economy Of Development in India*, Dihli, Oxford University Press, 1984
37. Kalinga Ranjan Qanungo, *Dara Shukoh, Volume 1*, Biography, Calcutta, 1934, p. 273.
38. Tabakat-I-Nasiri: *A General History of The Muhammadan Dynasties Of Asia,* Including Hindustan; from A. H. 194 (810 A. D.) to A. H. 658 (1260 A. D.) and the Irruption of the Infidel Mughals into Islam by Maulana, Minhaz-UD-DIN, ABU-Umar-I-Usman, transl. from Original Persian Manuscripts by major H. G. Raverty, VOL. 1, Oriental Books Reprint Cooperation, Book Publishers, 54 Rani Jhansi Road, New Dihli, 1970, p. this text notes honor coming in an embassy from Abbasi Khalifa of Baghdad to honour the ruler, p. 616. The event was celebrated in the city with pomp and show.
39. R. C. Jauhari, *Medieval India in Transition- TARIKH-I-FIROZ SHAHI, A FIRST HAND ACCOUNT,* SUNDEEP PRAKASHAN, NEW DELHI, 2001, notes the receipt of robes from the Caliph, deputy of the Eternal God. Jauhari notes

    'The edict of the Caliph, which signified that Sultan Firoz was the deputy of the Caliph, fully sovereign in his kingdom, with the title of Syed–ul-Salatin, was presented.' p. 160.
40. Dilip Hiro, op. cit. p. XXIV-XXV.
41. The Tuzuk-I-Jahangiri, or MEMOIRS OF JAHANGIR, op. cit. pp. 240-242.
42. Inayat Khan, *Shah Jahan Nama*, Hafeez Press, Karachi, pp. 105-108.
43. See Kalinga Ranjan Qanungo, op. cit, pp. 28-33.
44. K. S. Mathews, *'Akbar and Portuguese Maritime Dominance'* in Irfan Habib, fn. 23, pp. 256-265.
45. Tuzuk-I-Jahangiri, op. cit, pp. 255.
46. *Ibid.* p. 276.
47. Abdul Hamid Lahori, *Badshah-Nama*, , op. cit, pp 34-39
48. Alfred Thayer Mahan, *The Influence of Sea Power upon History, 1660–1783* (1890) online edition.
49. Ellison Banks Findly, op. cit, pp. 128-160.

50. Dilip Hiro, op. cit. pp. 262-263. The Mughal Army was a cavalry force maintained by Mansabs. The artillery was the dominant force. 'There were 40,000 infantry, 200,000 horsemen. Among the artillery were matchlock men, gunners, rocketeers and cannoneers. This gave a weapon of domination in urban power centers since the ruling class was urban. Athar Ali, *'Toward An Interpretation of the Mughal Empire,'* in Herman Kulke, op cit. p. 274.
51. Thucydides, *Peloponnesian Wars*. The author noted that given ego centric human nature wars were bound to happen.
52. It is interesting to note that similar religious action was taken by Babur when he was trying to consolidate his power against the Uzbeks. Dilip Hiro noted 'little wonder, Babur kept his part of the agreement with Shah Ismail Safavi, including stamping the names of Shia Imams on his coins. This offended his subjects. Being predominantly Sunni Muslim of the **Hanafi** Code, they considered SHIA Islam heretical. So did Babur. Yet Babur had to be a realist. He knew that, unaided, he was no match for the Uzbeks who were determined to attack him, and so he had no option but to maintain his alliance with Shah Ismail Safavi under Safavi suzerainty. This happened prior to his coming to India. Hiro refers to this as to prove Babur to be a man of principles. Dilip Hiro, op. cit., p. xxix. HANAFI SECT WAS FOUNDED BY Imam Abu Hanifa (699-766 A. D. He was a Persian basing his system on opinion and analogy. Starting from Quranic texts he developed it further. He also insisted on the right of preference (**Istihsan**) necessitating a careful study of actual conditions in legal thinking. For him Traditions related to Prophet were to be placed in the context of the times and space he lived in. They could not be applied indiscriminately to the new conditions. By the tenth century Islam had become a closed system since now only adherence was insisted. Khaliq Ahmad Nizami, Some Aspects Of Religion and Politics In India During The Seventeenth Century, IDARAH-I ADABIYAT-I DELLI, 1974, pp. 38-39.
53. Gul-Badan Begam, HUMAYUN-NAMA, op. cit. pp. 110-111.
54. Annette S. Beveridge, Introduction, *Ibid.* p. 43.
55. At the advent of Islam into India the country was witnessing centrifugal tendencies and small provinces came into existence. Anarchy prevailed with the decline of Buddhism, rise of Brahmanism and the coming into existence the lineage power of the Rajputs. The Rajput lineages did not centralise power.
56. Ahsan Raza Khan, '*Akbar's Initial Encounters with the Chiefs: Accident vs. Design in the Process of Subjugation,* in Irfan Habib, AKBAR AND HIS INDIA, op. cit. p. 4. A. R. Khan said that to win over the chiefs was a plan suggested to Humayun by the Persians.
57. *Ibid.* p. 13.
58. Stephen P. Blake, op. cit. p. 97.

59. Gul-badan, op. cit.

60. SAA RIZVI, *The Wonder that Was India, Vol. II*, Picador India, p.163. In the phase of the Dihli Sultanate Divinity under the Islamic order had an underlined fetish to describe a Sultan from Iyaltimish down to Firoz Shah Tughluq. Maulana, Minhaj-ud –din Abu Umar-i-Usman,, Tabakat-I Nasiri for Iyaltimish 'beneficence, inclination for mystic music as opposed to Muftis, military prowess, patronisation of monks, saints, soldiers, nobles, learned, building reservoir at Haus-i-Shamsi and liberality towards the people. pp. 496-523; Isami further elaborated on these aspects. His popularity among the people of Dihli was noted by him at the time of Iltyamish's death. Futus-I Salatin, ShahNamah-I-Hind of Isami, op. cit. p. 244 Similarly, there was a similar description of humility, beneficence and piousness about Firoz Shah Tughluq. The difference noted between him and the earlier Sultans was that he assigned land to the soldiers that provided stability to his rule. This measure had been rejected by Allaudin earlier. Jauhari recorded, '…for the benefit of the Muslim servants of the state, assigned all villages and towns to army men in lieu of their salaries. Since the Sultan was by heart, a slave of God and His favourite, God the Almighty kept his kinship and reign stable and permanent for forty years and the country was full of glory and light on account of his splendor.' Jauhari, op. cit, p. 73.

61. Sayyid Zaheer Husain Jafri, '*A Farman of Akbar (1558) from the Period of Regency*' in Irfan Habib, edited by, *Akbar and His India*, op. cit. p. 265

62. Satish Chandra noted these changes in the society and justifications of the State despotism. Satish Chandra, *Essays On Medieval Indian History*, Oxford India Paper Backs, ND, 2013.

63. *Ibid.* pp.42-49. Chandra noted that egalitarian notions and precepts coexisted with hierarchical order.

64. *Ibid.* p. 263

65. The problem with deploying the idea of social contract was of multiple nature. First it came up in England and France much later in seventeenth century in the writings of Hobbes, Locke and Rousseau. Secondly, it was an abstraction of understanding the new society's anarchy and the way out of it. Third, its rationalism (Thomas Hobbes, Leviathan, 1651), Empiricism (John Locke, Two Treatise of Government, 1689) and Romanticism (J. J. Rousseau, Social Contract, 1762) had different intellectual bases and had different *problematiques*. In case of Hobbes, the problematic was Liberty. In case of Locke it was Property and in case of Rousseau it was Equality. The solution for Hobbes was Absolutism, for Locke it was Constitutional Oligarchy, and for Rousseau it was direct rule of small commodity producers.

66. fn. 64, p. 466.

67. Many interpreted Hobbes' to be also a man supporting religion. Yet, his book was burnt on the orders of the Church. He had to run away from England and had developed mental instability.
68. He said, '...it is no wonder that Akbar's rationalism ended in mysticism'. Kalinga Ranjan Qanungo, op. cit. Calcutta, p. 389.
69. ABUL – FAZL, *THE HISTORY OF AKBAR, VOLUME 1*, edited and translated by Wheeler M. Thackston. Murty, Classical Library of India, 2015. pp. 215-219. See also Blockmann's translation, op. cit., pp. ii –ix.
70. Henry S. Beveridge, Preface, op. cit. p. viii.
71. *Ibid.* pp. 33-34.
72. *Ibid.* p. 244.
73. Fn. 64, p. ix.
74. Muzzafar Alam, *Political Language of Political Islam in India, 1200-1800* Permanent Black, Ranikhet, 2004. Alam refers to the idea of 'Akhlalq' based on justice, during Jahangir's times. 9. 73.
75. Stephen P. Blake, op. cit., p. 123.
76. Fazl examined his horoscope and indicated that the position of Jupiter and Mercury in the trine **'indicating 'great sovereignty, perfect intelligence, and justice**.' p. 91.
77. Aurangzeb stopped this practice after some years.
78. Dr. Tara Chand as quoted by Dr. C. Colin Davis, Foreword, Khaliq Ahmad Naqvi, op. cit. p. xviii.
79. Khaliq Ahmed Nizami, *ibid.*, pp. 66-67, 76.
80. Colin Davis Preface to *ibid.* p.xiii
81. Khaliq Ahmad Nizami, *ibid.* p. 33. For local resistance to Qutubuddin see Raverty's notes to Tabakat-i-Nasiri, op. cit, pp. 517-518.
82. *Ibid.* p. 323.
83. Futus-i-Salatin, op. cit. p. 239.
84. Ibn Battuta on urban life. Minhaz praised the majesty of Dihli as a center of world culture. Tabakat-Nasiri, op. cit, 598-99
85. Khaliq Ahmed Nizami, op. cit. p. 209
86. *Ibid.*
87. Kenneth Smith, *Emile Durkheim and Collective Consciousness of Society: A study in Criminology*, Anthem Press, A1 books.
88. This section follows the work of K. M. Ashraf, *Life and Conditions of People of Hindustan*, New Dihli, 1970.
89. op. cit, p. 253.
90. Tuzuk i Jahangiri notes the caste system as do earlier chroniclers like Ibn Battuta. Tuzuk i Jahangiri, op. cit, p. 244-46.
91. K. M. Ashraf, op. cit., p. 112.

92. S. A. A. Rizvi. op. cit., p. 199.
93. Abul Fazl op. cit, Thackston Introduction, p. 17 this was a very different scene of racial prejudices from the period of Dihli Sultanate. The racial infighting among the Dihli Sultanate Sultans caused instability of factions, rebellions, conspiracies, revolts and change of monarchs. Till the time of Humayun it meant that the Emperor was on the move either as a warrior or a fugitive. During Akbar's initial period he was engaged in subduing Punjab and Sindh.
94. Tuzuk i Jahangiri, p. 261; on Arjun Singh he says '...there was a Hindu named Arjun, (fifth Guru of the Sikhs and the compiler of the Granth Saheb), in the garments of sainthood...had captured many of the simple hearted Hindus...foolish followers of Islam...treated Khusrau well....I ordered them to...be put to death.' Meaning Arjun Singh.
95. *Ibid.* pp. 437-438.
96. Stephen P. Blake, op. cit. p.84 he described the city layout of Ahmadabad to conclude that the population lived in purahs or quarters of the ordinary people and elites as in Shahjahanabad. Since the reign of Qutubuddin construction work in and around Dihli city was recorded. Tabakat-I Nasiri, op. cit,p.599; Ibn Battuta, Op. cit., p. 194;Tarikh-I Firoz Shahi noted the money given for rehabilitation of townships and villages and construction of Hissar Firozah op. cit. p. 71, 91Eleven times the center of Dihli shifted between 13-16th century. Hamida Khatoon Naqvi, op. cit. p. 22.
97. Loyalty was the key to the Slave system that began with the Ghurids and continued through the Mughal period via the Dihli Sultanate. A slave could rise to the position of an Amir as per the system of Manumission. The Mughal court valued and promoted the culture by decorating men with state symbols of promoting them. These were the offering of robes, gems, rare kinds of swords, horses, elephants, daggers, jagirs, making them Mansabs and strengthening loyalty though marriages and using human milk to outsiders to cement loyalties.
98. Different locations of Dihli that came up during the Sultanate were owing to three perennial factors. The soil erosion and the river changing its course, the lack of water and the congestion of cities, Added to this was the belief among pre-Mughal rulers that if death took place in a fort the new Sultan did not stay there. He got a new one constructed. Also cities came up in relation to victories in certain areas as noted in every Chroniclers narrative. Other reason was the climatic conditions or natural condition's were good. Babur Nama was full of details about areas of natural beauty. So was Tuzuki Jahangiri.
99. Hamida Khatoon Naqvi, op. cit. p.73, 155-157.
100. *Ibid.* p. 171.
101. K. M. Ashraf, Op. cit. p. 140.

102. Irfan Habib, *Potentialities of Capitalistic Development in the Economy of Mughal India*, Irfan Habib, Edited, *Essays in Indian History*, Towards a Marxist Perception, MS, Tulika Publication, New Dihli, 1995, pp. 229-230.
103. Stephen P. Blake, op. cit. p.
104. M. Athar Ali, *'Towards an interpretation of the Mughal Empire'*, Herman Kulke, op. cit, p. 270.
105. Iqtadar Alam Khan, *'The Mughal Assignment system during Akbar's Early Years*. 'in Irfan Habib, Researches, op. cit. pp. 64-66.
106. Satish Chandra, op. cit. p. 130.
107. *Ibid.* p. 129.
108. Karl Marx, Pre-Capitalist Socio-Economic Formations, Progress Publishers, Moscow, 1979, p. 163.

Chapter - 2

Birth, Family and Personality of Dara

Birth

In his Memoirs Jahangir noted the birth of the eldest son of Prince Khurram, (Shah Jahan) and other royal personages, men and women, including his father, sons and grandsons. The mention was followed up by astronomical and astrological details and the exact timing of the day in terms of the phase of the day and the night. He noted the birth of Dara Shukuh thus,

'Two watches of the night had passed on the night of Monday, the 29th Safar (30th March, 1615), in the ascension of Sagittarius, when a boy was born to Baba Khurram by the daughter of Asaf Khan; I gave him the name Dara Shukuh. I hope that his coming will be propitious to this State conjoined with eternity, and to his fortunate father.'[1] (Jahangir's spellings of Dara Shukuh).

Sagittarius

The statement gave the ideas of relationship, astrology, naming and the desire for eternity. Let us look at the word Sagittarius first. It refered to the Greek mythology of a Centaur, i.e. half horse and half human.[2] The Wars of succession were nothing short of beastly. As for the person born with that sign, his characteristics were of an extrovert and arrogant, free, intelligent, happy, funny, honest, generous and proud along with being careless, rebellious, highly sensitive, quick to temper. In relation to Dara Shukuh (sometimes spelt as Shikoh or Shukoh), one could say he was a man of Akhlalq- man of the pen and the sword-intellectual and a warrior (aggressive).

Born to Baba Khurram

Jahangir notes his son's birth thus

> 'To Jagat Gosain, daughter of Mota Raja (the fat raja),was born Sultan Khurram, in the 38th year of my father's reign, corresponding to A. H. 999, in the city of Lahor, His advent made the world joyous (Khurram), and gradually as his years increased, so did his excellences, and he was more attentive to my father than (all) other children, who was exceedingly pleased with and grateful for his services, and always recommended him to me and there was no comparison between him and my other children, He recognised him as his real child.'[3]

We notice here no reference to astrology or time of the day. Secondly, we also notice that Jahangir praised him to be Akbar's son and who recommended him to Jahangir. It was here that astrology and religion came into play to give him the name that he got. Jahangir said,

> "The name Sultan Khurram was given by Akbar, meaning ('Prince Joy'), because his birth made the world glad. It was noted that the child was born in the first millennium, and also that, like his father, he was born in the same month as the Prophet."[4]

There was however a dispute about his date of birth. Some subsequent historians put it at A. H. 1000 while others put it as 5th January 1592. In both cases the names of mothers also found a place. We notice here an absence of any reference or analyses of their Birth Charts, like the discussions done by Abu Fazl of Akbar's horoscope that he mentioned in his first book.[5] Gul Badan's text mentioned the date of Babur's birth as the 14th of February, 1483 (*Muharram* 6th, 888H). There was no other detail given of his birth. She further noted that Humayun was born after the taking of Kabul. She said,

> 'The most-high God blessed the taking of Kabul, for after it eighteen children were born. (1) Of my Lady Akam who was Maham Begam there were born his Majesty the Emperor Humayun, and Barbul Mirza, and Mihr-jan Begam, and Ishan-daulat Begam, and Faruq Mirza.[6]

There was a mention of all the other children of Babur. On Humayun's birth she said,

> 'The blessed birth of Humayun, the first born son of his Majesty... occurred on Tuesday, Zul-qa'da 4th, 918H. (March 6th, 1508) in the citadel of Kabul, and when the sun was in the sign of Pisces.'[7]

We notice in this noting the astrological sign, as in the case of Dara Shukuh. Further she noted the propitious moment of Babur's Kabul victory as also Babur then adopted the prefix of His Majesty. Going by the birth sign values of compassion and over sensitiveness, adaptable and indecisive, accepting and self-pitying, imaginative and escapist were mentioned to be in a Pisces person. Right or wrong the fact was that all the first sons and other children's birth signs were mentioned and in some cases their horoscopes interpreted. This happened at least in the case of Akbar.

Mothers and Daughters

It was also striking to note that Babur's wife, and, Shah Jahan's wife, had off-springs in double digits, 18 and 14, respectively. All Mughal Emperors were fond of their first wedded wives and continued to love them dearly. An exception was Nur Jahan who was loved and doted upon by Jahangir, though not his first wife. Nur Jahan could not bear any children to Jahangir but had a daughter by Asaf Beg, her former husband. She was called Ladli. Apart from the strong emphasis of lineage and astrology the royal families had the practice of not letting their daughters marry outside the royal household. So most of them remained unmarried and in secluded compartments as Salatins. Two well-known unmarried daughters of Shah Jahan, Jahanara and Roushanara, were Dara's elder sisters. They were an exception. They lived like royal princesses with their own sanctioned finances, supporting their brothers-Dara and Aurangzeb, respectively. After Mumtaz Mahal's death, Jahanara was declared to be Padshah Begam and given the royal seal. This was unprecedented–an empress without being married to a King. After Dara's death she was made in charge of Aurangzeb's haram. A fictional account suggests that Jahanara Begum wanted the practice of not marrying the royal daughters to end. She, it is opined, was responsible for having taken Ladli, after Raushanara went into disgrace, by then a widow and a Salatin, to Lahor to enable her to live next to her mother, Nur Jahan's grave. She was buried there alongside her mother's grave.[8]

Mothers played multiple roles of engaging in foreign trade, owning ships, forming court factions, looking after children and grandchildren, protecting them in wars of succession, engaging in horticulture, facilitating patron-client relationships in the haram and the court, accompanying their husbands in wars, expeditions, holding parties, organising pleasure trips, and setting up parties for celebrations. Their diplomatic interventions helped monarchs to steer the ship of the State and make religious trek to Mecca.

Two names assume significance in terms of commerce and court politics. These were Maryam Makani (Akbar's mother) and Nur Jahan (Jahangir's most beloved wife, Ladli's mother, maternal aunt of Mumtaz Mahal, d/o Asaf Khan. Most of these women were also significant tourists to Mecca. Annette S. Beveridge noted the visit of women who had gone to Mecca. She regretted the fact that there was no record of what they thought of the religious rites expected of visitors to most important undertaking.[9] It is a significant observation but it did not make clear its import. Jodha Bai was mentioned as the Rajput queen and mother of Jahangir. It was of utmost significance since the policy was to strengthen the roots of the Empire through alliances with the Rajputs. Dildar Begam was the wife of Babur. She was held in highest respect as a lady. Five children were born to her. Among these was Hindal (b. 1519). The details of their families showed their royal lineage and education in the context of their times. In both these senses Gul-Badan Begam became a symbol of both education and high lineage and she left behind an important text about those times.

The haram was full of other ladies who were hierarchically placed in accordance with their relationship to the Emperor, lineage, education, and, endearment by the Emperor along with widows, daughters and concubines. It is not clear if the lovers lived in the haram too. Some of them did. Though not recorded, the story of Anarkali living in the haram of Akbar was considered to be a street talk. We do not know anything about the residence of Guf Safa, (whose painted portrait is recorded in Johnson Album, British library), a sweetheart of Dara Shukuh. How were such women placed is not clear. There seems to be no record about her. There is none in case of Anarkali during Akbar's time. The mothers, daughters, widows, concubines and consorts were balanced through the system of hierarchical administration with a head Eunuch being the spy master/ master general.

In this world of Mughal family there were jealousies, conspiracies and counter spying of and by relatives. Did women have a right to their own sexuality or to their nudity is difficult to say. An Islamic society in a Hindu populace – both patriarchal and promiscuous- there was hardly any evidence for a possibility of studying male gaze or views on nudity. Mukhia gave just one example of nudity on the basis of a painting of the sweet heart of Dara Shukuh.[10]

Jahangir noted that when a daughter was born to Akbar and she gained age, her nipples were pressed and the milk was given to Jahangir to drink, so that a mother son relationship could be formed between the two.[11] Further he recorded that Bayazid's mother was the first person who gave him milk for just a day.[12] His own father also had gone through this experience. What was striking is the fact that when Dara Shukuh made his wife wash her breasts (since milk was not coming out) and made him drink it to assure the loyalty of the Rajput prince, Rajrup.[13] Practically all the Emperors and Dara Shukuh loved their first or favourite wives notwithstanding their multiple relationships with other women, Jodha Bai (Akbar), Mumtaz Mahal (Shah-Jahan) and Nadira Banu Begam (Dara Shukuh) and Nur Jahan (Jahangir) to mention some.

The women were also the cause of jealousies and conspiracies of the Emperors. The case of Jahangir's interest in Nur Jahan was in point. She was married to another man, Sher Afgan, who was killed as a result of a conspiracy hatched by Jahangir. She was finally brought to his haram. He ultimately married her. She had earlier not responded to his overtures when he had seen her in the bazaar before her betrothal to Sher Afgan.

Gul-Badan Begam also noted another example of a woman who refused to respond to Humayun's overtures.[14] Strong women and women of great skill and sensibility but marred by the fact of not being the ruling Emperors wives led a difficult life of taboo and tragedy felt especially acute owing to high degree of their sensibilities of aesthetics expressed in art and architecture. Many became *Salatins*. There was this contrasting remark that Jahangir made about Muslim women while he noted the Rajput women practising Sati, or dying for the men they loved. He referred to the act of poisoning herself by a concubine of one Lal Kalawant, who was in the service of his father, Akbar. He recorded,[15]

> 'Few women among the Musalmans have ever shown such fidelity.'

The practice was seen in the context of those times. Even earlier Ibn Battuta described (with prejudice) this practice among the Hindus.

Eternity

The desire for eternity was common to mankind and took men of royalty to idiosyncrasies. Pharaohs of Egypt and their terra-cotta mummies were famous sign of this desire. Paintings and photography follow the same utility path in subsequent history. Others like Tarkovsky, the Russian film makers believed that four generations sitting at the dinner table symbolised eternity.[16]

Religionists, royals and ordinary individuals belonging to different Cultures longed for *afterlife* since they feared death. So the idea of eternity would be fated to be linked to the desire of kings as an imperishable being. It was so held that the being in the world howsoever complete or incomplete was like a fetus to be delivered to the next world to fully bloom and return after meeting the being who was not annihilated. The afterlife ideas in Islam looked at the issue. The *afterlife* world was described as *Barzakh*, i.e. a place of meeting angels, Munar and Nakir, the delights of paradise in Islam.

The belief of communication between the dead and the living, assuming the direct proportion and performance of good deeds in this world the rewards granted in the next world, was upheld. Ibn Abi al-Dunya (d. AH281/ 894 CE) narrated tales of people who were dead, or lived near the dead or came alive for a few minutes after death. These anecdotes created a physical contact between the two worlds and alluded to the fact that death was not the final stage of life. The living and the dead were in a dialogue and that the former could gain from the latter. Thus, the fear of death was overcome.[17]

The Kings of feudal England and France believed in mysticism and eternity. Bloch Noted,

> 'The happiness of the king and the realm in the present; the salvation of the royal ancestors and of the king himself throughout

> Eternity: such was the double benefit which Louis the Fat declared that he expected from his foundation when he established a community of Canons Regular at the Abbey of St. Victor in Paris. "We believe" said Otto I, "that the protection of our Empire is bound up with the rising fortunes of Christian worship."[18]

This kind of evolution was mystical[19] and had nothing to do with the ideas of science and modern way of understanding evolution. In case of the Mughals we noticed that their building activities had given them an afterlife existence with its pros and cons. Further their contribution to evolving popular-culture and memory thereof made them eternal up to the point when time turned their contributions into a negation. Therefore, the word eternal remained within the four walls as does the fetus in the human body in Islamic theosophy to which Dara belonged.[20] The two authors refered to the importance of the city of Ajmer and the Silsila of Moinuddin Chisti's influence from the time of Akbar to Shah Jahan. Jahangir and Shah Jahan's birth was related directly to Ajmer and the blessings of Chisti. Dara was born in Ajmer. He describes it thus in his work titled Safinat-ul-Awliya,

> 'As in the house of my respected father three daughters had been born and there were no male issues and (as) the age of His Majesty had reached twenty four, he, on account of the faith and devotion that he had for the Khwaja prayed, with thousand presentations and supplications, for the birth of a son. And with His grace God, the Most High, brought his meanest slave of his life (i.e. Dara Shukuh) into existence who hopes that He will grant him grace of doing good and will bring to his host His good will and that of His friends. Amin, Oh Lord of the world'.[21]

Dara on Eternity

In most of Dara's works there were indications of his ideas on eternity. He described eternity in cyclical terms as beginning and ending with the Prophet. In his book of Tariqat-Ul-Haqiqat (a text printed only in the mid-nineteenth century) he stated,

> 'On the abstinence of ignorance and the acquisition of knowledge, for which the value of time as an "internal felicity" is an essential factor.'[22]

Internal felicity was linked with natural elements-great element, wind, fire, water, and dust. In his work on Mingling of The Two Oceans, He stated how natural elements were created by Him. Then he came to annihilation to conclude the section on elements thus,

> 'Everything is perishable but His face (i.e. He). And there will endure the face (i.e. the person) of thy Lord, the Lord of Glory and honour.'[23]

To complete the cyclical argument he wrote in one of his quatrain,

> 'I tell thee the secret of Tawhid, if thou wert to understand it alright,
> Nowhere exists anything but God,
> All you see or know other than Him
> Is separate in name, but in essence one with God.'[24]

We further notice that for him and his Sufi master, Shah Muhibullah, eternity was also *infinity*. His master wrote to him,

> 'Mind has access to the Infinite, for, it is endless in its own end. And if this fact is not comprehended properly, it would not be possible for human mind to contain Infinity.'[25]

This was very close to Aristotle's 'nisus', or, views of nature where potentiality exists in embryonic form and finds fruition as an end (tree). All this movement ends with the idea of the Creator in Aristotle. Here ended his empiricism of forms. The last idea was picked up by St. Thomas Aquinas to embellish Christianity with by the thirteenth century.

In his work, Risalai Haq Nama, Dara said,

> 'The first is the theory of the heterodox Sufi views. The first is the theory of the spirit transforming into matter. The spirit in its essence is Divine, as the seed in its essence is the tree. 'know of friend that...the reason, why the essence of man has entered this frame-work of body, is that the seed of perfection, which lies latent may become patent; that which is potentiality may reach actuality and may return enriched with all experiences to its original source.'[26]

Dara- What is in a name!

Abul Fazl noted that Akbar's name was calculated on the basis of numerology. Ḥumayun, well versed in mathematics, had himself calculated the influence of the ascendant on his son and agreed that most of the horoscopes were mutually consistent.[27] Abul Fazl's brother, Adul Fazl Faizi had done a numerological assessment. He wrote,

> 'One of the strange characteristics of the mysteries of the letters that form exalted words, the effects of which appear in differing degrees in isolation and combination, is that the 'indications' of the letters in *aftab* (sun), which are 223, agree with the numerical value of 'Akbar'.[28]

Therefore, this linked with the quality of the signs made Akbar shine as sun does, was the author's conclusion. The same idea could be further buttressed by the Sufi teachings of initiation to annihilation in the practice of meditation. We will take that up later.

Letters of Dara Shukuh/Shikoh as signifiers

According to a Vistara Official website Shukuh is also spelt as Shikoh. It goes into the letters to say that S stands for real charmer, i.e. strong feelings, starter, magnetic attracts money, energetic, in positive sense and impulsive in negative sense. The letter H stands for somebody who has business acumen and negatively is self-absorbed. The letter I stands for genteel, impulsive, elegant, compassionate, humane with negative qualities of quick to anger and timid. The letter K stands for strong-willed and discontented negatively. The letter O stands for good student and negatively with uncontrolled emotions. The Ruling Planet was *Neptune* which emphasised green, color, gem stone and spiritual and philosophical characteristics. The name Dara meant possessor and a sovereign. In Hebrew it meant nugget of wisdom. In Biblical terms it meant name of a descendant of Juddah for wisdom. In Gaelic the name means oak tree. Therefore in astronomy and astrology it meant creative, intuitive, secretive, wealthy with uncontrolled emotions, timid, and self-absorbed.

Chroniclers' Assessments of Dara

The contemporary records had characterised his qualities. Manucci said of him that he was dignified in manners, comely countenance, joyous and polite in conversation, ready and gracious in speech, had most extraordinary liberality, kingly and compassionate, over confident, deaf to the advice of friends, highly self-regarding, mad about his object of love. He fell for a dancing girl called Ranadil whom he wanted to marry. On being denied permission by Shah Jahan, he pined for death and finally was permitted to marry her.[29] Bernier confirmed most of these qualities thus: courteous in conversation, quick at repartee, polite, and extremely liberal, high opinion of himself, very irascible apt to menace, abusive and insulting to Omrahs, had momentary anger and heathen.[30] He put faith in miracles, loved music, composed poetry (lyrics and quatrains). He believed in astrology and astronomy.[31] Muhammad Kazim gave a critical view of him and called him unworthy and frivolous with over weaning ambition and a heretic.[32]

Some of Dara's teachers expressed their assessment of him. Mulla Shah reposed great confidence in Dara's sagacity and farsightedness of mind and love for truth, warned him about the evil breath of his foes, and warned him further about heedlessness.[33]

Akbar, Dara, Shah Jahan and Aurangzeb

Going by numerology and astronomy the great grandfather (Akbar) and the great grandson (Dara) did not have any commonality in terms of the shining star. The former was full blast divine brilliance while the latter a lesser mortal even though Dara carried with him the legacy of Akbar: desiring a concord among communities. One created the root and fruit of Mughal Empire's glory and passed on the legacy to posterity. Dara basked under it during his life time cut short in ignominy. Qanungo considered Akbar to be in the tradition of the then prevalent scientific temper while Dara was a mystic. Both were committed to composite culture.[34]

He compared him to Shah Jahan and considered him to be his father's liberal part of the character but not the killer part in politics. Aurangzeb had inherited the other part of real politik in terms of deceit, diplomacy, maneuverability and tenaciousness to get the throne against all odds.[35]

Celebrations

Every occasion had similar festivities. Births, New Year day (Nauroz), victories, forming of marriage alliances, marriages, getting of honors, promotions, yearly solar and lunar weighing and annual occasion of accessions were celebrated. The expanse of celebrations could be delineated by the invitees' number, days of celebrations, money spent and forms of events. Abul Fazal described the festivities at the time when Humayun heard of Akbar's birth thus,

> 'After executing the duties of thanks, he went to the imperial camp. There celebration of joy and happiness was renewed, drums of festivity and jubilation were sounded regally, and the court was held with splendid pomp and circumstance.'[36]

The use of the drums here is not metaphoric signifying only the sound of announcement but an indication of the music filled enjoyment and celebration of birth as imagination and reality. The mention of use of the drum goes back to Prophet Muhammad Himself. In his Compass of Truth, Dara recalled this

'Once they asked Muhammad, "in what manner does revelation come to you?" He replied, "I hear a sound, sometimes like the sound of a boiling cauldron and sometimes like the sound made by the bees, and sometimes I see an angel in the form of a man, who talks with me, and sometimes I hear a sound like silvery bells or the beating of a drum."'[37]

The next paragraph quoted above Abul Fazl said it thus,

> 'Enchanting musicians and singers turned their various instruments and adopted diverse modes; harpists plucked the right strings from the locks of desire; hot-breathed flutists blew in correct pitch; rebec players charmed hearts with strands of desired strings; tambourine players held up mirrors of fortune.'[38]

The Ulamas in the sixteenth century, according to Edmund Burke[39] were opposed to music and celebration and joy. The beating of the drums, the playing of music and generally celebrations was less Islamic and more Sufi. Of Sufism, Robert Graves said they practice love. They respected the rituals of religion in so far as these furthered social harmony. They linked love with enlightenment. That led to ecstasy as was the Sufi belief. They were poets of re-edification so that man came back in this world after he was reconstituted as a better being in comparison to his earlier life in *Barzakh*, or paradise.[40]

The celebration of births is thus in line with the Sufi poetry, music and dance of love. For Graves this could be traced back to eighth century world and different cultures from Arabic to the European and Asian worlds. To understand this one had to be in the path (tarika).

The process of celebration around births began here in India with the return of Humayun from Chunar for Gul-Badan Begam. She says

> 'My lady, Maham Begam gave a great feast. They lit up the bazaars. Before that time people used to illuminate the bazaars (only). Then she gave orders to better class and to soldiers also to decorate their places and make their quarters beautiful, and after this illumination became general in India....
>
> 'Festivities lasted several days extending to a fortnight.'[41]

Jahangir noted a different spirit of festivities on the occasion of weighing of Khurram when he was 24 years of age. He said to his son,

> 'Baba thou hast become the father of children, and kings and king's sons have drunk wine. Today, which is the day of thy being weighed, I will give thee wine to drink, and give the leave to drink it on feast days and at the time of the New Year, and at all great festivals.' [42] He went on to quote Avicenna on its use in moderation that was profitable.[43]
>
> Saqi Mustad Khan noted of Aurangzeb's second coronation
>
> '...he ordered his officers to make preparations for the coronation celebrations, and they did their best.....

'The courtiers bowed to do honour, and sang the praises of and prayed for the Emperor. The doors of imperial treasuries were opened to people....

> 'The Emperor with open handed liberality gave grand rewards to the princes, begams and imperial households; every one of the nobles and faithful servants received promotion and the title according to his rank; pious and religious men, poets, musicians and singers received suitable rewards and gifts.'[44]

In this very year he abolished the celebration of Nauroz (Persian New Year) and started the celebration of the first day of Ramazan and those celebrations ended with Idul Fitr.[45] The first day of Ramazan was the day of his accession. So, it became a state festivity coinciding with his religious persuasion negating the earlier Shi practice.

Fathers

Dara himself noted that his father took him to Chisti's headquarters in Ajmer since Dara was born after two daughters.[46] He was especially favored by his father as the first born son. His grandfather had also taken a trip to Ajmer for the birth of Prince Khurram. His great grandfather, Akbar, had similarly made a trip to Chisti's silsila for prayers to beget a son. They were thus faithful to the Chisti's Centre. At the same time it was also a product of a blind faith to propitiate the supernatural powers for mundane/political desire for continuity of the dynasty. For such divine intervention they resorted to transference owing to their capacity for following the path of mysticism.

Miracles, Myths, Magic

The Mughal fathers were not immune from the ideas of miracles, myth magic, superstition and nature rites found in the first stage of feudal society in Europe. In the second phase Christianity and translation of texts was followed.[47]

In Aini we noticed the *miracles* performed by Akbar in his eight month with regard to his wet nurse.[48] Jahangir was known to be superstitious. In his Memoirs he mentioned the appearance of a star and the negative events that he soon witnessed. He further noted, in the context of the failure of medicines to cure Shah Shuja's flatulence, in his fiftieth year he gave up hunting with bullet and gun and not to injure any creature with his own hands,

> '...it were possible that his life would become the means of preserving the lives of many animals, and God Almighty might give him to me.'[49]

A similar exercise was done by Shah Jahan, it was reported, with regard to his son, Dara's treatment of an illness, by which time the latter was an adult, at Ajmer.

Circumbulation, Intervention of Magic or Blind Faith in Mystics

Recorded events in the Memoirs of Babur, Gul-Badan Begam and

Jahangir's show their pining for their eldest sons and desired giving their own life for the sake of saving their son's life. Yet fathers were also Emperors. This dual role made fathers like a coconut with its hard outer crust of sovereign power of the State and the soft inner core pulp of love, The outer crust was expressed by Jahangir thus,

> 'Kingship regards neither sons nor sons-in-law. No one is relation to a king.'[50]

Mughal Emperors as fathers were kind and generous to sons especially to the first born but strongly critical of their sons in revolt. The first made them give costly gifts, robes as form of transferences, fiefdoms, governorships of provinces, privileged sitting arrangement at court near the throne as per the court etiquette. These attributes were both an expression of kingship, and kinship with the sons. Dara sat on Shah Jahan's right and Aurangzeb on his left.

Kinship-Kingship

The sovereignty that was symbolised by the Emperor's person was used to the hilt in face of challenges to his authority. These Emperors were Janus faced in that they offered to give their lives away or as Transference-Babur for Humayun. They went across to Chisti walking bare-footed all the way from Agrah to Ajmer for miracle transference to get a son, e.g. Akbar. Rebellions against them by these very sons made them use the sword to humble their son's rebellion. Records of the reigns of Akbar, Shah Jahan, and Aurangzeb are replete with both these sides of the Mughal Emperors. Jahangir recorded that when he found his eldest son to be hostile to Nur Jahan or when he revolted, he was called a '**Bi-daulat**'.

Further, when brothers and fathers and sons fought amongst themselves their respective children were also kept as surety against their rebellions. Kamran, Jahangir and Shah Jahan did this as a routine. It did not matter to them what their ages were. Akbar was a babe when in custody of Kamran. Dara and Aurangzeb stayed with Jahangir up to the age of thirteen under the supervision of Nur Jahan once Khurram had revolted. Kingship and kinship Messed and many times it was the sword that decidedly resolved the conflict.

Gratis, Popular and the Populist culture

The Emperor and his children were weighed in gold, silver and other forms of wealth according to the solar and lunar time. The practice was started by Akbar and was observed till the early years of Aurangzeb's reign. The money thus given was distributed among the high and the low in and out of court. This was an old practice in India and linked with a popular belief that at the time of stress giving monies as gratis to the poor helps. So the popular and the populist also met. It was of cultural closeness among the poor and the rich as well as between communities. The practice of giving alms to ward off impending ill fate was universal and common to all classes.

Example of transference practiced by Hindus and Muslims

Waseem narrated, Shaikh Shams Uddin Darayai, celebrated for his marvels, and was buried in Deep Dal, in the province of Lahor. Among many miracles attributed to him there was one about a person called Depali, who was an orthodox Hindu but at the same time Daryai's disciple.

> 'Once he got Daryai's permission to go on a particular occasion, to bathe in the Ganges along with his co-religionists. The saint advised him to remind him of his desire on very day fixed for the sacred bath. Depali did this. 'Close your eyes,' Daryai asked him. Depali closed his eyes. On opening his eyes he found himself on the bank of the Ganges and there he bathed in the company of parents and friends. Again he closed his eyes and when he opened them, he found himself in the presence of his spiritual guide and this surprised him greatly. When his co-religionists returned and found him there they thought he had come back earlier, but when they came to know how all that had happened, they were plunged in an ocean of admiration....What is most striking today is the fact that the guardians of his tomb are the Hindu descendants of Depali'[51]

The example suggested the role of miracles and transference brining people of different communities together. Qanungo narrated how Dara during his campaigns against Qandahar invoked *magic* and *miracles* for his success. Those who engaged in these activities were Hindus or Hindu pretenders. The practice was followed at all levels and fell within the framework of micro and macro consciousness links in politics. Which informed and influenced what is the issue discussed by Mukhia who said that *folk culture* influenced court culture. He said,

> 'If transference is central to the working of folk culture, it has an equal place in the functioning of the imperial court culture.'[52]

The point illustrated our position in Chapter one where we stated that politics at the micro levels through laws was determined by power. The cultural hegemony that evolved happened to percolate or go up to the court level. The veils of superstition were used by the powers that be in their own interests. This was genuine connect since the court and the folk were on the same feudal ideological format. The giving of alms was prevalent in all societies since pre-monotheism and / or paganism. The fact of pleasing pagan gods by the Greek people through, painting their bodies, performing dance, drawing colored pictures on sands to please totems with festivities were the source of subsequent developments in each society. These early forms of celebrations to propitiate totems were post tribal. In India the profane sacred and the symbols were linked to the tribal and agricultural communities from pre-Vedic and Vedic ages.

Education

The education of Dara deduced from the *education system* of his times traced since the thirteenth century and his *accomplishments* in theology and translations, interest in astronomy and fine arts, music and magic and the military campaigns. Very little was available directly about his education in formative years or during the time he spent, along with Aurangzeb, at Jahangir's court with Nur-Jahan. These were generally very significant years since the longevity of the warriors and rulers was generally short, with exceptions.

Nasiriya College, thirteenth century

The advent of the Dehli Sultanate was noted to be an inauguration of Dehli becoming the center of educated and literary world of the then Islamic civilisation. Nizami talked about the Islamic revolution in World history. This signified for him abolition of slavery and urbanisation among other things. Under urbanisation he wrote about the school, khanaqs, education and Friday Mosques.[53] All claims about equality by Nizami were negated by subsequent development of unequal Islamic societies. We are concerned about education here which was Islamic and given the early stages of feudalism incorporated trends of early flowering of science with the advent of Islam. Beginning with Iyaltimish, the Dihli Sultanate established the centers of education and welcomed and promoted intellectuals. Minhaj noted that during the reign of

> 'Sultan Raziyyat committed to the charge of this servant (the author) the Nasirryah College at the capital....'[54]

Akhlalq

During Akbar's period the fame of Abul Fazl and his elder brother Abul Fazl Faizi, was well known. Both Minhaj and Abul Fazl were historians during their times. Both were administrators in addition. In case of Fazl, he was involved in apotheosising Akbar.[55] History writing was a significant theme apart from ecclesiastical overtones. Minhaj wrote more on the entire history of the Dihli Sultanate up to the Shamsi period in contrast to Abul Fazl's work on the period of Akbar. Both histories undertook to delineate the dynastic lineage in two very different phases. By way of complexity of understanding a changing reality during the reign of Akbar Fazl's work was far more variegated and deep cutting across disciplines which were prevalent then. Fazl's work was not just a history, it was also a description and analysis of intellectual nuances, politics and culture of its times and the churning of the society that had long term effects. The memoir writing (Babur, Gul Badan Begam and Jahangir) and commissioned writing, Akbar, Shah Jahan and Aurangzeb's reigns was the process through which intellectual life was shaped and governed. The system of education was accordingly framed. These were men of Akhlalq at the top.

Nasiral Din Tusi (1235) mentioned that Akhlalq referred to maintenance [56] of harmony. Abul Fazl also mentioned men of pen and men of sword. He refered to Ghazi Khan Badakshi, an Amir who came to India from Iran in the nineteenth year of Akbar's reign. He was a Sufi, well read in the sciences under Mulla Isami, had a thorough knowledge of Sufism and a man of the sword in battle. Such men were 'great Amirs'-about seventy to hundred people during 1639-1739. Dara fit this bill even if he was defeated in the war of succession and martyred for his gnostic views for harmony among communities.

Schooling

During the Sultanate phase, curriculum was on theological studies in the two tier system of education (Maktabs) and there was private or mosque teaching where theology was emphasised. At the second level were the *madrasas*: institutions of higher learning where fee was charged. The poor were given a stipend. There were a thousand schools in Dehli.

Curriculum (thirteenth century)

During Firoz Shah Tughluq's time exegesis, jurisprudence, tradition and grammar were taught. The secular disciplines were literature, logic, mysticism, scholasticism and art of poetry. Students were trained in Calligraphy and Accountancy.

The science subjects were medicine, mathematics, and astronomy. Quite common was the training and skill in medicine with vocational practice. Yunani treatment was superimposed on indigenous medical systems.

Persian medium of instruction was introduced. Local dialect of *Hindavi* made popular by Amir Khusrau developed. In subsequent centuries it found its expression in *Urdu/Hindustani.*

Mental Culture

On the eve of Akbar's reign, Ashraf negatively commented on mental capacities of elites and people, after noting the achievements of Dihli Sultans, specially Firoz Shah Tughluq, Allaudin Khilji and Muhammad Tughluq,

> 'The life of the vast majority of common people was stereotyped and unrefined and represented a very low state of mental culture.'[57]

About the rich and the powerful he noted negative opinion of Nicolo Conti who observed the riches of the people and then said, how could it profit the observer

> '...since the people are beasts who wear them.'[58]

He commented on the intellectual culture thus

'...did not progress beyond the stage of folklore. Folksongs and ghost stories.'[59]

It was a country without charm, for Babur, despite its riches.

Education under Akbar

The Mughal system of education was available to both males and females at an early age within the precincts of the family. In-house tutors provided instructions. Other family members could study with the children of the nobles.

Higher education had the *madrasas*. The families and cities had public libraries by the sixteenth centuries. They ignored Akbar's code on education.[60] The codes were drastic innovations in their content and teaching methods. As per the codes, boys were to read books on morals, arithmetic, measurement, geometry, physiognomy, household matters, the rules of government, medicine, logic, mathematical and religious sciences, and history. When studying Sanskrit, students were to learn grammar, logic, and Patanjali's *Yoga Sutra* on Yoga philosophy. The impact of his teachings on the madrasas was not noteworthy. But the seminaries set up under the influence of Fatullah Shirazi (d. 1589) were far reaching. His work combined Greek sciences with religious sciences.[61]

During his reign history of Islam (Mongols and Timurids of Iran), the learning of Persian ethico-political works, Persian poetry, accountancy and al Ghazali's works were underlined. Abul Fazl preferred the reading of historical works to ethico-political and Sufi literature.[62] Athar Ali noted that the history that was hitherto taught was of royal dynasties but now the history practiced was that of the country, involving pride in the country as a matter of faith.[63] This new way of writing history had begun with the work of Isami, he said. Abul Fazl looked at India as a cultural and geographical unity.[64]

The reign of Akbar focused on translations of Sanskrit and Persian texts and got a building *Ibadatkhana* (dialogue-building) constructed for dialogues among spokesmen of different religious persuasions. Delvoye noted his contribution in promoting Indo-Persian and Indian music.[65]

The education system that settled as a routine by the end of the sixteenth century was in the direction of unity of India and cultural and religious synthesis of the peoples of India. These values continued till the reign of Bahadur Shah Zafar in the nineteenth century, despite the aberrations in the reigns of Jahangir and Shah Jahan and the antithesis in the form of orthodox Islamic interlude of Aurangzeb, before the British captured Bahadur Shah Zafar in 1857.

Science and Religion

The scientific paradigm available then was determined by culture-areas. The Islamic world was one connected such area. Here rationalism-Greek-Byzantine and Arabic science flowered. Yet specific areas remained unevenly developed. Many texts were translated for the benefit of Arab, Sanskrit and Persian scholars. In mathematics, medicine and literature cooperative developments had taken place. The use of sciences for religious purposes was the practice, i. e. use of science for *Zakat* and *Sidak,* or of geography in finding the direction of *Qiblah* (direction) and astronomy for working out the calendar and timings for prayers. To separate the two in both the Arab world and India was a difficult task. Among many factors that Rahman mentioned was the philosophic and theoretical framework being different in India. The Vedic logic on one hand and the Ptolemaic, the Euclidean and the Aristotelian ideas on the other became a major bloc, since both were associated with religion. The processes of assimilation and exclusion were complex and had an impact on the development of science. As a result India could not benefit from either Shiraz or Sawai Jai Singh to create an indigenous base of Indian science.[66]

During Akbar's reign Indians knew about the discovery of America. Technological ingenuity of the Firangis (foreigners) was known. European physicians had established themselves here in the seventeenth century. Bernier had noted the knowledge about the circulation of blood, but zinc and science was not known in Islam according to Abul Fazl. Dara rejected traditional sciences, rationality and focused on mysticism, astronomy, astrology and the world of magic and miracles.[67]

Dara-Mind

Dara inherited this broad paradigm of Akbar's education system and its Syncretic dynamism which had a limited though important reaches. Mulla Abdul Sultanpuri was his teacher. Dara studied *Quran*, *Persian poetry*, *history* of *Timur*, *calligraphy* and *cultivation of letter writing*. His calligraphic instructor was perhaps Abdur Rashid Dialemi. He learnt languages since he engaged in translations. Unlike the orthodox Islamists he showed interest in Greek-Arab ideas of science, rationalism and Mysticism. A Sunni and Sufi, he was a poet and collector of art, congenial and haughty, logical and superstitious, a historian of select Sufi saints' biographies and translator of Hindu texts. His mind was complex amalgam of congruent-conflictive trends.

Development of his Mental Make up

Haq noted the development of his mind from common place to the sublime. Haq stated,

'His is a mind that advances from the common place to the sublime.'[68]

The concept of sublimity has its own history. Since antiquity it was an expression of grand and noble passions, e.g. Homeric poetry and great classical tragedies. These brought into play the *emotional involvement* of both the *creator* and the *perceiver* of the work of *art*. This idea was revived in the seventeenth century undergoing changes in the subsequent centuries.[69] The idea of *ecstasy* (love) could easily be related to the Sufi core i. e. of love between the seeker and creator present in all cultures and religions. Robert Graves in his Introduction says

> 'The absorption with the theme of love leads to ecstasy, all Sufis know. But Christian mystics regard ecstasy as a union with God, and therefore the height of religious attainment, Sufis admit its value only if the devotee can afterword return to the world and live in a manner consonant with his experience.'[70]

Experience, not experiment, was significant here that started from *Initiation* (under an instructor) to adopt the Sufi path and ended with *Annihilation* merging the self into Him so that He was me and me was Him. Idries Shah mentioned about this by narrating the story of grapes.

This story showed how despite difference of languages words mean the same thing, as was pointed out by a linguist, whom he equated with a Sufi teacher and grapes' essence, i.e. wine with God's love. Grapes were different religions and their essence was the same-mingling in Him with love.[71]

Rationalism

Qanungo suggested Dara's attachment to the teachings of Plato and Aristotle.[72] In mystical teachings there was not much scope for allegory. In rationalism there was as in Plato, e.g. his allegory of the cave. It seems Dara being a part of Akbar's legacy carried this as well in his mental make-up. In order to understand Dara's mind the two values mentioned by Qanungo need elaboration. Let us look at the two aspects here, viz. *allegory* and *rationalism* and yet practiced mysticism which does not allow for allegory.

Ernst said about Dara Shukuh that he combined intellectualism with mysticism,

> 'Though born into the ruling dynasty, Dara Shikoh from an early age showed the proclivity to be an intellectual explorer and spiritual seeker....he was an accomplished scholar and author, despite his administrative and military responsibilities as crown prince and governor of several provinces.'[73]

These two descriptions pose a dilemma since both Islam and Mysticism did not permit allegory while Sufi poetry in some countries used allegory. Dara combined the two as a bold and even audacious explorer.[74]

Allegory/Simile/Mysticism

The *etymology* of allegory is both in Latin and Greek. In Greek, 'allos' means

> 'Another, different and 'agoreu' means 'to harangue, to speak in the assembly'

Originated from agrarian assembly, it was an extended metaphor. It had objects, persons and actions in a narrative. It was equated with the meanings that lie outside the narrative. The underlying meaning had moral, social, religious or political significance. It had a hidden or a symbolic meaning.

Immanuel Kant and Goethe distinguished it from symbol associating allegory with rational abstraction and symbol with the attempt to grasp the divine. The rational cannot comprehend or express the divine. To do so some scholars look for imagination (Spencer). The famous example of an allegory is that of Plato's cave. Plato focused on reason based abstraction of knowledge of Goodness through an allegory.

Classicists

Aristotle defined allegory as an extended metaphor. There are two approaches to the category of the metaphor, the classicist and the romanticist. The classicists regard it as a hindrance to understanding since it is *transference* from one domain to the other. The transference is from one field to the other, i.e. from (a) genus to the species, (b) from the species to the genus, (c) one species to another and (d) a matter of analogy. The Classicists consider language and reality to be different. Quintilian, who started the field of Rhetoric, held that transferences were the following: (a) from animate to inanimate e.g. the enemy is called the sword; (b) from the inanimate to the animate, e.g. he gave his feet the rein and (c) from the animate to the animate e.g. Scapio was barked at by Cato.

Romanticists

In contrast, the Romantics regarded it as constitutive of new reality and not just an appliqué work. Plato conveyed ideas through metaphors, e.g. of equality of women through a metaphor of the watchdog and of knowledge through the allegory of the cave. Romantics recognised a link between imaginations similitude's. Metaphors combine different processes. It was a way of experiencing and living a perceived reality.[75]

Communication

It had a functional utility in *Rhetoric.* McClelland said,

'Metaphor is a very effective means through which potential leaders can communicate with the voice "within" because it creates evocative representations of the speaker and their policies by arousing emotions and forms part of the process by which an audience reconstructs causal relationships of an argument.' [76]

16th and 17th century

In the 16th and the 17th centuries allegory was related to religious morality. It was used to transfer moral and ethical qualities onto the visible figures who accompany the main figure. In the seventeenth century *emblem* became the new allegory. It combined Christian meaning to classical myth.[77]

Allegory is a form of interpretation in all religions.[78] The teachings of scriptures were interpreted in (a) historical, implied reference to incredible statements to supposed events, in (b) the allegorical, which gave an intellectual meaning to stories which were supposed previously to have been taken as history. Lastly in (c) a spiritual meaning for the man in whom the divine light was unfolding who was neither in need of history or allegory. Being beyond the pale of mysticism allegory was also not a symbol as we noted above. In mysticism one sought an internal illumination the many-sided truth, glimpses of which have been caught by many people at different stages of evolution; and endeavoring to see the truth, in its fullness, so that all the scattered truths may be found to form a coherent whole.[79] It would then appear that both allegory and mysticism are allied to convey the totality of the spiritual light to the speaker.[80] Dara himself described his position as one committed to mysticism in the text referred to above. He was also a poet. Here came the dilemma again between mysticism and allegory. He combined metaphors, similes and allegory to put across his ingenious method to convey generic views of Sufis, Sunnis and cosmopolitanism.

Allegory in Islam

In Quran verses related to allegory were regarded as misleading and only the perverse give their own interpretation to the verses. In Islam there are clear and allegorical verses. Those who do not distinguish between the two are the *confused* and follow allegorical verses. The Islamic verses and their Sufi variants seem to be at variance. On this aspect there was no agreement.

Idries took a negative view of allegory in dealing with Sufism and considers it to be a burden of cabbage in the journey (sea) of love to Him.[81] There is some difference of opinion on this. The Arab and Sufi poetry had the forms of *Odes*, *Lyrics*, *Quatrains* and *Epic* in their Arabic set meters and themes. The Persian Sufi poetry borrowed from profane mystical poetry and subjected them to, he says,

> 'Allegorical interpretation, transformed according to rules outside the text of verses. Wine was no longer the stuff poured by Caliphs' servants but now became the intoxication of divine love.'[82]

The ideas of cup, wine and beloved underwent a change from within Arabic, Turkish and Persian poetry. They became also symbols of the Sufi teachings.

Persian Poetry and Dara

Even if one conceded that there was scanty positive evaluation of allegory in Arabic poetry, it existed in Persian poetry, as noted above. The person who discovered Persian Rubai's (quatrains) meter is Rudaki (d. 941 Ad). He was considered as the father of classical Persian Poetry. It was a four line composition with the first three lines as the preface. The fourth line reached the point of being sublime or pithy and clever.[83] They appeal to the classes and the masses giving rise to ecstasy. *Wine*, *Cup*, *Lover*, *Saqi* were used as metaphors with changing meanings in pre-Islamic, Islamist Arabic, Persian, Turkic and Indian poetry to convey the ideas of love of Him with the exception of the Pre-Islamic poetry that had the themes of war.

There had been a close link between poetry and dissemination of Sufi positions. Nizami, the Persian Sufi writes,

> 'Under the poet's tongue lies the key of the treasury.'[84]

Graves mentioned the inquisition of Ibn El-Arabi at Aleppo where he pleaded that his poems were metaphorical, the basic message being God's perfection of man through divine love.[85] His poetic name derived from the same root as the noun 'saw' and was chosen in accordance with Sufi usage. "Sawing wood" was also taken to refer to the effort which was put into the life of the Sufi, as well as production of something new (saw dust) from the material worked upon (wood).

It referred to transmutation. The allegory was of human change as flexible in other societies was attributed to alchemy and transmutation. In other words, it meant transforming man through divine love.[86]

Further we also noticd that in consonance with Dara's adherence to Islamic religious beliefs he was an experimenter, unorthodox scholar, and assimilator of different cultures. Being a Sufi meant he was an insider of the faith since Sufism is embedded therein, i. e. all religions. It was thus possible that he used various forms of aesthetic categories in his otherwise **didactic verses**[87] and not very profound written texts like Majma-Ul-Bahrain. It was in line with his work, to hold, that he did use allegory and simile for conveying abstract spiritual ideas.[88] His quatrain, randomly chosen, underlined Him. It showed the meter and also its metaphorical aspect. It ran as follows,

> 'The mystics keep going into a new state of ecstasy:
> They are leaders of religion not followers...you see?
> Lions are only eating what they have prayed for...
> What's left out in sun the fox eats, unthinkingly'[89]

Dara's unwavering search for Him led him to identification of truth in all religions at one level i.e. syncretism and he looked for values of loyalty in his own demeanor.

Rationalism

It focused on deduction as a method of arriving at knowledge. It ignored focuses on experience and induction. It assumed a-priori the existence of an idea-God, Good, Form, Spirit- and deduced the real which was but a carbon copy of the abstract idea. Its representatives in the seventeenth century were Descartes, Spinoza, and Leibniz. In theology rationalism was a trend according to which only those dogmas of faith were acceptable which the mind considered to be in conformity with logic and the natural light of the intellect.[90] In Dara's quatrains there were innumerable examples of shadows of reality that were part of the ocean of divine knowledge. At one place he said,

> 'Things other than He have their existence of God is like boundless ocean-Men are like forms and waves in its water.'

Loyalty

Alongside his literary quality he shared the value of loyalty common with Muslim rulers of India since the Slave system of the Dihli Sultanate. In the Dihli Sultanate a slave could rise to the position of an Amir (noble), even to the position of a successor of a King. The Mughal period was replete with emphasis on loyalty of the family (independent of filial ties), friends and collaborators in political, military and personal matters. This was of utmost importance to all Emperors who recognised and profusely rewarded it with gifts, positions and promotions. Many practices were developed during the Mughal rule.

Sense of loyalty could be gauged by a brief account of the happenings since Babur's time. Thrown into a cauldron of intrigue and power play after the assassination of his father, Omar Shaikh Mirza and educated by his mother, Qultuq Nigar Khanum and her mother Aisan Daulat Begum, he took to the sword at the age of eleven, he was a man of high degree of loyalty. On an advice to betray his near and dear ones, on one occasion, he said,

> '(It) was not my habit to cheat and play false. After making promises how was I to break them?'[91]

Instead of betrayal, he chose alliances with Safavi ruler. The most significant example of rewarding loyalty came at Agrah in 1528 A. D. Dilip Hiro noted that at the grandest feast of his reign in Agrah Babur invited the tribal leaders in the Kabul region who had given him sorely needed refuge a quarter century earlier, and rewarded them generously.[92]

Annette S. Beveridge, otherwise critical of Humayun's fidelity to women, observed on his sense of loyalty in the context of conflict among sons of Babur-Humayun, Kamran, Hindal, Askari during the period of Humayun's escape from India as a fugitive,

> 'Humayun was urged to put further mischief out of Kamran's power by his death. He refused a refusal which would be upheld in the haram, ever faithful to the injunctions of Babur, and knowing these better than the real risks caused by Kamran's disloyalty. Penetrating everything was the irritation aroused by Kamran's opposition to the royal march for Kabul,-irritation which diffused itself and barely missed the sequel of bloodshed.'[93]

During Akbar's times his team that upheld court culture, his faithful historian like Abul Fazl and his collaborators among Rajput Kings proved of mutual loyalty. His adherence to the treaty with the Portuguese (despite their piracy) in Goa and Surat, with regard to sea trade show this in respect of foreign powers. In his Memoirs Jahangir noted many personal episodes of this strong sense of loyalty that Akbar had and engendered among others. In his own reign Jahangir gave evidence of the premium he put on loyalty. His Memoirs began with his birth, and go on to detail his ordinances followed by the appointments he retained from the nobility of his father. One of the significant part of that nobility were the Rajput families. His description of loyalty and the Rajput shows up his sense of justice and magnanimity. He narrated,

> 'As the reality of the loyalty of my father's servants had not yet become apparent, and certain faults and errors and unbecoming intentions which were not approved at the throne of the Creator or pleasing to His creatures had shown themselves, they of themselves became ashamed. Though on the day of my accession I had for given all offences and determined with myself that I would exact no retribution of the past deeds.'

He further mentioned the services of the family of Amiru-I-Umara, his guardian and protector, and of Raja Man Singh. Man Singh's grandfather (Raja Bihar Lal, father Raja Bhagwan Das) he praised for loyalty during the early Phase of Akbar's reign. And Raja Man Singh's brother's son, Madho Singh. He described the Rajputs as the confidential servants of his father.[94] Shah Jahan's reign was full of nuggets about his contribution to Indo-Muslim architecture and the making of the Peacock Throne. Therein lay his loyalty to his deceased wife Mumtaz Mahal. Taj Mahal, now known as the wonder of the world, was Shah Jahan's, otherwise not known for fidelity to women, contribution to architecture and a symbol of his memory of his wife.

Much of the texts by Hamid Lahori and Inayat Khan (in their abridged form) about his reign do not tell us much about his attitude and loyalty to his allies. They do refer to the two gems of his reign, namely the Taj Mahal and the Peacock Throne, his love for Dara Shukuh whom he had given the title of Shah Buland Iqbal. During Dara's flight as a fugitive from Agrah to Lahor and Multan after his defeat at

Samugarh Shah Jahan had helped him with treasure and soldiers (from Dihli's treasury) during the war for succession. Love of the first born had kept him next to Shah Jahan in the Imperial Court. His throne was always on the right side while that of Aurangzeb was on the left side of the Emperor's throne when attending the Court. He was inclined towards Dara Shukuh by all accounts and surely as one in Aurangzeb's hostile perception.

The punitive actions visited revolting sons. Shah Jahan, who was part of the Junta under Nur Jahan during 1611-1620,[95] after he turned against her and his father was called Bi-daulat. As a surety of his loyal behavior, after his defeat, he sent his two sons, Dara and Aurangzeb in their childhood, to Nur Jahan's care. His other son Shah Shuja was already under Nur Jahan's care. Jahangir noted Shah Jahan's mischief with regard to Nur Jahan's fiefs. It was only much later when Shah Jahan's enthronement was inevitable (in the wake of Jahangir's imprisonment and death) that he was able to get his sons back, with the help of Mahabat Khan (Nur Jahan's brother). Akbar was with Maryam Makani at Kabul with Kamran when Humayun and Kamran were fighting it out amongst themselves. The role of Maryam Makani saved Akbar during Humayun's siege of Kamran's fort.

Loyalty to Factions

Loyalty was highly valued and frequently defiled during that period. Dara was no exception to this practice of blood being thinner than sinews of politics of power and succession. He was more a victim of this practice. There was no record of the period of the growing up of the formative years of the three brothers at Jahangir's haram. Ruchir Gupta maintained in his fictional account of Jahanara that Aurangzeb grew up under the Islamic influence of Nur Jahan while Dara was allowed a more liberal atmosphere. As we had mentioned earlier the reliability of this interpretation of their formative years is as good as Gupta's fiction.[96] There was however no doubt that Dara valued Jahanara's loyalty and Aurangzeb depended on Roushanara. There was partisan atmosphere among these four. If one extended this to the political field within the patron-client relationship of the Mughal Courts there were political parties.[97] His other brothers were Murad Baksh (b.1624-1662) and Shah Shuja (1616-1660). All the three had turbulent dispositions, hated each other, entertained ambitions to be rulers, and were Governors of different Provinces. All of them maintained independent armies and were capable of declaring their principalities independent.[98] Both Murad Baksh and Shah Shuja became allies of Aurangzeb owing to his deceit. Both of them were let down by the latter and killed.

Dara's sense of loyalty and fair play

The sense of loyalty made him do unprecedented things like making Raja Rup Singh drink the water with which his wife had washed her breasts since she could not deliver milk any more. At the time when Aurangzeb was the governor in Punjab on the former's request for a transfer to the diamond rich Dakhyn, Dara interceded with his father to transfer his younger brother there. Shah Jahan had agreed to that. On one occasion impressed by the loyalty of Manucci he promised him to get a Church constructed if he came to power. He supported his sister in personal matters. Manucci also benefitted in other ways too.[99] At one stage owing to his liberal attitude he made Shah Jahan restore a Hindu temple that had been destroyed on the latter's instance.

Both at the personal and the intellectual level he evinced a cultivated mind with a broad outlook, free of intrigue, ready to explore within the dominant paradigm of his age. The necessity of his age, since Babur's victory over Samarkand and then India, was syncretism and continued to be so for the next four centuries. In this regard he was considered to be the enunciator of Akbar's embryonic vision of Din-i-Illahi.[100] Despite the fact that he was narrowly local and dated, his mental make-up, determined by the dominant ideology of his times, produced results that proved to have longevity surpassing the end of the empire and colonialism into free India. It is his sense of curiosity and experiment that made him look for monotheism in Islam and Upanishads though of Sunni identity which he never gave up and combined his birth marks with Sufi wisdom, described as source of Freethinking/Masonry.[101]

Marriage and Family

Qanungo mentioned two wives of Dara, while Manucci mentioned three. The first wife of Dara Shukuh, Nadira Begam, originally named as Karim-un-nisa, matched in beauty with Mumtaz Mahal, was his first wedded wife and gave him all his children. She was his late mother's niece and daughter of Shah Jahan's half-brother, Parviz. He had set his eyes on her in Meena Bazar. It was like history repeating itself. Jahangir had also set his eyes and heart on Nur Jahan at Meena bazaar. Nadira had medium height, green eyes and serene temperament. He married her two years later.

His elder sister and close associate, Jahanara, resumed the organisation of the wedding ceremony, after Shah Jahan assumed the throne. He personally participated in these ceremonies enjoying hospitality at Dara's house, attending mehndi in the Court and partaking in the music that he permitted to be played on the occasion. The mood of gaiety was charged with damsels putting the red color on the hands of the luminaries and tying them with a golden embroidered handkerchief. Gifts to the bride were sent and they amounted to about two lakhs.

Dara mounted a charger, accompanied by his three younger brothers and female relatives of Mumtaz Mahal, he proceeded in a procession from his house to the Court which was the venue of his marriage. This must be an unusual procession for a Crown Prince belonging to the Sunni family. An orthodox Mulla by the name of Qazi Muhammad Islam performed the ceremonies. The kabin of the bride was five lakhs. A total of thirty two lakhs of rupees were spent with half the amount being contributed by Jahanara. Dara must have been quite an attractive sight on this day. He had sharp features, was wearing the same sehara that Shah Jahan had been made to wear by Jahangir, and his neck and chest being adorned by a pearl necklace given by Shah Jahan, His hands red with henna, or 'mehendi.'[102]

Ranadil and Udepuri

Ranadil, a dancing girl was his other wife, and was very loyal to him. Manucci narrated a story about her loyalty to Dara. After the latter's death Aurangzeb wanted to marry her. She asked the reason for it. He said he liked her hair. In response, she removed her hair and got them sent to Aurangzeb. Again the latter asked for her and again on being asked the reason for it, he said he liked her face. She slashed her face, collected the blood and then sent it to him to enjoy her face. Thereafter Aurangzeb made no effort. Dara's third wife was an Uzbek woman, called Udepuri, a Georgian by race, who married Aurangzeb, and gave a son by the name of Prince Kam Baksh.[103] It is possible that

Dara had other promiscuous relationships if one went by the fact that he had had a girl, called Guf Safa, who was his friend, as mentioned earlier in this chapter. The other reason to mention this aspect of comfort of other women is the character of Shah Jahan who liaised with his nobles' wives to disastrous effects for Dara. We describe this later when dealing with Dara's battlefield let downs by his associates.

Love for Nadira Banu

Dara's love for Nadira Begam, his first wedded wife was well known, and was in line with the Mughal Emperors' love of their first wives. Like Mumtaz Mahal, Nadira Begam never left Dara's side and travelled with him in happy and unhappy parts of his journey. Three episodes stand out about his loyalty to her. One, he had got an album of paintings and his own calligraphy for his wife as a present. This was just love sublime. This album is in the British Museum and is reported to be badly maintained and in many of the paintings his signatures erased. On her death, owing to a wound and stomach ailment that she contracted during his flight to Punjab after his defeat at Samugarh, he was grief stricken and for days he was inconsolable. Third as per her desire, she was buried in India, i.e. in Lahor.

Children

Dara's children were three sons and five daughters. First, fourth, fifth, seventh and eight were daughters and second, third and sixth were his sons. The sons were Suleiman Shukuh, Mihir Shukuh (born July 4, 1638 and passed away within three months), and Siphir Shukuh (born October3, 1644). The first daughter died in a few months after her birth (nineteenth January, 1634).The fourth daughter was Pak-Nihad Banu Begum (Jani Begam mentioned by Manucci) was born on 26 August, 1643. The third was Mumtaz Shukuh, born October 3, 1644, the 7th child was Jahanzeb Banu and the last was Amal-u-nisa. Qanungo mentioned that their dates of birth were difficult to ascertain owing to confusion of names and the lack of records of their births in various Shahnamas/Padshahnama. We have deal with Sulaiman and Siphir later for the valiant role of Suleiman in the war of succession and the latter's tragic separation from Dara Shukuh.

Dara was a representative of the ideas of his times in practice and articulation. The predominance of ideas was determined by the powers that be since ruling ideas were the ideas of the ruling class. The system of symbols, rituals, practices, beliefs and signs at the organised and the discursive level were products of their times. They coloured that power and society. These ideas were a cementing factor and produced divisive actions. Since the thirteenth century the ruling ideas as cementing factor increasingly gained in strength from their fledgling emergence.

The predominant racial divisiveness within Islamic identity had its other in the Sufi co-mingling within and Hindu world view without. By Akbar's time the ethnic rivalry and scientific disposition of the Ptolemaic and Avicenna's rationalism within the feudal society increasingly played a role to cement the society as against its divisive propensities in orthodox Islam and Hinduism. The religio-rationalist paradigm determined the social consciousness as well as dominant ideological movement. Astronomy, astrology, magic, miracles, numerology, divinity, mysticism, meditation, medicine, sense of loyalty, ideas of kinship and kingship, matchlocks, knowledge of ship building the Persian wheel were part of this ideology.

The camp-court culture and the popular culture started to find common ground in the liberal Sufi-Bhakti movements (a trend started by Amir Khusrau in the thirteenth century with Hindavi) on the one hand and the reaction against it in Islamic bigotry of a Sunni Maulvi, orthodox Naqshbandi Sufi identity of an Aurangzeb. Any ideology has two dimensions. One, the cementing and the other that created cracks.[104] Dara the man of Akhlalq represented the man of the pen and the man on the horseback, even if defeated by the deceit of friends and foes but not by lack of military valour. He was the man of Akhlalq with a vision of cementing society. His discriminating sense of justice even in war was represented by the slogan he gave during the civil war against his younger brother:

> "To the Humble, pardon, to the haughty, death."[105]

In contrast Aurangzeb's war cry was

> "I will lose my own, or take my adversary's."[106]

For all practical purposes his entire life showed the predominant ideology of the times and his vision became a victim of the other part of the ideological contradiction, namely bigotry of Aurangzeb whose rule saw the geographical expansion of the empire but the weakening of the roots of the *Mughal* rule despite his long reign. Dara's life journey reflected the Janus face of his times: liberal religious trend and orthodox religious bigotry. He articulated the first and was lost out to the second. One was the emerging ideology to unite and homogenise the other was to assert previous times and denigrate the new within. Usually Dara Shukuh was negatively viewed as a horse man. That was too narrow a view. He was a writer warrior on a ship hemmed by the ill practices of the drift wood of destiny of his country.

End Notes

1. In similar astronomical and astrological terms Aurangzeb's birth, the sixth child of Mumtaz Mahal, was so noted,' ...in the thirteenth year from my accession, corresponding with the fifteenth Zi-l-Qa'da of the Hijri year 1027, in the nineteenth degree of Libra, the Giver of blessings gave my prosperous son Shah-Jahan a precious son.... I hope that his advent may be auspicious and blessed to this everlasting state'. *Ibid.* Vol. 1, p. 282; Vol. 2, p. 47.The date of birth was 20-10-1618. The fourth child was Muhammad Shah Shuja and the tenth son was Murad Baksh. Abdul Hamid Lahori, op. cit. p. 29.
2. Niccol Machiavelli used the expression Centaur to describe politics in his book Modern Prince. The feudal politics was surely almost literally centaur like, with Man being on the horse back. Nicole Machiavelli, Prince.
3. op. cit., pp. 19-20.
4. *Ibid.*
5. See Chapter 1.
6. Gul-Badan Begam, op. cit. pp. 88-89.
7. *Ibid.* p. 90.
8. Ruchir Gupta, The Mughal Intrigues, The Mistress of the Throne, Shristi Publications, New Dihli, 2014.
9. Annette S. Beveridge, 'Introduction', op. cit. p. 70.
10. Harbans Mukhia, The Mughals of India, Wiley-Blackwell, September, 2004.
11. Tuzuk i, op. cit. Vol 1, p. 36.
12. *Ibid.* Vol. 1, p. 32
13. Waldemar Hansen, op. cit. p. 288.
14. Gul-Badan Begam, op. cit. pp. 116-119
15. Tuzuk i , op. cit. vol. 1, p. 130
16. Andreai Tarkovsky, Seulpting in time - Tarkovsky, the great Russian film maker discussed his art.

17. Leah Kinberg,' Afterlife', in Josef W. Meri, editor, Medieval Islamic Civilisation, An Encyclopaedia, Vol. 1, A-K, Index, Routledge, Taylor and Francis Group, New York and London, eBooks.
17. Marc Bloch, op. cit.loc. 2240, e-book's.
18. Bloch quotea nineth century text, by Rabanus Marus, who wrote in his treatise that enjoyed a long time popularity, 'I conceived the idea of comprising a little work..., which should treat, not only of nature of things and the properties of words...but still more their mystic meanings.' Ibid. Loc 2160.
19. See Bikrama Jit Hasrat, Dara Shikuh, Life and Works, Munshiram Manoharlal Publishers Pvt. Ltd. New Dihli, 2014. P. 2; Kalinga Ranjan Qanungo, Dara Shukoh, Vol. 1, Biography, Calcutta, 1952, pp. 1-2. Both of them refer to the history of Shah Jahan's reign, Padshahnama. Vincent A, Smith described him as having unorthodox views of pantheistic mysticism in Gopal Gandhi, Dara Shukoh, A Play, Preface, Tranquebar, New Dihli, p. viii.
20. 'Quoted in M. Hahfuz-Ul-Haq, M. A. Introduction, *MAJMA-UL-BAHRAIN or The Mingling of the Two oceans*, The Asiatic Society, Calcutta, p. 5.
21. 'Bikrama Jit Hasrat, op.cit. p. 116.
22. Fn. 21, pp. 40-41.
23. *Ibid*, p. 152.
24. *Ibid*, p. 98.
25. *Ibid,* p. 28.
26. Abul-Fazl, op cit., p. 70.
27. Quoted in ibid. p. 77.
28. Nicolao Manucci, *Storia Do Mogor or Mughal India, 1653-1708, vol. 1,* transl. and notes by William Irwine, Indian edition, Calcutta, 1965, pp. 213-215.
29. Francois Bernier, op cit, P. 16.
30. Niccolao Manucci, op. cit.213
31. Muhammad Kazim, *Alamgir-Namah,* in Elliot and Dawson, History of India *By Its Own Historians, Vol. 1* and 2,*letters as nam pp. 178-179.
32. Bikrama Jit Hasrat, op. cit. p. 91-93.
33. Kalinga Ranjan Qanungo, op.cit. p. 387.
34. Loc. cit.
35. op. cit. p. 75.
36. Paul Smith, Introduction and translation, Dara Shikoh, Life and Poems, New Humanity Books, Victoria, Australia, 2014. p. 21.
37. *Loc. cit.*
38. Edmund Burke, The Annual Register of World Events: A Review of The Year, Volume 57, England, p. 460.

39. Robert Graves, 'Introduction', Idries Shah, The Sufis, Anchor Books, New York, 1971, pp. vii-xix.
40. Gul-Badan Begam, op. cit. pp.113-114. Here the author talked about festivities in the tents decorated with brocades from Europe, from inside, Portuguese cloth was outside, the tents were of Gujarati cloth-of-gold, evers of rose water, and candlesticks, and drinking-vessels, and rose water sprinklers- all of jeweled gold. The practice of decorating bazaars and houses was very old. 'There was a problem of accuracy here. Minhaz noted these during the time of Iyaltimish. He said, 'The city was decorated for this occasion....' The note to this line adds 'When inhabitants of this city are ordered to decorate their houses on the occasion of rejoicings, as such as indicated above, the trades people, in particular, deck out their shops by hanging out rich shawls, brocades, fine dresses, all kinds of costly articles of merchandise, and even the ornaments and trinkets of their women. Lamps and flags, attached to cords, are drawn across the streets, and the doors and lower parts of private dwellings painted in the gayest colours procurable." Domes and arches were also erected. Tabakat-i-Nasiri op. cit. p. 616. Gul – Badan Begam's account showed a possible ignorance of this practice of decoration of bazars in the 13th century.
41. Tuzuki, op. cit. p. 306.
42. *Ibid.*
43. Muhammad Kazim, op cit, pp. 13-14.
44. *Ibid.*
45. Bikrama Jit Hasrat said that Dara mentioned it in his first exercise as an exemplar, i.e. (Safinat-ul- Awliya).
46. Marc Bloch, op. cit. Vol. 1&2, pp. 2680-94.
47. Abul Fazl, op. cit. Transl. Thackston, op. cit. pp. 566-67.
48. Tuzuk-i-Jahangiri, op. cit. Vol. 2, p. 45.
49. *Ibid.*
50. Gracin de Tassy transl. and edited by M. Waseem, OUP, 1997, pp. 102-103. The author tells us that the tomb is not with any solar or lunar fete.
51. Harbans Mukhia, op. cit. p. 163.
52. Nizami, op. cit.
53. MAULANA, MINHAJ–UD-DIN ABU-UMAR-I-USMAN, Vol. 1, Oriental Books, p. 644.
54. Wheeler M. Thackston, Introduction, op. cit. p.ix
55. Stephen P. Blake, op. cit. pp. 148-149.
56. K. M. Ashraf, op. cit., p. 275.
57. Loc. cit.
58. K. M. Ashraf, *ibid.*

59. SAA Rizvi, op. cit. p. 218.
60. SAA Rizvi, loc. Cit.
61. *Ibid.* p. 219.
62. Athar Ali, in, Irfan Habib, edited, *Akbar and His Times*, op. cit. pp. 218-219.
63. *Ibid.* p. 221.
64. Francoise 'Nalini' Delvoye, 'The image of Akbar as a Patron of Music in Indo-Persian and Ver He was religionist-secularist, mystic-rationalist, Secular Sources, in Irfan Habib, *ibid.* p. 214.
65. A. Rahman, '*A perspective of Indian Science Of Tenth-Eighteenth Centuries*', in Science Philosophy, and Culture-Multi Disciplinary Explorations, edited by D. P. Chattopadhyay and Ravindra Kumar, New Dihli, PHIS PC, 1996 pp. 396-426.
66. Athar Ali, *Towards An Interpretation of The Mughal Empire,* Herman Kulke, op. cit. p. 276.
67. M. Mahfuz-Ul-Haq, M. A., *Majma-Ul-Bahrain or The Mingling of Two Oceans* By Dara Shikuh, Asiatic Society, Calcutta, Reprinted, 1982, p. 5.
68. Umberto Eco, Ed. *On Beauty, A History of Western Idea.* translated from Italian, Alastair McEwen, Machlehose press, London,2004, p. 278.
69. Idries Shah, Sufis Introduction by Robert Graves, Anchor Books, A Division Of Random House, New York, 1971. p. xiii-xiv.
70. Idries Shah, pp. 24-25.
71. op. cit. 4-6.
72. Scott Kugle, edited by, Sufi Meditation and Contemplation, Timeless Wisdom from Mughal India, transl. by Scott Kugle with Carl Ernst, Preface by Syed Mohammad Rasheed-ul-Hasan Kaleemi, Suluk Press, Omega Publications, New Lebanon, New York, 2012. P. EBooks, 14 per cent.
73. Loc. Cit.
74. Terence Hawks, *Metaphor*, General Editor, John D. Jump, Methuen, London, 1972.
75. J. S. McClelland, *The Crowd and the Mob, From Plato to Canetti*, Unwin Hyman, London, 1989, p. 11.
76. Jane K, Brown, *The Persistence of Allegory, Drama and Neoclassicism from Shakespeare to Wagner*, University of Pennsylvania Press, Pennsylvania, 2007.
77. Annie Besant, op. cit. p. 78 per cent kindle books
78. *Ibid.* p. 80 per cent kindle books
79. Fn 74.
80. Idries Shah op. cit. p. 11.
81. Carl W. Ernest, Ph. D, *Sufism, The Shambala Guide*, South Asia Editions, Rupa, New Dihli, 2000. p. 157.

82. Paul Smith, op.cit. pp. 35-37.
83. Quoted by Robert Graves, op. cit. p. x.
84. Loc. Cit.
85. *Ibid.* p. 435.
86. Bikrama Jit Hasrat, op. cit. p. 135.
87. To recapitulate an allegory is a representation of an abstract or spiritual meaning through concrete or material forms; figurative treatment of one subject under the guise of another. This style is evident in Dara's writing.
88. Paul Smith, op. cit. p. 57.
89. M. Rosenthal and P. Yudin, edited by, *A Dictionary of Philosophy*, Progress Publishers, Moscow, 1967, pp. 378-79.
90. Dilip Hiro, op. cit. p. xxix.
91. *Ibid.* p. xxx.
92. Introduction, Humayun Nama, op., cit. , p. 33.
93. Tuzuk-I Jahangiri, pp. 14-17.
94. Ellison Banks Findly, op. cit, pp. 43-62.
95. Ruchir Gupta, op.cit.
96. Kalinga Ranjan Qanungo, op. cit.
97. Niccolao Manucci, op. cit. pp. 15-15.
98. Niccolao Manucci, ibid. p. 295.
99. Dr. Roma Chaudhuri, Introduction, A critical Study of Dara Shikoh's "Samudra Samagam", Institute of Oriental Study, Calcutta, 1954. p. 4.
100. Robert Graves, op. cit.
101. Kalinga Ranjan Qanungo, op. cit. pp. 12-15.
102. Niccolao Manucci, op. cit. p. 343.
103. Goran Therborn, *The Ideology of Power and the Power of Ideology*, Verso editions and NLB, London, 1980, p. 7.
104. Niccolao Manucci, op. cit. p. 256.
105. *Ibid.* p. 253.

Chapter - 3

Qadiri Scholar

Sect

In a thousand years history of Sufism (starting with the five companions of Prophet Muhammad in the Madina Mosque) Dara Shukuh came practically after seven hundred years of its history in India, with the identity of a voice from the Qadiri Silsila (Order) that merged with the Chisti Silsila much after his life time. So enamored was he of the Qadiri silsila that he assumed his *nom deplume or pen name* to be *Qadiri* when he composed his *ruba'i's* or *quatrains*. The symbol of Qadiris was Rose of Green and White cloth with six point star in the middle made into a cap that was worn by Qadiri dervishes. Robes of black felt were also customary. It was widespread in India, though was one among many sects of Sufism.

Sufism was born of plural influences from abroad (Arab-Turkic, Persian and Central Asian) in addition to the influences in India of the Bhakti movement. Bhakti movement was not a mass movement. It had conservative and radical trends and could be traced back to Mahayana Buddhism. It inspired people to fight against tyranny in Punjab; in the Dakhyn it supported caste system.

By the fifteenth century it reached its zenith with Kabir and his popular monotheism and popular *Vaishnavism,* upholding the worship of Ram and Krishna in the first half of the sixteenth century. He was a new mystic. Tara Chand listed seventeen sects who substantiated the same doctrines as Kabir's doctrines.[1]

Between the seventh and the fifteenth centuries Bhakti movement arose in North India owing to the decline of the State, economic setback, alienation of land to the Brahmans and Rajputs, and arose in the backdrop of the local heterodox movements of dissidence as the spread of Tantrism and Shakti movements, rise of *Nathpanthis* in UP, Nepal, and Bihar, and the growth of *Sidhas* and *Yogis*. The emergence of the Dihli Sultanate produced Amir Khusrau (born in India) in this tradition. It was a multiclass movement assuming conservative stance during Akbar's time owing to the zamindars.[2] It helped in developing music, dance, painting and sculpture and love of God through devotion-a dominant trend in mystic thought whether Sufi or freemasonry springing from other faiths.

Sufism promoted *syncretism*. Sufism, like Islam, could not be painted with a broad brush in a single framework. It was like calligraphy-smaller strokes even though both Islam and Sufism spread across the large canvas of the three kingdoms of Caliphs, Safavis (Persian dynasty) and the Mughals. The beauty of it lay in the specific smaller, sometimes miniscule strokes to understand the two broad swathes of identity and ideology in Islam cutting across other religions as well. There were at least thirty three sects of Sufism[3] in India by the sixteenth century.

Sunni and Shia

Islam had the predominant sect of Sunnis (followers of the Path) and a minority sect Shia who were followers of His Holy Self Prophet Muhammad. The twins of Islam and Sufism have had many sects with peculiarities of each in terms of content, codes, orientations, message, practices, preachers, institutions, support systems and way of life. The political community of Islam had two sects, viz, Sunnis and Shias owing to differences of interpretations over the *Hadis* or (corpus of traditions) about Prophet Muhammad's sayings and doings. Their views on traditions differ as to their doctrines upon the succession and on His sayings and doings.[4] Sunnis[5] were and continue in majority in India who did not believe that He appointed any successor to him. The Shia's[6] were spread all over, especially in Bijapur and Golconda.

Islam's culture was challenged without getting overtaken for the Sufi and other mystical thoughts always came to its rescue in the face of dogmatic preaching since mysticism was based on Quran and its traditions as well.[7] Quran itself is an extended metaphor with a mystical touch. Sufis differentiated the teachings of the Prophet and the Book. Mysticism meant *interiorisation* in the rites of worship, Prophet himself used to retire to the cave of Hira to meditate for a certain period of time every year. Some seventy people lived in the mosque of the Prophet (called Ahle Suffa) and prayed day and night during his life time. They had no early attachments or worldly engagements. The Sufi dictum began 'Look into the mirror of the heart for there is no book better than this.'[8]

There were **three stages** of the growth of the movement. These were period of Quietists (661 AD to 850 AD). There were individual Sufis. They were Imam Basari, (720), Ibrahim B. Adham (777), Abu Hashim (777), and female Sufi Rabia Basari (776). These were followed by sects based on special topics in Arabic. By the twelfth century there were twelve sects. They had introduced pantheism. The **second stage** was the period of mystic philosophy from Ghazzali (111AD) to Rumi (1273), who gave complete philosophy of mysticism. Owing to the unsettled conditions in Baghdad **third stage** was marked by setting up of Silsilas (Orders) preaching charity and philanthropy. Among these were the Chisti, the Suhrawardi, Sattarri, Naqshabandi, and Al Fathur Rabbani's Silsilas. They came into India only in the twelfth century. The last one came by the seventeenth century.

Sufis

There were four epochs of Sufism. One that began with Muhammad implying, *zikr,* fasting and prayer. Second implied intuitive insights and intense spiritual experiences. Third, Spiritual tawajjuh (telepathy) overcame worldly constraints and four stages of descent of the necessary Being, i.e. essence of primal Being, unity of God, sphere of finite forms, similitude of Angelic forms and bodies of physical world. Edmund Burke made an observation on plurality of Sufi sects. He said,

> 'The Soofees are divided into innumerable sects, as must be the case in a doctrine which may be termed the belief of the imagination.'

Etymology and Concept

Different sources point to different etymology of the word Sufi. In Arabic *Suf* meant wool and referred to the woolen garments of the mystics. The word Sufi meant in Arabic tajawwuf meaning 'the process of becoming a Sufi." In Greek it referred to the word Sophos meaning wise man. The main formulator of this concept was Abu Abd al-Rahman al-Sulami (d.1021) from Iran. The word was after Prophet Muhammad, to reflect on the increasing specialisation of Muslim religious vocations. Ansari (1089) who translated Sulami's biographical work pointed out that the first person who bore the name Sufi was a Syrian named Abu Hashim al-Sufi (d. 767) and added that he was preceded by many ascetics trusting God and the path of love.[9]

Sufism as Freemasonry

Robert Graves expanded the scope of Sufism to all religions. It was spiritual freemasonry for him. He did not even consider Sufism to be a sect for they has no city, no monastic organisation, and no religious instruments. 'We friends' or 'people like us' is what they call themselves recognising each other by certain natural gifts, habits, qualities of thought. Significantly he traced it back to the second millennium B.C. Sufis had their maximum impact during the eight and the eighteenth centuries. It had gained an oriental flavor owing to its link with Islam. A natural Sufi whether in the West or the East may come as a general, a peasant, a merchant, a lawyer, a school master, a housewife, anything.' He was 'to be in the world, but not of it. They promoted social harmony'.[10]

In Central Asia

In Central Asia, Khwaja Yusuf al-Hamadani (1048-1140) was the initiator of the Sufi tradition with his two books, namely, 'Stations and Travelers' and 'Stations of Wayfarers'. His basic position was all human beings have shared the intimacy of God's presence and have been born witness to God's lordship before their creation, and each must now strive to remember the resonance of that moment, which forms the basis of faith. This is the goal of Zikr or (meditation).[11] They recognise the role of the Path in attaining mystic knowledge.

Special quality

The special quality of the Sufi sects was that they were not sectarian, despite their nuanced differences. A follower of a Sufi sect could adopt another sect and its practices. The key to the sects was the initiator or teacher or Pir or Khwaja or preceptor. The smaller Sufi sects were numerous and went to the roots of the land they were in. They became the voice of the people and their travails. So, the high priest needed the Sufi even if he derided him for debasing religions. Annie Besant's analysis of mysticism's contribution upholds their value for the existence of the official priesthood.

Elements

- The earliest Sufi settler in India was Hujwiri, also known as Data Ganj Baksh (d. 1088) and author of celebrated manual of Sufism entitled Kashful Mahjub.
- It believed in the principle of Islam being *exoteric*. It underlined individual's aim to realize in his living personal experience the living presence of God.
- Sufis transformed from retired exiled life into a corporate system of their own ideas and practices borrowed from Christianity, Buddhism, Neo Platonism and Upanishadic concepts. Different influences were incorporated into Islam so that these influences became part of Muslim life.
- Most early authentic text was Risala (Epistle) of Abul Qasim Al-Qushairi (d. 1074).
- Change in the life of Abu Hamid Ghazali (1095) who left the Nizamiya Academy of Baghdad influenced the development of Sufi life and message.
- The influence of poetry shaped Sufism.
- In the twelfth century Sufis were divided into Silsilas (orders), each with its Pir (preceptor), also known as Shaikh or Khwaja, as an infallible guide.
- The process of acquiring knowledge was to have a Pir as a teacher with whose help you practiced Mysticism, Meditation and Mediation. The aim of the Sufi was to move from the direction of initiation, then reach the stage of light of the soul

and the world of nature and finally reaching a point of zero or merging with the divine. This point was called annihilation the completion of the process that began with initiation.

- The Pirs established Khanaqs (hospice) for Sufi mendicants, travellers, prayers, followers, and lived either with or without State patronage. Most of these khanaqs initially were set up near the poor inhabitants in the rural settings. All people of different religious persuasions were permitted. The rules of pollution and purity in serving of water and food, housing and shelter were followed depending on the individual's identity.
- Networks of Khanaqs were set up in Central Asia, Iran and India.
- In Central Asia the Sufis had no belief in being and becoming, no belief in contradictions, focused on changing perception through love and ecstasy, annihilate (fana) one self and die daily death to be immortal. Their belief was in non-existence of the physical world in the Sufis of the north (Aryan and Turanian sages in Transoxiana, Khurasan, Iran, and Azerbaijan). The Southerners (Iraq, Syria, Arabia, and Africa) focused on secondary notions like existential monism, union and love manifestations and visions, unification and so on.[12] These spiritual dynasties lasted for five centuries.
- In Mughal India, as per Scot,[13] the Sufis began with a verse from Quran: "Remember God, that I may remember you." Memory was practiced through Zikr or Dhikr. This led to meditation and contemplation and antidote of the Sufis for self-righteousness, which was the sickness of most often spread by religious institutions. Religious institutions taught hypocrisy, self-righteousness, fanaticism and the pious condemnation of others.
- Three major categories of Sufi works were *hagiographical*, *discourses of teachers* and *letters of masters*. Other manuals described code of conduct as adab.
- There were three timeless Sufi texts of the Mughal period by Shaykh Khalimullah, second by Dara Shukuh, and the third attributed to Chisti, The first had an interesting title Alms Bowl,

The second The Compass of Truth, and the third treatise of Human Body. All of them gave interesting metaphors.

- All three of these upheld the values of *Mysticism*, *Meditation* and *Mediation*. They followed the path set by the Pir, and the philosophy of initiation to annihilation covering different stages of consciousness of the Holy One.[14]
- Mysticism meant direct knowledge, not based on experiment which was external to an individual. Rather it was knowledge based on inner realisation or experience, the knowledge of the spiritual world which was reproduction of the spirit of man. This was in Christianity, Hinduism and all other religions.[15]
- All Sufis knew that love leed to ecstasy. Christian mystics regarded ecstasy as a union with God, and therefore the height of religious attainment, Sufis admited its value only if the devotee could afterward return to the world and live in a manner consonant with his experience. Western literature recognised the role of love for spiritual tempering under the influence of many Spanish Arabs.[16]
- The Sufi movement despite its peculiarity was cosmopolitan and specific in its methods to unite with divinity.

Soofee *doctrine*-Burke, 1815

Sufi doctrine

'teaches that there are four stages through which man must pass before he can reach the highest, or that of divine beatitude; when to use their own language "his corporeal veil will be removed, and his emancipated soul will mix again with the glorious essence, from which it had been separated, but not divided.' 'The first of these stages is that of humanity, which supposes the disciple to live in obedience to the holy law, and an observance of all his rites, customs, and precepts of the established religion, which are admitted to be useful in regulating the lives, and restraining within proper bounds the vulgar mass, whose souls cannot reach the heights of divine contemplation, and who might be corrupted and misled....The second stage, in which the disciple achieves power, or force, is termed the road, or path...the third stage is that of knowledge of the supernatural...the fourth and the last stage is that which denotes his arrival at truth, which implies his complete union with divinity.'[17]

Sufis in the Mughal Period in India

Social conditions and the language of India's thought at different time did not limit the universal character of mysticism. At the center of the polity was the Mughal dynasty promoting syncretism in the social conditions of heterogeneity through the process of dialogue and not pogroms of denial of identity. There were Mughal-Rajput marriages among the elites, conversions of Rajputs to Islam, co-mingling, adopting styles of fashion, modus Vivendi and modus operandi. Mira Bai's bhakti mysticism, allowed Hindu and Muslim devotees to co-mingle. Qawali singing started. Hindus entered in a dialogue with the Sufis. Guru Nanak who represented ecumenical spirit had friendly relations with Sufi teachers and the Mughals, no less was his friendship with Akbar. There was interaction among South Asians and Christians elsewhere. Their travelogues showed up the commerce and diplomacy and the European styles of paintings entered the Mughal miniatures and paintings and noted the multicultural polity of the Mughals.[18] The trend started then increased under the British in the future. Many British painters made a name in England by paintings from India of Indian Bazaars for example, even if they were of indifferent quality.

The dialogues among different religious personages under Akbar were well known and the translation works were trend setters for the future as much as they carried forward the tradition of translations of Indian texts into Persian or Turkish started earlier, especially in the realm of Buddhism, customs and religion.[19]

As extension of Akbar's translation of Sanskrit and other work's under Jahangir an Arabic text was translated into Persian which consisted of the maxims of the Greeks, the Persians, the Indians and the Arabs. In Persian it was called The External Wisdom. Its further version was Inti-khah-Shayista Khan. It contained pre Islamic and Islamic counsels focusing on skills, justice, prioritisation of policy and its execution, constant vigilance to prevent official negligence or oppression of the administrators, to the people and reward for excellence and efficiency and punishment of the wicked. Other books during his reign focused not on Islam but State administration. These books focused on non-sectarianism, justice, and harmony. Panchtantra was translated and found a place in Mughal political culture.[20] He observed that concepts of wahadut-ul-wajud and advaita mingled with Sufism and bhakti movement.

The Mughals patronised the Sufis, built monuments for Sufi saints of the past, implored the blessings of Sufi guides of their era (from Akbar to Shah Jahan blessings for the birth of male successors were sought after), some practiced Sufism in their devotional lines with more or less sincerity. Music, art, poetry, philosophy, commerce, agriculture prospered in an unprecedented manner. In the area of translations Dara's contribution was a continuation. His efforts led to the translation of popular works such as Singhasna Bahisti, Tota Maina and Panchatantra apart from seminal religious texts.[21]

Different persuasions of Sufism

(1) Orthodoxy of Islam;

(2) Those who challenged that Islam was the only means to salvation;

(3) Sufis who undermined their own traditions of their orders;

(4) Sufis who embraced music as the highest form of meditation;

(5) Sufis who rejected music as sensuous impiety;

(6) Sufis who mixed with elites;

(7) Sufis who rejected the rich and preferred to live with the down trodden;

(8) Sufis who explored the subtleties of theology;

(9) Sufis who boldly crossed the boundaries of confessional allegiance to find fellowship with those of other faiths like Hindus and Sikhs, and, *Yogis* and Christians. Dara was one such Sufi who delved into Hindu texts and established links with Christian priests, especially Jesuits and well disposed towards the Sikh guru of his time;

(10) Sufis who combined different orders and emphasized their common principles. They attempted to discover common principles of different religions and different sects.

Sufi Orders

In India there were four Silsilas (orders) which were prominent and were different in their orientation and linkages, namely Suhrawardi, Chistiyya, Qadiri and Naqshabandi. The first leading khanaqs (hospice) was under Bahaudin Zakarriya (1182-1262) who was the founder of the Suhrawardi order originally started by Shihabuddin Suhrawardi (1145-1234). The latter was the author of an Arabic manual on Sufism entitled 'Awariful-Ma'rif'. They associated with the rulers and the rich and their riches were symbolised in their financial aid to kings. Zakariyya financially supported Iyaltimish in the latter's fight against Qabacha. The Emperor gave him the title of Shaikhkul Islam (Leader of Islam). His grandson Ruknudin Abdul Fath (d.1335), in his own turn was respected by Sultan Allauddin and the Tughluq Sultans.

Under Shaikh Jalaluddin Tabrezi, who was the disciple of Shaikh Shihabuddin the order could not be established in Dihli, and so he retired to Bengal, where he established a khanaq and a 'langar' (common tables) at Lakhnauti first and then at Davatalla near Padua. It was responsible for converting a large number of Bengalis to Islam. The sect believed in forced conversions. It established itself in Punjab, Multan, Sindh and Bengal. They were evangelists and so travelled to foreign countries like Makhdum Jahamiya (1308-84) and Raju Qattal.[22] Being aligned with the powerful it had a conservative tinge to it and did not expand very much in other territories of India.

Their tenets were: enough money for offering sherbet to Qalandars, knowledge to counter Ulamas, and mystical enlightenment.

Suhrawardi was followed by his son-in-law, Shaikh Fakhruddin Ibrahim Iraqi, his son, Shaikh Sadruddin Arif, and his son, Ruknuddin, who died in 1334-35. Another of his follower was Sayyid Jalaluddin Bukhari popularly known as Jahaniya, his grandson Qutubi Alam (d.1553) and his son, Sayyid Muhammad known also as Shah Mahjhan.

This silsila declined with the rise of the Chistiyya silsila.

Chisti –Silsila

The centers were Ajmer, Narnaul, Suwal, Nagaur and Mandal in Rajasthan, Hansi and Ajodhya Punjab, and in some towns in Bengal, Assam and Dakhyn. Chisti (1140-1230) enunciated three principles in

Ajmer. First, in sphere of Oneness (Universe) all is one i.e. lover, loved and love. This *pantheistic* view brought Chisti close to Upanishads and extensive exchange of ideas took place. Second, higher form of devotion to God was to *redress* the *misery* of *those* in *distress*, to fulfill the needs of the helpless and to feed the hungry. Third, described the qualities that endear a man to God, he referred to first river-like *generosity*, sunlight *affection* and earth like *hospitality*.

His follower, Fariduddin (grandson) Mahmud patronised by Muhammad Tughluq who married his daughter to Farid's grandson, settled in Ajedhan, ramjamat Khanaq and died in 1265. Nizamuddin Auliya was his successor and settled in Dihli. He died in 1322 and remained estranged from Sultan Ghyasuddin Tughluq. His maxim was 'Do unto others what you would they do unto you; wish for yourself what you wish for them also.' Feed the hungry. He was hostile to philosophy's cosmological theories. He was succeeded by Chirag (Nasiruddin Mahmud) who came in conflict with Sultan Muhammad bin Tughluq and died in 1356. His tenets led to association with common people. By fourteenth century the doctrine of Wahadat al-Wujud (esoteric reality of creatures) was rooted in India. Identified with Masudi Bakk, a relative of Sultan Firoz, Ulamas got him beheaded. His tenet was From Masu I Bakk appeared all human qualities. Since He in reality was Essence, he ultimately became essence.'

The method adopted by the Chistiyya silsila led to its spread to non-Muslims with intuitive knowledge of their problems, then adopt some symbolic custom, led simple life, bowed before the sheikh, offered water, circulated zanbil (basket mound), shaved the head of the new entrant, audition parties and the chillah i makus (silent prayer of forty days/in Indian Sufism spiritual practice of penance and solitude). This was like first controlling the emotional life and then controlling behaviour. The Chistiyya orders were set up close to the neighbourhood of the poor and made tremendous appeal to them. The strategy worked for the populace. They converted on their own volition to escape the indigence suffered by them under the old society.

Naqshbandi Order

Rumi used the word NQSH implying form-making engraver. The name meant literally painters. These were on the analogy of the corporations and guilds of early classical Sufism, such as the builders. The order had an inner and an outer branch. Many Persian poets used the words naqsh (diagram, painting, map, etc.) to denote a relationship between these Sufis and the whole 'Plan' of development which Sufism was believed to be aiding. Khayyam, even earlier than Rumi, used it to denote the same. The outward form was the dervish school of austere appearance that helped to maintain the cultural identity of the environment. It was powerful in Turkey before the republican revolution and dominated both the Ottoman and Moguls Courts from time to time.[23]

This sect originated in Central Asia. Khwaja Baha al-Din Naqshabandi chose Khwaja Ala al-Din Attar, son of Muhammad al-Bukhari, made him his son in law, then asked him to go barefoot to travel to the bazaars of Bukhara carrying a tray of apples on his forehead to sell apples in the streets at the top of his voice, especially in front of the shops belonging to his two brothers who had inherited their father's property, which he was denied. This led to his initiation in the spiritual path. The elder considered him to be the 'House of Allah'. He told his disciple that the heart was like the moon when it was three days old. He further said that to know the heart was to know one's purpose, and to find the heart was to find one's purpose. The student believed that it was possible to see Allah in one's heart and be in ecstasy. For Allauddin it was more significant to be conscious than to be ecstatic. So after Naqshbandi's death his disciples took oath to follow Khwaja Attar. Muhammad Parsa, his disciple, wrote down some of Khwaja Attar's sayings. These were intended to be an appendix to Naqshbandi's biography. These sayings were

The purpose of asceticism was to repudiate material and physical attachments and to turn oneself in the direction of the real spiritual world.

It was most necessary for the novice to bind his heart to the guide. Since the spiritual guide and director was the mirror of the divine reality, communion with him led the pupil to annihilation and ecstasy. Ecstasy was the route to renunciation. For this a novice needed the director during the early stages till the stage of ecstasy.

Achievement of God was the absolute beauty. To reach the essence of being was to see oneself as a drop in the ocean, an atom in the sun. So one needed a guide endowed with the spirit of Prophet Muhammad, for by giving one's heart to him, and annihilating one's own being in his, one may reach the final stage of annihilation and so attain the ultimate goal of the quest.

Naqshbandi Sayings: Negation of Being

Finally he said that ceremonies and customs should be abandoned. The sayings of Naqshbandi were 'True prayer, fasting, spiritual exercises, and self-discipline led to the presence of the divine oneness, sanctified and Exalted is He, but in my opinion, the shortest road of all is the "negation of being". For this he upheld the values of *Vigilance*, *Contemplation* and *Examination* of conscience.[24]

In India Naqshabandi was the patron saint of the Central Asian Muslims (Turants) and was the oldest Sufi order that flourished in Transoxiana in the midst of Buddhist traditions in the region. They came up during Akbar's time under Khwaja Baqi Billah (1563-1603) who settled in Dihli in 1599.[25]

Qadariyya Order

Hazrat Abu Muhiyuddin Shaikh Abdul Qadir Jilani, of Prophet's lineage, and whose birth was predicted four hundred years ago, was born in Neef in Jilan in Iran in 1077-78 AD and founder of the Order. His contribution to Islamic studies was so important that he was called al-Ghawth al-Azam. His birth was accompanied by miracles like his mother being sixty years of age, the foot print of the Prophet was present and that in itself bestowed sainthood on him, on his day of the birth approximately eleven hundred males were born in Jilan and every one of them became a Wali of Allah, and Hazrat Abu Saleh Moosa, his father, dreamt of seeing Beloved Prophet who said to him 'Ó my Son Abu Saleh, Allah, Most high has given you a child who is my beloved son an also the beloved of Allah. His ranking among the Awliya is akin to my rank among Prophets.' He died in 1166.

In India this Order established a stronghold in the Punjab and Kashmir in the fifteenth century with coming of Shaykh Bandgi Muhammad Ghauth a renowned descendant of the originator of the sect, and he settled at Uch in Bhawalpur state. Its influence increased under a Sindhi, Miahn Mir (1550-1635) who advocated a broad humane outlook on life, urged Jahangir and Shah Jahan to be considerate to all groups of their subjects. His disciple Mulla Shah was both a mystic and a poet. He defined a believer as one who could reach God and behold him and a kafir who failed to do so. Mulla Shah was Dara's preceptor, and after the latter's execution Aurangzeb tried to harass him. Such was his popularity that the Emperor could only banish him from Dihli.[26] The harassment by Aurangzeb, in a sense, was a negation of Shahjahan's legacy who had introduced Dara to Mulla Shah to the saint for treatment of Dara's illness by the magic of supernatural powers. Aurangzeb, in recorded history, favored the Naqshabandi sect during his rule.

Impact of Sufis

Elites and masses breathed a sense of social harmony. Common customs, neighborhood living, and celebration of each-others' festivals, commonality of dress, purdah of women, inter-community marriages, common places of labor, sharing of each other's woes, bonding over issues affecting common interests related to trade and agriculture, collecting for local decision making, dialogue as a form of exchange of views on run of the mill issues and religious exchange to discover commonalities and decline in religious bigotry were all a product of this movement. This became the mainstream even if for some it was short lived. It created a syncretism relevant today for multiculturalism, even if Islam and Hinduism are regarded as fire and water, as some did.

Dara's Sufi Identity

In his introduction to Dara's work 'The Mingling of the Two Oceans' Haq called him a devout Sufi and the 'man of the path' throughout his life.[27] From early life he was given to study the Sufi texts and showed evidence of his familiarity with them. Dara himself wrote in the Introduction to the work titled Safinat-Ul-Awliya, written at the age of 25, that he was a follower of Hanafi code and a Qadiri, i.e. a follower of Imam Abdu Hanifa and a *Murid* of the order which owed its origin to Sheikh Abdul Qadir of Jilan. He further noted in his second work Sakinat-ul-Auliya written in his twenty eight year that he was dealing with a biography of Miah Mir, or Miya Jiv, the spiritual guide of his Pir and Murshid, Mulla Shah, called lisanullah (the greatest divine for Dara) and many of his disciples.[28] His intellectual prominence was underlined by Mulla Shah in a ghazal (lyric) and an advice to him to instruct other disciples. In the Ghazal Mulla Shah thus admired Dara

> 'The first and second Sahib Kiran (namely Amir Timur and ShahJahan) are the kings of grandeur, while our Dara Shikuh is the Sahib Kiran of the heart. From the universe of the two worlds, he has brought under his grip on account of the merchandise of his heart.'[29]

Under the influence of the orthodox Ulamas he did not impart instructions to the other disciples. So he remained a Sunni following Hannafi code while gaining Sufi knowledge and propagating the knowledge about the biographies of Sufi saints in his two works. These two early works were followed by two works on Sufism, i.e. Risala-i-Hak Numa or Compass of Truth discussing various stages of the Path, and Shathiyat or Hasanat ul-Afrin on sayings of earlier Sufi divines like Bayazid, Dhun-Nun-al-Misri, Junaid, Ghazali, Jilani, Ibn Arabi, and sayings of the Prophet and the Caliphs, and the great Hindu saint Baba Lal. In his forty second year (1657) he completed two major works on Comparative religion. These were the next two works Majma-ul- Bahrain in Persian and Samudra Samagam in Sanskrit. His seventh work- a translation of some fifty chapters, called 'Siri-i-Akbari' was completed two years before his execution.

He was credited for translating the Bhagvadgita the same year. He was the author of many letters, poems and ghazals and had collected an album of paintings and calligraphy for his wife, and credited with an anthology, collection of Sufi Aphorisms. He inspired others to write in his vein. His secretary Chandra Bhan composed 'Mukalima-i-Dara Shikuh Wa Baba Lal on various topics on Hindu religion and Ethics. A translation work was also undertaken on Hindu religion and Philosophy, viz., *Yoga-Vasistha* into Persian.[30] His personality was of a great scholar, a mystic, expert on Comparative religion, music, fine arts, believer in miracles, builder of unique monuments like his wife's tomb in Lahor, tomb of Hazrat Mian Mir in Lahor, the Dara Shikoh library in Dihli, the Akhun Mullah Shah Mosque in Srinagar and the building for astronomical observations and Parimahal Garden in Srinagar. In context of Sufi identity he was Punjab centric.

Rising Graph of an Intellectual

His personality evolved from Islamic orthodoxy (for the first thirteen years he was with the conservative Nur Jahan)[31] to a Sufi (preferred to call himself a *Faqir*) and described as a free thinker,[32]and, a dervish[33] to later become a scholar of Comparative Religion and a translator. He developed from looking at past of Sufism to its then contemporary scope and role followed by studies on Comparative Religions, undertaking translations, holding dialogues with Non-Muslims like Baba Lal, writing letters on points of religious and philosophical issues, holding dialogues about the commonalities between Upanishads and Islam and asked others to write on Sufi theme and befriending Sarmad.

That gave his personality a finished form of an intellectual with multiple dimensions-practically like the Sophists in ancient Greece. The periodisation of his growth was thus delineated in two phases: one his initiation into Qadiri order in 1640 and his close association with Mian Mir, Mulla Shah Badakshi and other contemporary saints in India. He brought out five texts on Sufism and mysticism as a result of this phase. The second phase was marked by his search for truth and study of Hinduism from 1650 onwards with his translation into Persian of the Yoga-Vasistha.[34] His album show his interest in Hinduism since of fourteen.

On his way he picked up the allied forms of literature and fine arts. His work Iksir-i-Azam-an anthology is extant with only one copy containing 28 quatrains and 133 ghazals which is not available to posterity. The appeal of both these forms was to emotion of pantheistic ideas.[35] His other Sufi works were influenced by previous Sufi poets like Rumi, Jami and Sana 'I'. There were 34 quatrains in Hasanat-ul-Arifin and 41 in Risala-1-Haqnama. These works have elements of Sufism and Qadirism with an undercurrent of didactic and ethical note.[36]

Sufi literature had at its core idea of love of God, the belief in God in the human form, and respect of all God's creation. Being spiritual and appealing to emotion Sufi literature was in poetic form among others since the time of Adam, the first poet.[37] The first Sufi dervesh who wrote poetry in the form of a ghazal was Hazrat Ali, the son-in-law of the Holy Prophet. His ghazal had a lyrical style and Summed up the Sufi message at the end of the lyric thus

> 'You are the book that of any fallacies clear,
> In you are all letters spelling out mystery,
> 'You are the Being, you are the very being…It:
> You contain That, which contained cannot be!'[38]

Rubai's meter, as mentioned in the earlier chapter was discovered in Persia by Rudaki. Commenting on Rudaki, two hundred years later Shams-e Qais said of its effect on the population

> 'This new poetic form fascinated all classes….Many a girl cloistered away, out of passion for the song of a ruba i broke down doors of chastity's walls; many matrons from love of ruba i let loose the braids of self-restraint.'[39]

Sufi love poetry had no earthly connotation of sensuous desires. It was desire to discover divinity within and merge with the divine. In India till the nineteenth century love poetry was for the Divine and not sexual or gender love of opposites. In Rumi love poetry or poetry was pointing towards seeking the Truth that could not be mentioned in words. So he used *rhetorical* devices. He used puns, and adorned his poems with symbolism of music and dance as also he used different language forms in its use of Persian and Arabic languages.[40]

Any emotional exercise needs to be rooted in the soil of the poet that is literary tradition; language and the society provided a context. Even for mysticism to be conveyed it became necessary to improvise with imagination poetic forms so as to give voice to both peoples' plight and doctrinal glue of love. In India, ridden with religious divides, a merging (melting) culture the function of love had to have an emotional appeal linked with meeting people's expectations and jelling them together with love.

'Sweet Fruits' 'Born of Clay'

Dara's writings full of aphorisms quatrains and *ghazals* have the same divine message. All of these are in the mystic tradition of Sufism.

In one of his rubai, he talked of the Divine representing a calm, desire, and goal in the form of four questions thus,

> 'Without You, what calm, what peacefulness.'
>
> Have We?
>
> As I' am lost in You, what desire, no less,
>
> Have we?
>
> Except our desire for you, what desire, no less,
>
> Have we?
>
> As You are our goal, we have no other, I stress:
>
> Have We?'[41]

This is Sufi thought but very bland, no symbolism, metaphor, allegory or a simile and the last line has no turn of phrase or idea. It seems to be for an audience already initiated or with poor understanding. The next suggests in a less bland form about how The One is the cause of nature's spin, craziness of the angels, and Earth's spread as a carpet before the One. At best it is a reference to the state of mind at the level of meditation that a Sufi reaches much before annihilation. Or that since the human is God's creation death does not matter for He in a person was eternal. There are many more ruba 'i' admiring God the creator of all things. He refered to the experience to ecstasy in another rubai and that implied a stage in the process of initiation to annihilation. Again it is bland and for the less initiated. He then talked about having faith in the beloved-meaning God. Very bland this was again.[42]

Would not help to change any one for it remains within the Islamic thought of the 'One'. He was critical of the priest as personified by Halaj who said *he was the truth.*[43]

Mystics in his poetry and borrowed Symbol

Another theme that his quatrains had was of the *mystics*. They underlined ecstasy, the Perfect One, humility, humans considered as a drop in the ocean, then he mentioned the pot filled with air that on breaking produces a sound like bubble bursting to be an ocean.[44] Here he was close to a metaphor and imagery. The imagery of a bubble bursting into an ocean was attractive. The allusion to it is reminiscent of an event in the life of the Prophet in the cave near Mecca before and after revelation.

Great Khadija, the most beloved wife of the Holy Prophet, narrated this. She informed about how revelation came to the Holy Prophet. He used to hear a sound. The result of hearing the sound in the cave was that form of Gabriel appeared before him, and that was the commencement of Revelation. Once Holy Muhammad was asked 'In what manner does revelation come to you?' He replied, I hear a sound, sometimes like the sound of a boiling cauldron and sometimes like the sound made by bees, and sometimes I see an angel in the form of man, who talks with me, and sometimes I hear a sound like silver bells or the hearing of a drum.'[45] In contrast to this reply his poem is not nuanced in explaining sound or air for that matter.[46]

In the context of the majesty of the Prophet's description this pales. On its own it stands as one of his better Rubai's. The poem where he appeals with his imagery and content is the following.

> 'Like an Ocean is the essence of the Ultimate being…
> Souls and things are like worms in water, shimmering,
> This ocean, heaving, stirring and expanding inside…
> Is transformed into drops and waves, bubbles rising.[47]

The content is monotheistic, the style is marked by a simile especially where the soul is likened to the fluidity of water and the rising of the bubble. The second reason for this preference was that possibly the residents of the countries with deserts have a special affinity with water and oceans that stir one's heart. Let us not forget that Dara was in Punjab-Lahor and Multan-in the midst of desert heat- as a Governor and had met his khurshids- saints Mian Mir and Mulla Shah and Mian Jiv. The paintings of Dara and the three saints are preserved in England. Lahor was significant also from the point of view of his military campaigns against Kandahar in his early life as also he raised a force during his flight there.[48] He repeated similar simile in his poem on God's existence.[49] In another poem he equated Qadiri with God.[50] His poetry reflected both on ideas of Sufism generally and Qadiri teachings, in particular.[51]

Qadiri Ghazals

A sampling of his ghazals brings out his faith in the Qadiri order firmly even though he was in his early years attached to the Chistiyya order owing to Shah Jahan who had sought the blessing of the Chisti saints for the birth of Dara born there. One quotation from his ghazal suffices to show how he equated Qadiri with God. He composed thus

> 'It's true that you'r Mohammed and God too:
> Such fortune on you was bestowed and it's set.
> Qadiri…O Qadiri...O Qadiri… O Qadiri…
> Into Beloved you changed yourself…no duet.'[52]

His Pir Mulla Shah commented on his poetry

> 'What sweet fruits cannot be borne by this pure clay.'[53]

There were other contemporaries who praised his poetry like Afdal-ud-Din Sarkhush. Bikrama Jit Hasrat said of his poetry

> 'In his Diwan, he is fond of giving voice to heterodox ideas and his poetic imagination transcends the limits imposed by religious convention. This he does by the use of the pun on the word Qadiri (Dara Shikuh) and Qadiri (God).'[54]

Dara's poetry was associated with his desire to bring out the Sufi and Qadiri identity among his siblings. Only one of his three sisters, Jahanara, came close to him in that craft by dedicating a work to Mulla Shah in which she talked about his healing powers. His other sister Roushanara was scheming with Aurangzeb, jealous and crafty. The third sister sided with Murad Baksh later. None of his brothers-Murad and Shah Shuja compare with him, both claimed to be Shias but the latter one adorned the tactical falsity of a devout during the war of succession owing to Aurangzeb's goading's. They were tipplers, failed schemers, rebels and power hungry. Aurangzeb was a cap maker turned into a king through deceit. He extended the empire yet ruined its roots with his divisive policies which were negated by his own men soon after his demise. The damage had been done though. This was ironical since a cap was also a symbol of dignity, for him orthodox State power. But subsequent symbolised the decline of the glory of the Mughal rule in the final analysis. Even the Sufi poetry of the last Mughal, Bahadur Shah Zafar,[55] jailed by the British could not save it or jell the differences among communities that were to be exploited by the British for their Divide and Rule policies.

Dara as Hagiographer (Tazkiras Writer)

His two biographical works at a young age we mentioned above. The biographies help to establish identities of the subject and the condition of the context of that object-event, literary piece, and personage. Such works during the Mughal period till the seventeenth century would reflect on the identity of Indo-Muslims. Till then they were written in Persian, only later were they written in Urdu and are found in Urdu translations. Later in the colonial period we find translations in Sindhi, Gujarati and Punjabi. These were helpful in establishing identities.

Hermansen and Lawrence underlined their significance thus,

> '...Indo-Muslim *identities*, since the range of elite literary reflection, is very broad, and Indo-Persian tazirikas encompass a wide variety of contexts. Above all, tazirikas traces memory through the lives of heroes, both lyrical and spiritual, and in doing so, it raises a number of interesting theoretical questions. How are its heroes selected, and who gets to tell their story for which audiences? While the heroes may display courage, evoke hope, and elicit loyalty, how do their lives relate to the unheroic, to the everyday, to the lives without traces?'[56]

Possible Motives of Dara

The motives of Dara were not very clear in writing the biographies that he undertook to write. He talked about his dream about writing. He stated that he wrote for personal clarification and not for the public.[57] He refused to preach Sufism when asked by Mulla Shah. The issue was how to understand his motivation. The reasons may not be far to seek. Given the ideology then of softening orthodoxy with Sufism and Bhakti movement through dialogues we find Dara as part of this State sponsored syncretism since Akbar to achieve harmony.

Second, whatever intellectual activity of the times, be it Sufi, mystic, Bhakti or hagiography, it ultimately got linked to the state patronage even though many sects like the Chistiyya sect did not covet

State patronage. Like the Confucian Mandarins at the lowest rung in Chinese literati, the Sufis here at the ground level were closer to the appreciation of the problems of the people and in a sense conduit to the authorities to respond in whichever way they thought it fit. Dara's accounts, in line with being an heir-apparent and sensitive to this need may have written the hagiographies and thus combined the need of the State with the tradition of writing hagiographies within the Sufi tradition. The attendant result was his gaining of popularity with the people of Agrah and Dihli. In this way he aimed at evolving a consensus on State policies or alleviation of grievances.

He was clearly conscious about studying texts of other religions and deployed many scholars of Sanskrit texts to translate and know about the Truth hidden therein once he was familiar with Sufi traditions mainly of Mulla Shah, Mian Mir and Mian Jiv, and the Qadiri order with the Chistiyya order as the main inspiration and compass and monotheism of Islam. It was natural for him to record his meeting with Mulla Shah in his first text though he details his life, teachings and miracles in his next work.

Safinat-ul-A'lwiya

Expressing his love and respect for all the Sufi saints he classified them in a *hierarchical* order given their attainments and expressed his desire to reach the position of these saints. Since he believed in the idea of **Path** that was enunciated also by the Sufis in Central Asia, he provided the logic of having guides to take the disciples on that path of going nearer God. These guides were next to the Prophet in their closeness to God. The hierarchical principle was based on the attainments of saints in terms of their individual spiritual powers indicating the existence of plural capabilities.

They were *classified* independent of their sects and the differentia of classification was functional as the following: those hidden saints performing miracles, some who performed under God's command, others who had worldly pursuits remaining in solitude even among the crowd and finally those who dealt with people who were of evil makeup so that they were not recognizable. They did not reveal themselves or break the law. All of them were to be considered above reproach and to be treated with faith in them with purity of heart. Further he recorded aphorisms and the names of smaller four hundred and eleven Sufi saints followed by an Epilogue.[58]

Sakinat-ul-I' Alwiya

This, being Dara's second work, was on the Qadiri Oder and listed twelve different groups with their corresponding attributes and fountain heads upholding the values of devotion, sincerity, truth, humility, resignation, contentment, generosity, faith, wisdom, love and seclusion respectively. These tenets he elaborated with his own personal experiences contrasting them with the practices of other orders that he mentioned admiringly. The three sections of the work dealt with the lives, miracles and practices of saints like Miyan Mir (first section), the life miracles and his sister Bibi Jamal Khatun (second section) and his disciples in two *firqas (categories)* namely those who died before the completion of the work and the then contemporary followers of Mian Mir. This work was full of evidence of Dara's affirmation of miracles, the supernatural, and was empty of any examination of the Qadiri doctrine and its links with Islam even if he was credited for recognising that the Sufi orders were not different from each other.[59]

The reference to the Qadiri practice Zikhr is called Dhikr in this work and to meditation[60] that is a part of the Path is in his next work, namely Risala'I Haqnuma. This was part of the process of true mystical knowledge beginning with sense perception (Physical plane of Dara) to divine light through the heart which had three centre's which led a person to the Plane of counterparts that was the gateway to the Astro-mental Plane. In this phase the rust of the heart would go and the heart would start to glow since the soul would. The imagery here was part of the larger Sufi terrain of symbols, metaphors, similes and allegory, especially among the Persians. Dara also refered to the idea of the sound[61] as we have noted above with the illumination of Prophet Muhammad.

This work detailed Dara's meetings, in company of Shah Jahan, with Mian Mir and Jahangir's esteem of this saint even though he did not care about saints. Dara mentioned about the work of Jahanara on Mulla Shah. The latter was called a free thinker and the most eminent Qadiri.[62]His literary writings and religious views made him a gnostic and heterodox and was accused of heresy.

Selective Biographer

Hermansen and Lawrence, as noted above, had raised questions with regard to the purpose of hagiography in general. With regard to Dara's hagiography more issues were raised in terms of his exclusion of many saints who did not necessarily belong to the Punjab where he was the Governor and had come in contact with Mulla Shah, Mian Mir and the Qadiris. They believed that biographies aimed at establishing Indo-Muslim identity. These incited memories through the lives of heroes selected to tell stories and determine which stories for which audiences. In this context they considered that Dara was selective and promoting only the Qadiri saints with a view to undergird his own authority vis-à-vis rival claims to Qadiri spirituality.[63]

Shaykh Abd Shaykh Adl-al-Haqq and Shaykh Abd ar-Rehman

In writing about the Qadiri order he was preceded by the formidable scholar of *hadith, himself a Qadiri adept, Shaykh Abd-al-Haqq Muhadith* Dihlawi whose work was completed in 1618 and was famous by 1640. Dara bypassed this line and selectively included Miyan Mir and Mulla Shah. He gave half a page to the giants like Rumi and Simnani (the Persian Sufis). He ignored the Dihli and Avadh based Qadiris recognising only the ones in Punjab-Lahor, ignoring saints of other regions like Avadh and other parts of eastern India. In contrast they refer to a text of one of his contemporaries, *Mirátal-asrar* authored by Shaykh Abd ar-Rahman. The author of this biography noted twelve family clusters into which Sufi brotherhoods could be parcelled and twenty three generations of spiritual exemplars to retell the saga of Persian and Indo-Persian Sufism as a single dramatic endeavor of the Divine for mankind's benefit. In this text the *Qutb* (Leader) of each age was shown to highlight the significance of both Persian and Indian Sufis (who found prime of place only after the 18th generation). The purpose of this was to give prominence to the handful of obscure saints, most of whom toiled and died in north eastern India, especially in the region of Avadh and also to show the links with the Persian Sufism.[64] This comprehensive approach put Dara in a narrow beam of light.

Dara's Letters

The letters that Dara wrote to others were interesting against the spirit of orthodoxy for search for mystical knowledge and the spirit of dialogue with his contemporaries. His letters to Shah Muhibullah, Shah Muhammad Dilruba and meeting with Sarmad showed his quest for mystical intricacies. The issue he discussed with them or sought clarifications ranged from the relation of duality to Unity of Being, limitations of knowledge being called the 'Great Veil,' Infinity. Perfection showed that the movement of ideas about GOD was cyclical. It started from Him and merged with him.[65]

Contact with Sarmad

In this process Sarmad, an American Jew who converted to Islam and came to India in 1654, introduced a complexity by saying 'I obey the Quran. I am a Hindu priest and a monk; I am a rabbi Jew, I am an infidel and I am a Muslim.'[66] He turned a nudist. In India he became a heterodox Sufi preacher. Dara, liked his company, considered him his *guide and preceptor*, recommended him to his father, and both Dara and Sarmad were condemned and executed for *apostasy* by the clergy under Aurangzeb. In his letter to Dara, Sarmad had said 'Whatever we have read, we have forgotten. Save the discourse of the Beloved which we reiterate.'[67]

Rebuffing the Orthodox

By the time he had reached his thirties, Dara had earned the accusation of apostasy as part of the ire of the orthodox clergy. His work on Aphorisms of saints, titled Hasanat-Ul-Arifin, written in his thirty eighth year was a rebuff to conservative interpretations of religion, namely, Islam, Hebrew and Christianity. He underlined the Unity of GOD attacked the Mullas as noisily spoiling the heaven by their *fatwas*, and wished a world free of such hypocritical asses.

With this intention he wrote about aphorisms of one hundred and seven saints and mystics of *diverse religious orders* and poets. He elucidated these aphorisms with personal experiences. He denied any idea of the gnostic denying God, or acquiring unity with God through uniformity of conception, praised guides like Shaikh Abdu Ansari as a God knowing Arif (mystic) performing miracles and his capacity to have premonition of his own death.[68] In defense of the gnostic, Dara composed the following ruba 'I'[69]:

'Never would a gnostic attribute God-head to his own self:
Never would he suffer separation from the Sublime Self.

For to be a slave is to become a master:

Since All is He: (the gnostic) will not act in vanity.'

In another ruba i he suggested that only by uttering a word does not take one to God, one has to be in the state (mental state through annihilation)[70]

In another posthumously published text belonging to the theme of his early writings, underlined in poetic forms the idea of Omnipotence of God in chapels, mosques and Hindu temples, and then he went on to explain the steps of the *tariqa* (method)[71] for the journey on the Path in thirty steps.

Detachment from the material world, acquisition of knowledge through understanding the eternal felicity, the removal of hallucinations of why and where in favor of fountain-head of heart and not succumbing to temptations, realisation of true self, knowing the ways of the men of path, contemplation, having faith in belief, inculcating the virtues of sincerity, love and fidelity and steadfastly merging the self in the universal Self, i.e. Annihilation. This tract was the sign of Dara's emotional and not rational approach. The mind must listen to the heart, he felt.

The same theme was found in Risala'I HAQ Numa' written in 1646 where the process described above is dealt with in the form of Grace and Action. The description undertaken for the uninitiated is simple, at times messed up and confusing. The more positive aspect was that it was interspersed with his own quatrains and delineated the steps for attaining occult knowledge and pantheistic doctrines pervading this text, written after he joined the Qadiri order. He narrated here the various exercises of the Qadiri order for the pupils (called '*yars'*– friends) to start off from the physical plane to reach the stage of the Divine communion.[72] He claimed this to be the text of a Divine who had acquired knowledge. He said of this text,

'The whole of this tract is a compass of Truth…' a work of kadir and not Kadiri. The latter name was Dara Shikuh.[73]

Sufi Scholar

Dara did not stop with being a Sufi 'Faqir' as he styled himself. He joined the illustrious company of intellectuals who were interested in learning about other religions here and especially in the Arab world where the knowledge of the Hindu texts helped even if it became difficult to measure their impact on the Arab world. Similarly the Arabs, like Alberuni[74] studied India and compared Hinduism with Islam to find similarities in philosophy, factual differences in society and custom. In Alberuni's tradition of finding similarities, Dara focused on similarities in Islam, Christianity and Hinduism. Six hundred years later, Dara, with the purpose of creating harmony fearlessly carried forward the tradition set by the likes of Alberuni who gave a comparative perspective on Hindu, Greek and Islamic tradition[75] of writing of religious laws. He showed how the Greeks, with the exception of Socrates, wrote the spoken divine word in hydes in Greek and Islamic tradition of writing them similarly including a treaty signed between the Prophet and the Jews while as the Hindu wrote on e.g. bark, on Papyrus wrote the Egyptian. Dara gave an Islamic, Hindu and a Christian perspective. Alberuni focused on the Bhagvadgita apart from other religious texts, while Dara concentrated on the Upanishads that was the essence of the Vedas.

Tradition of Syncretic Scholarship

The cross cultural movement and mutations remain marked by Greek, Arabic and Indian influences even though the Greek influence was all pervading around the world known then. The intermingling caused by wars and conquests and the scholarly movements brought cultures together. In this context the Arabic expansion was seen. The Sufi incursion into India became local tradition by the 18th generation, as noted above. So Dara was both part of and apart from the co-mingling of the Islamicate since he wrote at the time when Indian identity in the Muslim world was established as distinct Indo-Muslim part of the world of the Arab Muslim world that started with the Prophet, Caliphs and Ali Hussein known as Islamicate. Indo-Muslim identity had begun to take shape in scholarly works through the translation, writings, and commentaries.

Translations for Common Perspective

Works on medicine in Arabic, Panchatantra (reign of Al Mansur), a work of astronomy was translated into Persian (Sultan Firoz Shah's period), Mathematics in Persian (Akbar's phase) followed by the possibility of the two trends of Islam and Hinduism mingling into social harmony. At the philosophical level it meant looking at common points of religious and philosophical outlook. The work begun under Akbar had a long term significance since the study of Comparative Religion became a major preoccupation and finding a common religion became a life-long concern of the father of modern India, Raja Ram Mohan Roy who founded Cosmopolitan Religion after setting up the Brahmo Samaj. Both the will and paradigm of Akbar's Din-i-Illahi was much weaker though a strong precedent for co-mingling.

Fore Cry of Compositeness

This was still far from Composite Culture that Pandit Nehru and Mahatma Gandhi talked about though it was a culmination of the trend that began at least nine centuries ago. Nehru was an agnostic and a non-believer in mysticism. His focus implied reciprocal, mutual sharing and overlap of cultural practices, styles of life, a technological and economic world view of relations between nature and culture, shared practices of economy and technology, values and belief systems cutting across divides of space and religious belief systems and specifics of community differentiations.[76] These processes were furthered by reform movements by saints, poets, folk artists, and religious reformers. Cultural superstructures of the civilisational society further reinforced the emergence of composite culture.[77] All this happened much later than Dara Shukuh's efforts in furthering the process begun atleast in the thirteenth century by Amir Khusrau.

Multi-Cultural Society

The multi-cultural ideal is different from the plural society. The multicultural society is distinguished by a *public* and the *private* domain wherein the former includes single culture based on the idea of equality between individuals and the latter allows for diversity between private groups. The public domain includes the world of law, politics, and economics. It also includes education, in so far as this is concerned with selection, the transmission of skills the perpetuation of the civic culture. Moral education, primary socialisation and the inculcation of religious beliefs belong to the private domain.[78] The trend towards synthesis was both in the public and the private domain.

The Mughal period since Akbar was marked by a greater all-round push. Being a State directed move its focus was on the State parameters of public domain more directly. It was in the realm of cultural practice of families that the private domain was pushed in the same direction with varying degrees of success.

Public Domain: Scholar of Co-mingling

Dara Shukuh falls in this tradition even if a weak bubbling phenomenon. Not erudite but no less significant, his text Mingling of Two Oceans was both a metaphor and a pre-vision of compositeness wherein the shadows of different religious texts merge into the only One" in both religions (monotheism). He examined the Upanishads in his major work on translating the Upanishads with the purpose of finding commonality in the two traditions of Islam and Hinduism. He translated Upanishads, as Sirr - i-Akbari, the Bhagwat-gita and got the Yoga-Vasistha translated. He studied Hinduism and Islam in Majma-ul-Bahrain and a volume of seven dialogues with Baba Lal[79] on Hindu mythology and common points between Islam and Hinduism.

With Baba Lal and Chandrabhan

In the dialogues that Dara had with Chandrabhan Brahman the issues relating to monotheism were discussed around 1653 and common points about the creator and the creature, the one who orders and the order, the oneness of the moon and the sun despite their apparent differences, jivatma (man with senses) and paramatma (when he gives up his senses), discussion on Krishna and 'gopis' and the desires they represent need suppression in men, body was irrelevant and so one was indifferent to whether a body was cremated or buried since the men of knowledge were one with God, God existed in all, heart brought the dualism of life as one, and was like the breath of wind and such issues to underline the idea of one God in both religions.[80]

His earlier works show the influence of Indian Yogic practices related to control of breath, the heart and brain being the center of meditation and the process of meditation to mediation or initiation to annihilation showed parallels between both the religions. His work Majma-ul-Bahrain showed most of these influences.[81] He began by expressing his confidence in his knowledge of Islam, his quest to know the tenets of the religion of the Indian monotheists' and after his interaction with them he did not find any difference except the verbal one, in seeking and comprehending God. He quoted the verses that were inscribed by Abul Fazl on a building which Akbar had built for the common use of Hindus and Muslims. The verses were

> "Faith and Infidelity, both are galloping on the way towards Him,
> And are exclaiming (together): He is One and none shares His Kingship."[82]

Points made in defense of his position were[83]:

- Both Indian and Sufi monotheists talked about common senses, both external and internal ones.
- Showed similarity between the monotheistic cores of the Upanishads that underlay the religions of the Hindus with the unqualified monotheism of modern Islam.
- Compared the elements listed in Islam and Hinduism-wind, fire, water and dust of Islam with the *panchbhut* of Hinduism of sky, wind, brilliance, water and earth.
- Jibral was equated with Brahma the creator, Mikhail was equated with Vishnu the preserver and Shiva with Israfil, the destroyer.
- Further he identified water with Brahma and Jibral, fire with Mikhail and Vishnu, and air with Shiv and Israfil.[84]
- Mentioned the vision of God, the names of God.
- The apostles and saints in both religions.

This text is an early attempt at preparing the ground for subsequent development of religious compositeness first in Raja Ram Mohan Roy's Cosmopolitan Religion. An exercise a part, Jawaharlal Nehru's scientific temper to construct the vision of composite culture on the basis of tradition of compositeness and the reality of coexistence among different communities since centuries interrupted time and again by bigotry. Nehru had noted the differences but focused on the lived reality of peaceful coexistence of communities in villages and the cities till the coming of the colonial policy of divide and rule.

Dara said in Majmul-I-Bahrain that mysticism was equality and he found no fundamental difference between Hinduism and Islam.[85] This text was regarded as the most dangerous by the mullahs, who levelled the charge of free thinker and a heretic. Regarded as a feeble attempt at syncretism. Manen of the Asiatic Society of India[86] said that it was a point from which the movement could go backwards or forward. There was no such linear development. The mendering of life took to coexistence that had begun much earlier, strengthened under Akbar's push and Nehru's practice during the phase of independent India. Increasingly the public domain became secular and the values upheld by one and all were that of equality and toleration of cultural specificities of the private domain. Yet altercations on these issues never closed and new criticism had to deal with them carrently in far worse forms this is happening.

At the time of publication of another edition of his work done in his mature years, Amalendu De, General Secretary of the Asiatic Society noted the significant comments of Suniti Kumar Chatterjee of the Dara Shikuh- Raja Ram Mohun Roy Institute said 'that scholars would make 'a correct assessment of the place of Dara Shikuh in the history of India and a proper appraisal of his thoughts and ideas which are of great importance even today.'[87]

Dara's thinking remained the captive of the dominant ideas of his times marked by the then State ideology of Akbar. He expressed in his writings the essence in kernel form a possible future vision relevant for his country and suffered an untimely death for expressing it. He became a martyr at the altar of bigotry for expressing knowledge born of love from the heart common to all religious mystics as devotion to Him as Infinity of Cycles or eternity. He ended by noting this a work of his forty second year with a note of humility.

End Notes

1. Khaliq Ahmed Niazi, op. cit. p. xi.
2. Satish Chandra, op. cit. p. 285.
3. The companions of Muhammad who led a retired life living in the Madina mosque who started Sufism were an Ethiopian Bilal, Iranian Salman, Abu Ubayadah, Ammar bin Yasir and Abu Dharr Ghifari. Yet Ali was regarded by the Sufis as their Shaykh. Hasan Basari was the link between Ali and Sufi sects. He was both a Qadariyya and an ascetic. S. A. H. Rizvi, Islam in Medieval India, in A.L. Basham, The Wonder That Was India, Vol. 1, Picador, Indian Edition, 2004. pp. 281-283.
4. S. A. H. Rizvi, 'Islam in Medieval India', A. L. Basham, op. cit.

5. Majority in north India, had four principal faiths, viz. Hanafi after the name of Abu *Hanifa* of Kufa (c. 699-767); *Malikite* after Malik ibn Anas (d. 795); *Shaifi* iites after ash-Shafi of Baghdad and then lived in Cairo (767-820) and *Hanbalite* after Ahmed ibn Hanbal of Baghdad (780-855).
6. Asharis, recognised in Iran by Shah Ismail in 1501-1524. (Rulers in the Bijapur and Golconda kingdoms in the Deccan), were Shi There is disagreement over the number of successors beginning with Ali (6 / 11,).
7. Niazi, op. cit. p. 50.
8. *Ibid.* p. 51.
9. Carl W. Ernst, PhD, Sufism, Shambala, South Asia edition, 2000.
10. Robert Graves, op. cit. p.vii-vii.
11. Hasan Lutfi Shushud, op. cit.
12. Nevin Ergin, Foreword, Hasan Lufti Shushud, Masters of Wisdom of Central Asia, Teachings From THE Sufi Path of Liberation, transl. from the Turkish by Mukhtar Holland, inner traditions, Rochester, Vermont, Toronto, Canada, Ebooks.
13. Scot Kugle, edited by, transl. by Scot Kugle and Carl Ernst, Foreword, Sufi mysticism and contemplation, Timeless wisdom from Mughal India, op. cit.
14. Carl Ernst, The Shambala Guide to Sufism, op. cit; *ibid.*
15. Annie Besant, Mysticism, e-Books, Kindle.
16. Robert Graves, op. cit. p. xv.
17. Edmund Burke, edited by, The Annual Register of World Events: A Review of the Year, volume 57, p. 465.
18. Scot, op. cit.
19. Bikrama Jit Hasrat, Dara Shikuh, Life and Works, Munshiram Manoharlal Publishers Pvt. Ltd. New Dihli, 2013, p. 175.
20. This para is based on Muzzafar Alam, *Political Language of Political Islam in India, 1200-1800,* op. cit. pp. 72-74.
21. *Ibid.*
22. S. A. H. Rizvi, op. cit.
23. Idries Shah, op. cit. p. 433
24. Hasan Lufti Shushud, op. cit.
25. S. A. H. Rizvi, op. cit.
26. S. A. H. Rizvi, op. cit. p. 289
27. M. Mahfuz-ul-Haq, M. A., op. cit., p. v.
28. *Ibid.*
29. *Ibid.* p. 8.
30. Roma Chaudhari, M. A. D. Phil (Oxford) F. A. S. *'Dara Shikuh's Achievements in the fields of Learning and Culture'* in A Critical Study of Dara Shikoh's "Samudra-Samagam", Calcutta, 1954, p. 2.

31. Findly, op. cit. Ruchir Gupta, op. cit.
32. Reynold A. Nicholson, Foreword, Bikrama Jit Hazrat, op. cit. p. xvii-iii.
33. Paul Smith, op.cit.
34. Bikrama Jit Hazrat, op. cit. p. xxiii-xxiv.
35. *Ibid.*
36. *Ibid*, p. 135.
37. Paul Smith, op. cit. p. 31.
38. Paul Smith, Ibid. p. 32
39. *Ibid.* p. 36.
40. Carl W. Ernst, Ph.D. op. cit. pp. 166-68.
41. Quoted in Paul Smith, op.cit. p. 41.
42. *Ibid.* p. 46.
43. Halaj Said 'I am the truth'and got killed, Didn't he? Really it is the evil and malicious spirit of this priest: Every saint and every prophet he tormented. Didn't he?' *Ibid.* p. 57.
44. *Ibid.* p. 63.
45. *Ibid.* p. 21.
46. Inside and out, the clay pot was filled by air…

    Inside is the sound and noise vibrated, a blare: like bubble bursting to the ocean…everywhere.' *Ibid.* p. 63.
47. *Ibid.* p. 73.
48. We will return to this Punjab centricity latter in the chapter.
49. Op. cit. p. 81.
50. *Ibid.* p. 88.
51. Bikrama Jit Hazrat, op. cit, p. 135.
52. Paul Smith, op. cit. p. 92. See also his ghazal Realisation of the Self, in Bikrama Jit Hazrat, op. cit. p.144. In this ghazal the last lines are 'Qadiri found his Beloved within his own self:

    Himself of Good disposition, he won (the favor of) the Good.'
53. Bikrama Jit Hazrat, ibid. p. 131.
54. *Ibid.* p. 137.
55. Zafar (meaning Victory) was a Sufi Pir (unlike Dara) and a prolific Sufi Urdu poet and Calligrapher in captivity of the British against whom he wrote 'As long as there remains the scent of faith in the heart of our Ghazis, so long shall Talwar of Hindustan flash before London.' Like Dara he believed in magic, charms, transference of remedies through spiritual powers. His poetry embodied a multicultural composite Hindu-Islamic culture.
56. Marcia K. Hermansen and Bruce B. Lawrence,' Indo-Persian Tazkiras as Memorative Communication in David Gilmartin and Bruce B. Lawrence,

Beyond Turk and Hindu, Rethinking Religious Identities in Islamicate South Asia, University of Florida, Gainsville, Tallahasee, Tampa, Boca raton, Pensacola, Orlando, Jacksonville, Ft. Myers, 31 December, 2000, p. 149.

57. Bikrama Jit Hazrat, p. xxv.
58. Bikrama Jit Hasrat, op. cit. pp.48-63. The last part had subjective statements about his own life. He talked about his Qadiri identity, a dream, a tribute to Mulla Jami, a spiritual experience, his birth, Jahangir and visits to the tombs of various saints.
59. *Ibid.* pp. 61-70.
60. We noticed in the earlier chapter that the Path had three characteristics, mysticism, meditation and mediation.
61. Bikrama Jit Hazrat, op. cit, p. 75.
62. We noticed in the previous chapter that Sufis were regarded as belonging to Freemasonry cutting across religious divides on the basis of their mysticism, focus on heart and love meaning transcendental love.
63. Op. cit.
64. *Ibid.*
65. This was reflected in the cycle of initiation to annihilation to be achieved with mediation to mediation to mystical knowledge under a guide.
66. Bikrama Jit Hazrat, op. cit. p. 101.
67. *Ibid.* p. 103.
68. *Ibid.* pp. 103-106.
69. *Ibid.* p. 109.
70. Parenthesis is ours.
71. Parenthesis is ours.
72. Bikrama Jit Hazrat, op. cit. pp. 121-128.
73. M. Mahfuz-ul Haq, op. cit. p. 10.
74. Born in 973 Ad in Khiva, or Khwarizmi then so called, a scientist and literature, became a prisoner of war in 1017 AD, the reputation of astronomer, dedicated a book to a prince–Sultan Mahmud who caused much destruction to India, enjoyed royal patronage under Masod, the successor to Mahmud, stayed in different parts of India during 1017-1030 when in royal disgrace, studied India without anyone's patronage. He appreciated the Hindus for the knowledge of mathematics and astronomy, was positive about Sanskrit metrics, but all these views he held with the air of superiority. He had strong inclination for pure theories of the Bhagvadgita. 'As a Muslim though he does not escape the assertion of superiority of Islam over Brahmanic India, decrying caste, upholding superiority of matrimonial law of Islam in contrast to Indian laws and the cleanliness of Muslims against the filthiness of Hindus.' Yet he upheld the Hindu customs in contrast to the Arab society. Stylistically speaking, he did not

denounce the Hindus, opposed the priest who tried to convert them, not let any room to missionary zealots, and described Hinduism dispassionately. To quote Sachau, 'He gives a repertory of information on Indian subjects, destined for the use of those who lived in peaceable intercourse with them and wished to have an insight into their mode and world thought.' Dr Edward C. Sachau, Preface, Alberuni's India, Rupa, New Dihli, 2015 pp. xi-xxv.

75. The earliest Arabic scholars were interested in Greek and Islamic studies. The development of this trend took quite a few centuries. The interest in Islamicate studies involving Indian contribution to knowledge came much later. By the sixteenth century it transformed into Indo-Muslim interest in Hinduism. The water shed for this was Akbar's period preceded by Amir Khusrau's (Indian Turk) interest in Indian music, philosophy, logic, astronomy, physics, mathematics and metaphysics; the works of Abul Fazl and his brother, Abdul Faizi who were helped by Hindu Sanskrit scholars of Akbar's period stand out as a major boost to the study of comparative intellectual studies with a political purpose. Bikrama Jit Hasrat, op. cit, pp. 174-189.
76. Yogendra Singh, *Composite Culture, Community and Identity: Interface with Social Change in India in* Bipan Chandra and Sucheta Mahajan, edited, Composite Culture in a Multi-Cultural Society, Pearson, Longman 2007.
77. Satish Chandra, *Secularism and Composite Culture in a Multicultural Society*, in *ibid.*
78. John Rex, *The Concept of a Multicultural Society*,'Montserrat Guibernau and John Rex, edited, The Ethnicity Reader, Polity Press, pp. 205-219.
79. A follower of Chetan Swami of Lahor, a yogi, and with powers of performing miracles and built a hermitage for himself and began to initiate his creed of one God borrowing from Vedanta philosophy and Sufism, among his followers called 'Baba lalis', Dara was one. Dara described him as a man with clean shaven head and attached to the Kabir panthis. Kalinga Ranjan Qanungo, op. cit, pp. 332-333.
80. *Ibid.* pp. 334-347.
81. Op.cit. p. 212.
82. M. Mahfuz-ul-Haq, op. cit. translation, p. 37.
83. See Murad Ali Baig, Ocean of Cobras, tara, New Dihli, 2015 pp. 174-175.
84. Op. cit.
85. Bikrama Jit Hazrat, op. cit. pp. 217-218.
86. Johan Van Manen, Foreword, fn. 79.
87. Amalendu De, Preface, fn. 79.

Chapter - 4

Trajectory of Heir Apparent

Dara Shukuh was an adept scholar, a competent man of arms, preferred by his father as an *Heir Apparent*, a popular one at that in Agrah and Dihli, supported by his elder sister, Jahanara, herself esteemed by the people. She shared with Dara Sufi persuasion as a follower of Mulla Shah, a biographer of Sufi Saints and powerful court personality. Being the eldest and the most cherishedson, Dara was rivalled by and an eyesore for his other siblings-sister Roushanara and younger brothers, namely Shah Shuja,[1] Aurangzeb, and Murad Baksh. The third sister and the last of Shah Jahan's children, Guharara-at whose birth Mumtaz Mahal passed away-was committed to the triumvirate of brothers through Murad Baksh. Every rise and recognition of Dara by his father caused greater heart burning to his siblings. No royal family of medieval times was spared this kind of malaise in the absence of a firm law of primogeniture owing to a complex web of family relationships. Most rulers suffered intrigues, incarceration, wars and assassinations here and elsewhere causing turbulence and instability.

No Civil War or Class Struggle

In case of the Mughal dynasty the ailment existed from the time of Babur. Babur's struggle within his family in Afghanistan, Humayun's oppositions by his brothers, one of whom even used his son (infant Akbar) as a shield on an occasion of a siege laid by Humayun, the travails of Akbar, Jahangir and Shah Jahan and Dara Shukuh showed up real politik of the empire and the household of the Mughal Emperors. It was no less than a Kingship earthquake or power politics shaking the country. There were no class struggles that determined the future course for no section of the common people took to arms either in the city, qasbas or villages. There were no civil wars among the rulers and the people, who revolted spontaneously/episodically for this or that wrong of a governor of a province. The class struggles of the time did not rock the cradle of the Mughal Empire not with standing the severity of Shia Sunni fault lines' inter-play within the nobility.

Politics was coloured blue by royalty's blood that saw the dawn of every Emperor's reign, except that of Akbar who was groomed by his Regent[2] for the first years of his boyhood. Prince Salim's revolt was a short lived cracker for Akbar. Shah Jahan's successful entry to the court of Bulaqi (the puppet king) was through the subterfuge of a coffin, after he had established himself militarily a victor. Different levels of fear seized the minds of brothers and sisters with regard to royal disloyalty owing to the insecurity of their respective future under changed circumstances. This was indeed ironic for here was a Monarchy that put a premium on loyalty but negated by atomic kinship.

In the earlier period of the Dihli Sultanate it was the loyalty along with arms of the slaves that had made them 'Amirs' and finally some rose to be Kings. The life curve of Qutubuddin Aibak and Iyaltimish who had to fight Qabacha to become a King prove it. The last two mentioned were not blood relations. Famous is the haram conspiracy against Raziya in favour of Ruknuddin-Raziya's brother. She became the Sultan later where the role of the people of Dihli made a contribution to foil another conspiracy.

In case of Dara and Aurangzeb, if there was anything that bound them together it was mutual hatred, ambition and intent to go for each other's scalp. Their living together under Nur Jahan's stewardship ironically as surety of their father's good behaviour added no brotherhood. In fact Shah Jahan's family was unique in the fact that there were no older ladies to exercise restraint nor was there any one, like Jahangir who was considerate towards older ladies. Shah Jahan's own record in this case is not worth an ounce of value since he had put Nur Jahan behind bars and sent her to oblivion of Lahor after her brother[3] had arrested her. Her daughter Ladli was made a Salatin. It was not sure if Jahanara helped Ladli to go to Lahore and be buried next to her mother in Lahor though one fictional account mentioned this. In fact a Chronicler then considered it to be Shah Jahan's leniency-surely not clemency. In his opinion she should have been killed.

Shah Jahan's own conduct can be described in Machiavellian terms as that of a Prince in revolt for quite some time. For this he was called a Bi-daulat and his children were kept as surety by his own father.[4] He was both a fox (cunning) and a lion when it came to capturing power. This seems to be the trait he passed on to his own son Aurangzeb, who seemed to him to better his example by being a menace to his (Shah Jahan's) own authority by 1657, as he had feared for quite some time.

His rule was evidence of justice, prosperity, growth of art and architecture (construction of the Taj Mahal, Red Fort and Jama Masjid in Dihli and its Bazaars, e.g.) balanced by his Sunni identity, foreign policy of isolating Shia Persia by being with the Turks and Transoxiana and destruction of temples (that he restored owing to Dara's intervention) and getting the peacock thronoyade. His benign aspects reflected the political values bequeathed by Akbar through Jahangir. These were reflected in his,eldest son, Dara Shukuh. Qanungo suggests this bifurcation of Janus faced Shah Jahan's traits between Dara and Aurangzeb with Murad and Shah Shuja being variants of these features.

Politics and War: *Implosion*

The dramatis personae were the family members up in arms against one another involving younger ladies of the household despite the sobering role of the revered older ladies.[5] The military camp, the royal court and the haram were marked by real politick and politics by other means i.e. War, as Clausewitz put it. In chapter one we noticed that the Mughal Empire was not an extension of the household rather it was the other way round. Both were arenas of politics and war since kingship knew no kinship. The betrothals, animosities, friendships, sense of loyalty, family alliances, promotions, recognition, assassinations, and celebration of births[6], burials and martyrdom, grant of jagirs and Mansabs linked to zat (salary) and sawars (soldiers), and, party politics at the Court were part of the game of politics that ultimately proved to be a zero sum game for the empire. The victory of Aurangzeb and the defeat of Dara Shukuh turned out to be the undoing of the Mughals and a regression for India's politics of compositeness after 1857. The turn of events against the *crystal tower*[7] *owing to the treachery of*

Khalilullah Khan signified the implosion of the Mughal dynasty. On communal schism in the subsequent period and eventual partition of India and subsequent problems Waldemar Hansen says,

'The enduring nightmare of Aurangzeb's schismatic intent had triumphed over Akbar's and Dara Shikoh's dreams of unity.'[8]

Scholar-Soldier

The journey of Shah Buland Iqbal Dara Shukuh was a journey of a Man of Letters and Man of Arms. Dara, the scholar-soldier, was an attractive star by any standards of Akhlalq. An Army that was impressive and feared in the country, avoided conflict with the Mongols[9] was less than a match for the Persians.[10] The Army was parcelled within provinces, accompanying the Monarchy that was regularly on the move with the peripatetic court and Monarch with his haram. It had no formal training for recruitment except learning through wrestling, hunting, riding horses, wielding swords and small arms[11] supported by European artillery. It had no regular drill, practicing hand to hand fighting and exercises managed with tactical moves using the terrain of the battlefield. The element of surprise of the speed of the horseman and personal stamina to withstand woes of war made *war heroes*. By being on the move was another form of training, drill and discipline.

The points of surprise, speed and individual valour were emphasised by Babur and practised by every successful Emperor among others. So did Dara and Aurangzeb in different degrees at different times of battles they fought. In case of the war of succession that was fought between Dara and his siblings, great role of *deceit (called finesse by some commentators)* as his master quality made Aurangzeb a winning horse against his brother though he himself had a record of losing to the Persians at Kandahar earlier. He was cast in ignominy to a small Multan as a punishment by Shah Jahan for this, even though in Balkh and Badakshan earlier, he along with his general, was honoured. Dara subsequently had been successful (owing to their own difficulties of Persians in some measure)in getting Bust and Zamin Dawar. This enabled Shah Jahan to form the subah of Kandahar. Earlier Murad Baksh had failed to get this coveted prize.

The fight for Kandahar was off and on since 1522 between the Timurids and the Safavis involving the game of musical chairs during

Akbar and Jahangir's reigns. Where Aurangzeb and Murad had failed Dara had succeeded even if it was hardly a full engagement with the Persians. Qanungo notes the significance of this victory as part of Shah Jahan's foreign policy. He says,

> 'The characteristic feature of the Indian foreign policy during 16th and the 17th centuries had been the diplomatic isolation of heretical Persian by a coalition of the Sunni rulers of Hindustan, Turkey and Transoxiana.'[12]

The criticism of Dara as a failed soldier and a weak/scheming man was misplaced and partisan since it came from the pen of Bernier who had depended on Danishmand Khan (a learned man) the supporter of Aurangzeb. The worst expression of this jaundiced view was represented by Muhammad Kazim the writer of chronicle of Aurangzeb's reign, Kafi Khan and Muhammad Salih Kamba joined by Bernier. Kazim considered him a heretic.[13] Kafi Khan too regarded him a Sufi heretic.[14] Amal i Salih called him narrow minded, blamed him for causing the disturbances.[15] The context of these remarks was the politiking by the partisans in Shah Jahan's court. That court was, as were courts of earlier Emperors, rife with party politics involving the religious divide between the Islamic orthodox and Sufi liberal, a divided nobility and the changing colours and contours of loyalty among the Hindu (Rajput) and Muslim turncoats. The villain of the peace was deceitful acts and betrayals of disgruntled nobles in favour of Aurangzeb rather than the personality or bravery of Dara who was more of a clean man. Waldemar Hansen aptly put it thus,

> 'Caught in the court of the Moghuls, he makes a stab as coping with the practical details of statesmanship of war. But he is too naive, too credulous, he is fine and ingenious where others were coarse and cunning.'[16]

Shah Buland Iqbal

On February 3, 1655 Dara Shukuh appeared at the Court (durbar) of Shah Jahan in a special robe of honour conferred on him by his father. His vest was gold embroidered, the collar was studded with a fortune in diamond, the sleeves and skirts sewn with endless pearls. Shah Jahan, on the occasion of his sixty sixth lunar birthday, removed a turban fillet set with a great ruby and two wide rings of pearls, and attached it to the head of Dara Shukuh addressing him with a new title as Shah Buland Iqbal, formerly bestowed on Shah Jahan by Jahangir. The father required the son to sit on a golden chair made for him next to the throne of the Emperor, i.e. the Peacock Throne. He became a co-ruler.[17] His brothers were jealous if not restive, to put it mildly. This resulted in conspiracy on their part.

Earlier Appointments

This coveted position came after a long list of positions that were conferred on the first born by Shah Jahan causing constant heart burning among Dara Shukuh's brothers. Dara Shukuh's appointments and titles began very early. They were, as listed by Qanungo[18]:

(1) First Mansab given on Oct 5, 1653. Punjab was given to him as a fief on a high salary and soldiers as a signal to make him the heir designate.

(2) Within five years his Mansab was increased to such an extent that in terms of the cavalry and money, his command was more than the combined strength of Shah Shuja and Aurangzeb. Both of them were far off controlling Bengal and the Dakhyn, respectively. Both had joined hands against him subsequently.

(3) He was made the viceroy of Allahabad and assisted by Shaista Khan with the additional charge of two imperial forts, Chunar and Rohtas on 15 June, 1645. These were governed by his subordinate (Baqi Beg) for the next twelve years. During the civil war when Dara Shukuh was on the run, he used these areas to facilitate Aurangzeb's son, Sultan Muhammad when he was revolting against his father and had joined up Shah Shuja during the war of succession.

(4) He became the viceroy of Punjab in March 1647. After his defeat at Samugarh, leaving Agrah and Dihli he took to Lahor (Lahore) and Multan in the Punjab.

(5) His military rank was high and his salary was Rupees 75,000 annually apart from his forces.

(6) He had fiefs in Kashmir, Kangra, and Punjab and jagirs of Sadullah Khan who was the prime minister and ally of Aurangzeb by 1656.

(7) He had two rich sinecures of *Kaul* (Aligarh) and the Rahdari (guardianship) of the region between Agrah and Dihli with the total income of twenty two and a half lakhs of rupees. Once Dara lost at the Samugarh he came to Agrah. From there he moved to the Dihli region. Shah Jahan helped him from the treasury of Dihli at this point in time for him to muster forces.

Early Signs of Hostility sans Religion

Despite Dara, Aurangzeb and Shah Shuja being kept as hostages under Nur Jahan's care in Jahangir's court owing to Prince Khurram's (later Shah Jahan) failed rebellion against his father, there was not much childhood bonding among them. This was a fair reporting by default of chroniclers giving no evidence to the contrary. There were early signs of their jealousies as they were growing up, especially of the younger brothers towards their elder brother. The prime of place of the matrix of jealousies without, any frills of religious odium, was occupied by Aurangzeb who was joined by Shah Shuja[19] and Murad Baksh[20] and other disgruntled bellicose elements of the nobility who had their own grouse against either Shah Jahan (Khalilullah Khan, Asaf Khan and Jafar Khan) or Dara (Jai Singh, Rup Singh, Jaswant Singh) and Mir Jumla. We deal with these disgruntled elements later.

Incidents Relating to Aurangzeb's early Hostility

Two incidents showed this up.[21] One related to an elephant fight and the other to a visit of Shah Jahan to the quarters of Dara Shukuh. There was an elephant fight in 1633 on the sandy plains of the Jamuna behind the Red Fort in Agrah. Dara, Shah Shuja and Aurangzeb moved closer to one of the elephants. That particular elephant had made its opponent to flee. Then made a move towards Aurangzeb's horse and flung it down. In his fifteenth year, Aurangzeb showed courage of steel and came out victorious against the elephant. On this occasion Aurangzeb gave vent to his ill will against his brothers. Maliciously commenting on Dara he said to his father "If the fight had ended fatally for me" "it would not have been a matter of shame.... The shame lay in what my brothers did." He implied unjustifiably Dara Shukuh in this insinuation for Dara Shukuh was on the other side and was not in proximity to the location of Aurangzeb.

The second incident related to the visit of the royal family with the Royal Highness to the then recently constructed mansion by Dara at Agrah. The party was organised at a cool underground room bordering the river. Everyone entered but Aurangzeb. He kept sitting at the entrance gate. He did not reply to Shah Jahan's query about this strange behaviour. For this strange behaviour he was forbidden by Shah Jahan to enter the court. Seven months later he shared his behaviour with Jahanara that since the room had only one door he had feared lest Dara should close it and murder his own father and the rest of the family. So he sat as a sentinel to prevent such an eventuality. This malady was an early example of his thinking as well as his ill will for Dara. This was in the view of Qanungo a revelation of Aurangzeb as a future murderer of his brothers son's and gaoler of his father.

Shah Jahan's Tactical Postings of his Sons

Shah Jahan's astute administrative handling of the evident signs of future fission and Aurangzeb's personality was that he had kept his sons far apart and provided pride of place to the heir- apparent, Dara Shukuh. This strategy may have *delayed* but *failed* to *prevent* the subsequent implosion that he most feared keeping in view Aurangzeb's ambition and character, which was more significant as a cause than Shah Jahan's preferential treatment of Dara. He had warned Dara against Aurangzeb much earlier at the time when Dara had pleaded on Aurangzeb's behalf to shift him from Multan to the Dakhyn. In this effort sister, Jahanara (to whom Aurangzeb had written separately) had supported Dara. Dara understood Aurangzeb well as a Namazi.[22] Shah Jahan had warned Dara about this snake and cautioned him about the consequences of Aurangzeb's poisonous qualities. On another occasion Shah Jahan, not impressed by Aurangzeb's subterfuge of a faqir, warned Dara Shukuh as reported by Manucci

> 'You are acting on behalf of a venomous snake, and you will have to suffer from its poison.'[23]

These were prophetic views since the consequences of Aurangzeb's actions were murders of his brothers and some of their children, including his own, Sultan Muhammad, among others.

At the time of Shah Jahan's accession the revenues of Hindustan and the Dakhyn, were reckoned as the largest of all the countries, divided into fourteen subas of the provinces.[24] Subsequently after Dara's taking over of Bust and Zamini Dawar Shah Jahan had made it the suba of Kandahar. Bernier reported about Shah Jahan's tactic[25] against his sons thus,

> 'He was indeed in perpetual apprehension of their having recourse to arms, and either erecting independent principalities, or converting the seat of government into bloody arena, in which to settle their personal differences. To save himself, therefore, from some impending calamity, *Chah-Jehan* resolved to bestow upon his sons the government of four distant provinces. Sultan Shuja was appointed to Bengal; Aurangzeb to the Deccan; Murad-Bacshe (Baksh) to Gujarate; and Dara to Caboul (Kabul) and Multan.'

Shah Jahan kept the apple of his eye close to him resulting in Dara's participation in the central administration more as and when the need arose. This naturally caused both alarm and envy among the brothers. Aurangzeb was posted to the insignificant area of Multan while Dara was looking after Lahor (spelt as Lahore later). It appears that Aurangzeb did not acquit himself well there in the eyes of his father. During his governorship of Multan (1648-1652) Ismail Hut, the subordinate of Dara Shukuh in Lahor, did not wait upon Aurangzeb since they belonged to two different territorial entities. On being asked he showed a letter of Dara who was then with his father in Kabul. This was evidence of the dispute over jurisdiction of the two viceroys of contiguous provinces- a dispute which the Emperor justly decided in favour of Aurangzeb.

Once the charge of Multan came to Dara Shukuh he wrote to the Emperor about the misdeeds of Aurangzeb whose servants had destroyed many buildings in Multan. More regrettably Aurangzeb indulge in some unsavory incidents. On his way to the Dakhyn, alighted in the neighborhood of Lahor. Dara's official came out of the city to receive him apparently. Aurangzeb did not acknowledge this courtesy, walked past him and re-entered the city without visiting him. This had the intent of lowering the Prince in the public eye. The injustice to Dara Shukuh at his hands was in suspecting that Dara's servant had insulted him at his master's biding even if because Dara was staying with his father at Kabul.[26]

Dara's Administrative Skills

Dara's administrative acumen need to be seen in the context of the administrative machinery that was originally set up by Akbar, carried forward by his successors and the negative growths therein. As noted earlier in Chapter One Akbar's administration involved the Mohammadans and Hindu jagirdars and the mansabdars on salary (including the royal princes), the restrictions on them not to over tax the peasantry below them to tune in the financial system, and an efficient correspondence system that meant excellent travel infrastructure with roads and sarais, based on the ideas of Sovereignty of the State residing in the person of the Emperor and not the Sharia but for Suhl-I-Kul. Property relations were codified through *Farmans (Edicts)*.[27] The pivot of state power was an alliance system between the Hindus (especially Rajputs) and Muslims –a system begun by Humayun under the Persian advice. There was also the befriending of the Shias and Sikhs in his times. This was in a sense the idea of popular sovereignty.

Dara Shukuh remained within this paradigm of the polity in every manner. Further he had befriended the Jesuits. Bernier remarked that his entire liberality was only a charade for this was a political tactic of alliances in an hour of need. His realpolitik was based on his alliance with the Hindus, in terms of power underwritten with marriage alliances. The marriages of his elder son, e.g. as noted above reflected this aspect. His endearing of Rup Singh working for common cord between the Hindus and the Muslims and Jaswant Singh also showed this up. His efforts as a scholar proved this to the hilt. This practice was followed by every prince. Aurangzeb had alliance with Sunni Muslims and Rajputs.

Indiscrete utterances and Shah Jahan's Sex forays

His cavalier attitude in dealing with the nobles created problems that did not go well with both his father and some of the nobles. His treatment of Raja Jai Singh invited talking back by Jai Singh at the time of Kandahar expedition. He made fun of some nobles at court for example Khalilullah Khan leading to court laughter, mistreating Mahabat Khan's soldier again in the court annoyed them all beyond repair. His praise of Jafar Khan in front of Izzat Khan during the Kandahar operation was indiscrete.

Shah Jahan's sex-escapades with the wives of Jafar Khan, Khalilullah Khan and his brother-in-law, Shaistan Khan cost Dara Shukuh heavily later. They were sneered by the other members in the court- an insult they gulped and remembered. All of them waited to take revenge and that came later during the war of succession. [28] The heir-apparent paid heavily for this.

Negatives of the Administration

A rot in the Moghul administration had set in by the seventeenth century. There were issues of salaries not being paid to the Mansabs,[29] revenue losses thereby and the drain owing to incessant wars, revolts by princes (Mughal and Hindus Rajas) and siphoning off of the moneys by the recalcitrant provincial heads and the nobility like Aurangzeb. At the time when Aurangzeb was dealing with Golconda and Bijapur, Dara had complained that he had not sent the entire booty to the imperial treasury, apart from other issues. Others were similarly involved in cheating the royal exchequer. There were revolts of the jagirdars for their ends which were part of court politics. There was an agrarian crisis brewing since Shah Jahan's times. Even though he sat on the Peacock Throne-the pride of the world for its Kohinoor[30] till date, his architectural marvels of the Taj Mahal, again a pride of the world as a wondrous symbol of love and death, though housed many dead bodies, the peasantry and the people were poor. There were revolts from time to time. Chandra observes,

> 'More germane was the growing gap between the real and the paper income of the jagirs, which had come to a head during Shah Jahan's reign, leading to a reduction both of zat (personal) salaries, and of the obligation of the number of troops and mounts to be maintained.'[31]

Administration and Marriages

Dara's administrative actions need to be seen in the context of criss-cross of marriage alliances that the household was based on. Same significant personages were related to more than one brother or relative in the entire history of the Mughal period. During Jahangir's time the members of the junta that ruled for a brief period involved Nur Jahan (Jahangir's wife), Prince Khurram (first born to Jahangir), Nur Jahan's father and brother, Asaf Khan (I and II), whose daughter was married to Khurram and Nur Jahan's daughter from her earlier marriage to Sher Afghan , Ladli was married to Jahangir's another son , Shahryar. Prince Khurram's wife was the daughter Nur Jahan's brother. Nur Jahan was at a later twilight stage of her power interested in helping Shahryar to be the Emperor. Her brother, Asaf Khan was interested in Prince Khurram becoming the Emperor owing to his daughter, Mumtaz Mahal being married to Prince Khurram.

Kinship underwrote power politics and vice-versa. It was also well known that Aurangzeb and Shah Shuja were in agreement to marry their children at the time when Shah Jahan had assigned to them far off provinces to deter them from being a threat to him. Marriages of Aurangzeb's children also had a significant role to play in the alliances he forged during the war of succession. Sultan Muhammad, Aurangzeb, his eldest son married Shah Shuja's daughter and the daughter of the king of Golconda. Sulaiman Shukuh was married to a Muslim noble's daughter (1654) as well as to the daughter of a Hindu Raja Jai Singh's niece for reasons purely of Statecraft and need in time for winning over a man whom he had alienated during the Kandahar campaign. Shah Jahan two years later took the initiative for a second marriage of Sulaiman to a daughter of a noble-a concession to the feelings of Moslem nobility in general.[32] These played out in the administrative chess board in lobbies, factions, and parties. Nobles like Shah Nawaz Khan had two daughters and they were married to Murad Baksh and Aurangzeb.

The administrative skills were subject to this complex web of kinship, kingship, and factional politics. Which way the scales tilted was determined by the person in power and capacities to intrigue. Long term interest and the realpolitik of the individual's short term aims wrestled along. There were no permanent alliance systems. They were shifting like the shifting sand.

Lobbies, Factions and Parties

The Kingship-Kinship cocktail was quite a bomb, almost a cocktail bomb of the present times. It built and destroyed power cliques and juntas. The bone of contention being administrative advantages, favours, appointments, attention of the Emperor, placating/hemming him, distributing favours or sheer rebellion to win power. The kingship-kinship syndrome was an unintended result of the Mughal practice of not marrying their women outside the royal blood initiated by Akbar for maintaining the blue blood. The factional struggle for power was thus centred within the charmed royal circle with frills of the nobility taking sides out of selfishness, conscience, valour, gratitude, loyalty, jealousy, the desire to take revenge and seek change in kinship network. Briefly put it was a reminder of Jahangir's dictum quoted in an earlier chapter that Kingship knows no Kinship. Loyalty knew no permanent patrons, friends or foes.

Junta during Jahangir's Reign

One example of such lobbying or the emergence of the junta was provided by Jahangir's reign itself. The rise of the junta was facilitated by three factors, namely, the propitious positioning of the family preceding the formation of the Junta, the meritorious service of the members of the family and the personality and beauty of Nur Jahan.[33] This was complimented by over-drunkenness of Jahangir who himself recorded that Nur Jahan had to restrict his drinking to five cups since he had gone up to 25, (the early revolts of Prince Khusrau and the wasteful, drunken interests of Parwiz and Shahryar (Emperor's two elder sons) and the respect, handsomeness and adroitness of Prince Khurram who was loved and preferred by Akbar and loved by Jahangir).

The *composition* of the junta was of five members all of them in blood relationship and forming a web of family interests. Nur Jahan's father, Itammaudduala (respected and promoted by Akbar and called 'pivot of the country' by Jahangir) hailed from Persia, his son Asaf Khan (II)'s daughter (later became Mumtaz Mahal made famous by Shah Jahan's love for her in the form of the Taj Mahal) was married to prince Khurram, Nur Jahan's daughter, Ladli Begam, from her first marriage to Sher Afghan, was married to Jahangir's son Shahryar. All this happened after Jahangir married Nur Jahan in 1611. Other promotions of her brothers, brothers-in- law and cousins were the work of Nur Jahan. The opposition to the junta came from Mahabat Khan, who had revolted against a brother-in-law of Nur Jahan and who often spoke to Jahangir against her.

The *functions* of the junta were to deal with the affairs of the country, the court and relations with the Europeans with the help of control over communications (this included weekly espionage system), vested interest of the nobility and protecting the King from unnecessary responsibility.[34] The kingpin of the Junta was Nur Jahan who was the route to any importance of meetings/and/or favours sought by the nobility or the Europeans/British Embassy. Mr. Roe's descriptions are many on this, especially since he found it difficult to get along with Nur Jahan (his expensive gifts to her did not cut much ice). He befriended her brother, Asaf Khan (II). Roe was having trade liaison with him and through him (pursued his country's interests). He was merely the conduit to her for final decisions, though with passage of time her brother outlived her importance in general during twilight years of Jahangir.

As her brother sided with Khurram whose activities of revolt, beginning in 1620s culminating in his accession fortunes by 1627, his importance increased. Asaf Khan supported Shah Jahan and Nur Jahan supported Prince Shahryar for Emperorship who was married to her daughter. She planned to extend her years of power thus. It was instead Asaf Khan (II) who got fresh lease of importance in the court of Shah Jahan. Mahabat Khan joined Asaf Khan (II) in this power politics. Earlier, the group had managed the ill fortunes of Khusrau in *protective custody*, dealt with Parwiz deftly till he passed away. They handled the Europeans for foreign trade and diplomacy with the Dutch, the Portuguese and the English. The genesis, structure and activities of the junta showed that this grouping managed the affairs of the state in domestic and foreign affairs till its fall and the emergence of a new blocks of politics.

Political Parties in Shah Jahan's Court

Shah Jahan's court was marked by parties involving the family members as the kingpin. There were two factions or parties with the same agenda: power: Who would take position of Shah Jahan's. The issue was raised during his life- time only. Waldemar Hansen[35] said,

> 'Though no one talked about the future, the unspoken question was: what would happen when the Emperor died. He himself had

occasionally discussed the future with intimates, and prognostications were gloomy.'

Succession Issue

The parties in this struggle for the Crown were Dara on the one side and Aurangzeb on the other. The struggle for power and parties had an added feature that was absent during the period of the Junta under Jahangir's reign. The issue was ideological in terms of Islamic religion for succession this time as a frill. Dara's group was for peace and Aurangzeb's group was for war. Peace perhaps owing to Dara's characteristic of being overconfident in this case about being at the centre of power. He always had been at the centre of power owing to his father's weakness for the eldest son and his desire of making him the heir apparent. The issue of war was added owing to Aurangzeb since he was away from the centre of power and was ill-disposed towards his father and hostile to Dara Shukuh. His ambition to be the Emperor was the pivot of his designs.

Religious Frill

The second aspect was Islamic religious fission between Dara's liberal attitude to religion and Sunni religious bigotry as a frill attached by Aurangzeb to it. It was a frill for a variety of reasons. First was that he had no problems in aligning with Shah Shuja who was a Shia.[36] Second, he used a Hindu astrologer to dupe Dara. Third he staged a farce in front of Shah Jahan about magical qualities about himself as a man of predicting future events.[37] Fourth, his posture of abstinence was exposed when he fell for a dancing girl, enjoyed music and drank.[38] Fifth, he posed his personal selfless religiosity with Murad (a Shia like Shuja) to trick him into an alliance with him by offering him the crown. Subsequently got him drunk and killed him since he was a threat to his own plans to wrest the Crown for himself.[39] He told Murad Baksh that he did not relish the pleasures of the table and wanted to make him the Emperor. The pursuit of power was his central goal. The use of Sunni bigotry was deployed further to eliminate Dara by using the Maulvi and nobles who were against Dara's liberality towards Hindus and Christians.[40] Pure and simple it was statecraft as was also reflected in the fact that he employed the Hindus to manage financial administration even though he imposed *Jiziya* and destroyed temples.

Composition

The core of the two parties was Dara, supported by his elder and capable sister, Jahanara[41] on the side of Shah Jahan and the other three brothers with less capable Rushanara[42] and very able noble Allami Sadullah Khan, the vizier at the centre. Hamid acknowledged him to be his patron.[43] He had been in company of Aurangzeb in the Kandahar's unsuccessful expedition (1648), successfully handled the Balk and Badakshan expeditions earlier earning him honours. He was successful in the campaign against Raja Jai Singh of Chitor (1653). He was peeved by Dara's intercession with the Emperor on behalf of Raja Jai Singh to get reprieve to defeated Jai Singh from Shah Jahan. He had been defeated by Sadullah Khan. He was the most trusted man of Shah Jahan. It was rumored that Dara got him poisoned and killed though Inayat Khan disputed this and alluded to colic as the cause of Sadullah Khan's death.

Sadullah Khan and Dara Shukuh

Sadullah Khan and Dara Shukuh's rivalry was similar to the one between Jahangir and Abul Fazl during the last days of Akbar. Both led significant factions in the court of Akbar and Shah Jahan and Sadullah Khan, the man of worldly affairs and astute insight, often found himself fuming over actions that were taken as a result of Dara's influence over his father. Qanungo refered to quite a few anecdotes about their rivalry.[44] Sadullah and Dara disliked each other for their learning and their sectarian views on Islam-one a liberal and the other a bigoted Sunni, an ally of Aurangzeb.

Mir Jumla: astute turn coat

In this grouping the significance of Mir Jumla cannot be overstated for it is his combination with Aurangzeb that brought two very able leaders (Berniers description of the two) together in the war of succession. Religion was not the cementing factor of the group dominated by Aurangzeb. Mir Jumla[45] was a Persian who after arriving in Surat became a precious stones' (diamonds) merchant. He had grown in wealth and influence with the Europeans, especially with the Portuguese.

He rose in power structure generally both in Shah Jahan's court[46] and in the Dakhyn (first as Wazir in Golconda and later captured

Karnatik now Karnataka especially), helped Aurangzeb with amassing wealth of Golconda by suggesting the plan of taking over the King of Golconda and promised Aurangzeb to pay the expenses of the operations. He rose in the court of Shah Jahan whose protection began in 1656, a supporter of Dara Shukuh initially and ultimately became a part of Aurangzeb's deceitful strategy at Bijapur and in the war of succession for which he was awarded the Governorship of Bengal after Aurangzeb ascended the throne.[47] The Dakhyn politics and his relations with the King's mother (Golconda) made Bernier observe that sex had role to play in the war therein. He was greatest of the turn coats changing sides like a chameleon changed colours.

The issue that the ideological resurgence raised was as to what was the need for the restoration of the old order that Akbar had, with the able Abul Fazl, discarded in this country. There were some emerging signs for it. First, both Jahangir and Shah Jahan who followed much of Akbar's religious liberality and community concord showed signs of Sunni bigotry in destroying temples. Though in case of the latter he corrected the mistake on the intervention of Dara Shukuh. Jahangir had come heavily upon the Sikhs at one stage-especially Arjun Singh who had treated Khusrau well as we noted above. Overall their regimes exhibited liberality and prosperity. Shah Jahan kept asserting his Sunni identity with regard to foreign policy and some internal issues even though he had been granted the freedom by the Ulema not to observe religious fast of Ramzan. Instead he disbursed charity since he had reached the age of sixty in 1650.[48] He got some temples in Benaras destroyed in the sixth year of his reign.[49]

The other reason could be the possibility of existence of poverty and economic and sectional crises caused by continual war, and siphoning off of wealth by unscrupulous rulers and jagirdars below the layer of opulence of the flourishing of art and architecture under Shah Jahan. These had not assumed the general crisis in need of an explosion even though there were the revolts in the Northeast under Bhim Narain.[50] So politics remained of the old kind: implosion within the family power politics or regicide taking on the colour of restoration of the Sharia and the breakup of the concord among communities that Aurangzeb's rule subsequently symbolised. His restoration was not very helpful since the Jaziya did not add to his revenue. His entire restoration was overturned soon after his demise by his own men.

Dara Before and During Shah Jahan's illness in 1657

The title of Shah Buland Iqbal was given to Dara after he had participated in the campaign to Kandahar. In the preceding unsuccessful one Aurangzeb was recalled from his campaign that did not produce any results. Inayat Khan's descriptions of the two campaigns were short and make the following points. Abu-l Hamid Lahori mentioned that Kandahar war included in Akbar's empire in the fortieth year of his reign.[51] Inayat Khan noted that there were problems about Kandahar during the 15th year of Jahangir's reign and 17th year of Shah Jahan's reign. Shah Jahan was able to get it only when Ali Mardan Khan was enticed to leave the Persians during the reign of Shah Jahan. However the fortress of Bust went back owing to abandonment of the fortress of Khaushi. In 1648 Shah Abbas II of Persia with his heavy weapons and sedition in the Mughal Army and the winter snow won it back. In this fight Sạdullah Khan (the man in Aurangzeb's party) and Aurangzeb were involved and were asked to return.

In the next campaign Dara was sent to Kandahar and after making three months and some days' preparations at Multan and Lahor marched and ultimately assisted by Rustam Khan, brought in Bust but could not successfully conduct the siege of Kandahar. The Royal Edict of His Highness instructed them to return. This was celebrated as a great victory of Dara Shukuh.[52] Qanungo's discussion of this Kandahar episode was revealing with regard to the preparations, Dara's dispositions and significance of getting Bust and Zamin Dawar back. He made the following significant points:

(1) Tantric sadhu performed black magic for his victory; a haji, who was a magician and hypnotist also failed to fulfil his promise' so did a yogi, south Indian sadhus failed. They all promised to help in the siege. A promise that brought them favours but no success.[53]

(2) Bust and Zamin Dawar were won over by the efforts of Rustam Khan who was then asked to join the siege of Qandahar.[54]

(3) Dara's treatment of and indiscreet timing of the praise of Jafar Khan alienated Izzat Khan, both important nobles of the Empire participating in the expedition. Raj Rup Singh, Raja Jai Singh and Mahabat Khan were roughly treated with insinuations and insults. Qanungo concluded

'...he embittered the feelings of the three most powerful nobles of the Empire (Mahabat Khan, Jafar Khan and Izzat Khan) but also sowed the seeds of mutual jealousies between his two confidants by his tactless praise of Jafar Khan in the presence of Izzat Khan.'[55]

The insults to Raj Rup and Raja Jai Singh cost him dearly in the war of succession. The campaign was marred by *inaction of Generals*, their disloyalty, dissensions and talking back of almost all the major commanders of the Army, especially Jai Singh, Raja Rup and Najabat Khan in front of Dara. The front that engaged in the fight was badly mauled with 1000 fatalities. The artillery and the army did not acquit itself well at all. The Afghans in the army helped the Persians with supplies to undo the siege and the Afghan neighborhood played havoc by the disruption of communication and supplies from Lahor and Multan and the Afghan tribes' harassment of the returning army.[56]

Steps during and after Shah Jahan's brief illness

But Dara Shukuh was received well, decorated and practically made a co-ruler. His acts hereafter showed his understanding of Aurangzeb's real intent, the strategy of making friends with Rajputs in forging alliances, weakening the opposition, strapping the Opposition's allies (especially Mir Jumla) so as to prevent Aurangzeb from becoming powerful and withholding of communications from the three brothers, sending army against Murad Baksh under Qasim Khan, against Shah Shuja under his son Sulaiman Shukuh under Jai Singh's supervision, and restraining Aurangzeb in Golconda and Shah Jahan's sending of Mahabat Khan, Salabat Khan and Najabat Khan against the Dakhyn to whet the appetite for riches of the Karnatik and Dakhyn though this was not liked against the wishes of Dara and Jahanara.[57] Similarly the three brothers were engaged in forming an entente to prevent the common Enemy–Dara-from coming to power. In terms of strategy it was difficult to find fault with Dara's steps during brief illness of Shah

Jahan and his recovery. The feverish activity of the three brothers had preceded Shah Jahan's illness. Dara was quite aware of it.

Dakhyn politics at this juncture (1665-1657)

The coming together of Aurangzeb and Mir Jumla was significant for subsequent events. Berniers' account, followed more or less by Manucci, considered this companionship to be of great men and decisive.[58]

Amir Jumla became a strong man with riches and European connections, Dutch artillery men, possession of diamonds and with the help of his gifts and position came in the good books of the Sultan of Golconda who was the sixth in line of the rulers. He made Mir Jumla the Chief Wazir and commander of the Army. The latter developed intimacy with the Queen and got his son and other persons in the administration. He decided to attack Karnatik, ruin it, destroyed the idols of temples and amassed the wealth and stones from there. While in Karnatik, he learnt that the Sultan of Golconda ranted against him owing to Mir Jumla's relations with queen mother. On this he requested his son to come and join him but in vain for the King of Golconda would not let this happen.

At this point he wrote to Aurangzeb to go to Golconda with four thousand cavalry men, spread the rumour that it was part of the forces of Shah Jahan, then move to Golconda and arrest the King once he came to pay his obeisance. He promised Aurangzeb to defray the expenses. The Governor of Dakhyn did exactly that though the last part of the plan could not be implemented since the conspiracy was revealed by one of the group. Aurangzeb spoilt the entire forest after the King fled and stripped it of costly contents, but sent the women to the country as the then custom was among the despots. He laid siege of the fortress for two months but had to abandon it on the calling of Shah Jahan. Both Mir Jumla and Aurangzeb obeyed though they knew that this order was given by the Emperor on the recommendation of Dara and Jahanara. The latter suggested this fearing that Aurangzeb might become very powerful.

Aurangzeb, however married his eldest son, Sultan Muhammad (who was killed by Aurangzeb later) to the Sultan of Golconda's daughter with the promise that his son would be the successor to

Golconda throne and got as dowry the fort of Ramgiri. Soon these two, Mir Jumla and Aurangzeb planned great enterprises, and during their return to the Dakhyn they besieged Bider (about 75 miles north-east of Hyderabad, earlier called Begampet).

Visiting Agrah on different occasions Mir Jumla had impressed Shah Jahan by his speeches and schemes of conquering the Dakhyn's wealth and extending the empire up to Sri Lanka. Once he finally reached Agrah he enticed Shah Jahan to follow the wealth of the South and not Kandahar. He gave the Emperor the Kohinoor. Bernier suggested that Shah Jahan was annoyed by the insolence of his eldest son and so he agreed to the plan of Mir Jumla.[59] The latter was made the Wazir-Azam, the commander, given the house earlier occupied by Sadullah Khan. Hereafter Mir Jumla was asked to go to the Dakhyn, as recorded by Manucci. While all this was done Aurangzeb was asked to remain in Golconda and not join the imperial forces. Mir Jumla invaded Bijapur and surrounded a place called Kalyani. But Mir Jumla's family was kept as a surety in the Centre.

These activities of Aurangzeb were an alarm for Dara Shukuh who was constantly interceding with Shah Jahan to deflect a consolidation of Aurangzeb's forces and imperial forces. For this he managed to intervene on behalf of the King of Golconda as well as recall generals of the Imperial army. Generals like Mahabat Khan did not listen to Aurangzeb and returned. Mir Jumla also had to do the same. Aurangzeb was restrained from going to Golconda and was confined to Ahmednagar. Qanungo did not consider this to be a mean intrigue on the part of Dara Shukuh.[60]

The mean act was of Aurangzeb who had withheld the imperial letters from the King of Golconda. Aurangzeb was playing false with the Emperor. He was telling Mir Jumla that the King's mother was waiting for him and that his son will be married to the King's daughter. Yet he wished to kill him. This plan was revealed by Aurangzeb himself. He later eyed Bijapur in the same fashion and through Mir Jumla got Shah Jahan to agree to this war (26th November, 1656). This led to the fall of Kalyani. (August 1, 1657). At this point the Imperial forces were asked to return. It was not soon after that the civil war was to begin (September 6, 1657).

Sex and War

We noticed above the role that Shah Jahan's acts in the haram alienated three significant nobles. Mir Jumla's escapades with Golconda King's wife led to Mir Jumla joining up with Aurangzeb and lastly before the war of succession began the slumping of Shah Jahan into sex orgies, despite his age, that caused strangury and urine infection that took away his attention from significant tasks ahead which may have helped the situation at hand. He was given to using the then versions of potency medicines for satisfying his lust for women from all sections of society-low. He had fallen for a woman of a lowly class. He had justified it by saying that a good piece of article is good no matter from which shop it came. That caused him to fall sick. This became a flash point for the implosion.

Little Entente

The entente between Aurangzeb, Shah Shuja and Murad Baksh was in the making before Shah Jahan fell ill. The indications were: (a) Aurangzeb's consolidation of money and army in the South, (b) establishing marriage alliances with Shah Shuja[61] and the King of Golconda, (c) promise to Murad Baksh of his being a future governor of large tracts in the north involving the Punjab, Sindh Kashmir and Afghanistan in a written agreement, (d) campaigning with them against the 'infidel' Dara Shukuh, (e) giving disinformation about the condition of Shah Jahan and spreading the rumour that Dara had captured Shah Jahan and had blocked all communication in and out of the Court at Agrah, and (f) communication from Agrah to the provinces was being blocked by Aurangzeb and forcing his brothers to revolt while he himself did not engage in action to prevent any suspicion of his father. He was in no mood to face the combined forces of Dara and Shah Jahan. The reason for the last position was to rest any fears of Shah Jahan against himself to gain time to settle his own affairs in the Dakhyn i.e. relations with Mir Jumla, Bijapur and Golconda.

Motivations causing the Little Entente

There were no high minded principles of religion or morality but only ambition that was the central motivation and rest of the reasons derived therefrom. The welfare of the country, the uplifting of the people, and the future of the empire did not occur in their mutual correspondences or for that matter their correspondences with their father Shah Jahan. The eldest of the three, Shah Shuja, was interested in appropriating Bihar to his realm of Bengal. This was denied to him and given to Dara, hence the hostility to Dara. We will come back to this in just a while.

Similarly, Murad the youngest brother had only one desire. He wanted to be immersed in life-long amusement[62]-drinking, music and whatever else despite his inordinate thirst for dominion.[63] He had no intellectual assets to plan but only the desire to *expand his dominion* and imagined Emperorship for himself. For this he had no problems of conscience in conspiring against his own father by inviting the King of Persia to invade the country with the hope to deflect Dara's army to the North. This was suggested by Aurangzeb but Persian King did not oblige. His second step was to attack and loot Surat[64] of its riches and merchants on instigation of Aurangzeb who was very tardy and cunning with him, despite their being married to two sisters.[65]Aurangzeb ultimately, after Murad's insistence, gave him in writing, the assurance of making over the northern states of Punjab, Sindh, Afghanistan and Kashmir and asked him to adorn the camouflage of orthodoxy on the plea of convincing him of Aurangzeb's own loyalty to him and not Shah Shuja. Murad allowed himself to be played around. It was only on Murad's reticence to move his troops towards Narmada in February 1658 Aurangzeb had given this promise. Shah Shuja similarly did not have any imperial designs but was in a hurry to move towards Banaras in November 1657 and thus invited a military reaction from Shah Jahan. Aurangzeb made no precipitate move at this point.

Absence of vision and mental incapability

The second and fourth brothers did not appear to be mentally capable of fashioning a strategy to become emperors even though they got the coins minted and khutba read in their own name. The difference between the two was that one assumed a humble title of Maruwwajuddin and the other assumed the title of Abdul Feniz Nasirrudin Mohammed, Timur III, Alexander I, Shah Shuja Bahadur Gazi'. The other difference between the two was that Murad was more suspicious of others and in his semi drunken condition assassinated by piercing a spear in the chest of his only honest advisor, Ali Naqi, on a mere hearsay of a conspiracy that the latter was alleged to have hatched, as per the word of dubious and jealous courtiers of Murad. Thus was silenced a lone sane voice of advice that Ali Naqi was giving him. The advice was not to fall prey to Aurangzeb's plans of suggested actions. At every step of Aurangzeb's trap Murad did not listen to the advice of caution.

Both the brothers played into Aurangzeb's action-plan to start a War of succession. They had no plans of their own and their desires and actions could be nipped in the bud. The ultimate fate of both these brothers at the hands of Aurangzeb showed this convincingly. Both appeared to be Shakespeare's comic tragic figures in the royal drama of war of succession.

Acumen

Aurangzeb alone had the acumen among the three to outwit them. He prepared for the ultimate show down by garnering his resources-arms and money, spread the network of communication from the court to the battlefield camps among the nobility and kept a track of Dara's dubious friends. He pierced through the wall of secrecy (his own imagination) that was imposed on the fort for three days when Shah illness was rumoured, court entry restricted (even of Dara and Jahanara's entry) and the developments in the Mughal court were a serious subject of rumour, conjecture and calculation, political and tactical moves at the court and the three provinces at least. The three brothers regarded Dara to be the king-pin in all this veil of alleged or perceived secrecy and conspiracy, though in fact an over-evaluation of Dara's powers. Even the fact of Shah Jahan's *jharoka* appearance at the window was shrouded in a rumour of putting up a counterfeit act. They had set up a chain of communications between the three provinces of Bengal, Gujarat and the Dakhyn.[66]

Shah Shuja versus Sulaiman Shukuh

We noticed earlier of the rift between Dara Shukuh and Shah Shuja over the assignment of Bihar that came to Dara though the younger brother claimed it for himself. The three days of ailment of Shah Jahan were over despite the rumours continuing unjustifiably about his being a captive. He decided to send imperial forces against Shah Shuja with Sulaiman Shukoh under the leadership of Raja Jai Singh.[67] Shah Jahan instructed Jai Singh not to kill but to deter Shah Shuja. This combination was very unlikely since the young Sulaiman, Dara's eldest son, handsome and eager to prove his mettle in war, was vigorous and eager to pursue Shuja. Raja Jai Singh was engaged in delaying tactics. The imperial forces had 20,000 cavalry and 100, 000, elephants and supplies in infantry in contrast to Shuja's 45,000 cavalry and innumerable infantry along with river boats and artillery.

The race was to reach Banaras first. Shah Shuja had made the move first. Sulaiman was eager to reach there first to gain tactical advantage by the river crossing. Jai Singh made him drag his feet. In this battle Shah Shuja resorted to communication to his father asking him the fortress of Monghyr. Shah Jahan was on Dara's request prepared to do so on the condition that the fortress be dismantled. Shuja did not agree. The war continued. Once this position was clear, Dara, in contrast to the position of Shah Jahan, wanted Shah Shuja's head through a decisive action.

On Sulaiman's insistence the Army was made to cross over the river after building the bridge. This amounted to winning the first round of battle. The victory was Sulaiman's who stayed in the vicinity of Banaras for next four to five days. His forces were joined by Afghan troops under Dilir Khan whose behaviour was more akin to Jai Singh's. In this period Shah Shuja had become indolent and lax, sleeping till mid-day under his mosquito net while his soldiers restlessly moved around. Sulaiman imposed on him a humiliating defeat. Shah Shuja's rout was described as hilarious-while his army was in disarray he took to escape and the imperial forces looted his deserted camp.[68] This news reached Agrah in a month's time. Shah Jahan gave credit to Jai Singh for it and so Sulaiman Shukuh was deprived of it.

Raja Jai Singh's Treachery

Jai Singh[69] at this time played a treacherous role. He allowed Shah Shuja (with Dilir Khan's connivance) to flee by adopting the tactic of snail's pace for his army that was to follow him despite Sulaiman's impatience. The distance that Shah Shuja covered in five days, was covered by the Imperial forces in two months, which were crucial for Dara and Shah Jahan. The truce at Monghyr sealed Shuja's fate.

Raja Jai Singh's Rationale

The first reason of this stratagem of Jai Singh was that Shah Jahan still lived and would in due course release Shah Shuja. That would amount to the Raja gaining one more enemy at the imperial court. The second reason was orders of the King had been to avoid a battle. The third reason was that he had a grievance against Dara for having called him a musician. Since he wanted Shah Shuja to escape he advised Sulaiman Shukuh to return to court. To be ready for any other rising.[70]

Sulaiman wanted to pursue Shuja. The whole episode ultimately led to preventing Sulaiman Shukuh from joining his father for the battle that was secretly brewing in the South. It was secretly brewing since Aurangzeb had blocked all news to Agrah about his plans. He let Murad's battlefield activities to be followed by the Imperial generals. In fact the move of Murad Baksh from Gujarat was so zig zag that it was confusing to one and all. This was not Murad's plan. It was his eccentricity and hid Aurangzeb's moves.

Victory Undone

By the time Sulaiman caught up with Shah Shuja in two months' time it was March and April, 1658-the time of Aurangzeb and Murad's march to the North and the battle of Dharmat, near Ujjen (Ujjain today) that was conclusively won by them on 14th April, 1658 against the Imperial forces. Both Shah Jahan and especially Dara wanted Sulaiman's forces to return to Agrah to augment Imperial forces. Both knew that the real danger was Aurangzeb. It did not happen. The advantage that Sulaiman had won in Banaras and the treaty at Monghyr was negated by this defeat of the imperial forces.

Dress Rehearsal of Treachery

There was an incident in Shah Shuja's Bengal with regard to the surfacing of the cobras, including the one with a white hood. They brought ill omen to the Monarchy, as per the astrologers' prediction and wise men's opinion, and that Shah Shuja may become the King. They were referring to the emergence of the white hooded cobra.

The bad omen ultimately visited Shuja for he lost his governorship and being on the run had gone to the present Burma (a strip of land adjacent to Burma, now part of it) where tribes existed then and their king brought an end to Shah Shuja. The manner of the end is a matter of conjecture and mystery. The snake brought bad tidings as per the then views of the time. Aurangzeb was compared to a snake by Shah Jahan who meant to warn Dara Shukuh. The time of the warning was, as noted above, when Dara had, along with Jahanara, prevailed upon Shah Jahan to transfer Aurangzeb to the Dakhyn on the latter's request. Aurangzeb had done so for the material attraction of Dakhyn in contrast to the insignificant Multan where he had been posted as a punishment for his failure in Kandahar.

Cobra and Snakes

The odious implication of the cobras not only applied to the three brothers of Dara. It could easily be applied to the nobility of the Mughal court-both Muslim and Rajput-for they were unreliable and self-seeking as it was proved during the battles of succession among the royal brothers. It was observed at the dusk of Shah Jahan's rule that began with his illness (1657) of three days. The nobility was changing sides before the next battle was fought. They had their own personal and/or party reasons. Whatever they were it was lack of gratitude to Shah Jahan who had brought them up into the ruling nobility from indigence. In the sense of betrayal the battle between Sulaiman Shukuh and Shah Shuja was only a dress rehearsal.

As per the chronicler of Aurangzeb's reign the villain of the piece was Dara for he had caused the raiyats to revolt, and seed of rebellion sown on all sides.[71] The Nobles forgot the rule of their master Shah Jahan for more than thirty years, and the good acts of getting reprieve to nobles and others that Dara Shukuh undertook as well as his intercession with the Emperor for these. The Hindu nobility also forgot Dara's liberalism for their own petty thinking and self-interest accompanied their valour, courage and sense of loyalty. They behaved slimily. The battles that followed and the last phase of Dara Shukuh's life proved this to the hilt. The role of the Afghans in the episodes of conflict also went to show their treachery from time to time in Kandahar, in Banaras as elsewhere. The very composition of the Mughal Army had a potential of centrifugal tendencies.

There was an interesting case of a snake being a good omen for Aurangzeb at Mandu near Narmada where he was praying in the woods before the start of the battle at Dharmat. Manucci recorded it in a long paragraph. He observed:

> 'Once at ten o'clock at night, after Aurangzeb had arrived at Mandu, he being in his tent reading the Quran, there appeared at his right hand a hideous snake, which advanced towards him. Without being perturbed or losing his head, he drew with greatest calm a little sword that he always carried about him. By one sudden blow he separated the snake's head from its body, and, seated as he was, the blood splashed all over him. Getting to his feet, he shouted for his servants, and they finished off the snake, for they struck it all over its body. After it was dead he ordered it to be weighed. They made out a weight of sixty pounds.... He declared that this was a sign that God would give him victory, for the Mohammadans are very superstitious.'[72]

Aurangzeb considered this to be symbolising God's intent for him to be the King before the impending battle near Narmada.

Before the Battle of Dharmat

Apart from Shah Shuja's thrust and defeat Murad's antics in Gujarat were such that Aurangzeb had to control his behaviour. He started to meet up with Aurangzeb's forces with his royal bag and baggage of the nobles' families. He was restrained from doing so by Aurangzeb and he therefore deposited them at Champanir. Again too eager to travel North and give battle to Dara he found himself restrained by Aurangzeb on the plea that it was necessary to know if the Emperor was alive or not. Aurangzeb did not wish to take a precipitate action if the Emperor was alive. He therefore kept up the pretence of loyalty till the very end. Both decided to meet at Narbada in February, 1658.

Communication Network

The three brothers also wanted to have a cordon of communication[73] from Bengal to Gujarat with the Dakhyn in the South at this point to get information by posting their own spies and to stem any news going north to Agrah and Dihli. The news from the court was being received on a regular basis through the channels that they had with the court-Raushanara, Guharara close to Murad, and other nobles. This gave Aurangzeb the felicity to doctor the news and spread rumour to Serve his own purpose.

Blocking information and winning over the Nobles

The blocking of the letters from Agrah had another purpose. The Generals of the Imperial army who were advised by Shah Jahan to return were won over by Aurangzeb on the basis of disinformation: he spread the rumour of Shah Jahan's death and asked them to shift their loyalty rather than suffer under Dara Shukuh on the promise higher rank. A loyalist, Mahabat Khan refused to do so and without paying any heed to him or taking his leave moved northwards. Most of the Generals shifted their allegiance though.[74]

Aurangzeb and Mir Jumla

While Aurangzeb was blocking news from the South and forging his alliance he won over Mir Jumla to his side while returning from Bijapur to Aurangabad on the plea of paying attention to his children since he had lost his senior most wife, Dilras Bano. He had gained from his links with Mir Jumla who had come to the Dakhyn as the envoy of Shah Jahan to settle the matters there and restrict Aurangzeb. As surety Shah Jahan had kept his son and family in the Court we noted above.

The letters of Aurangzeb to Mir Jumla showed their close and confidential linkage and also that Mir Jumla was privy to Aurangzeb's desire to be the King after Shah Jahan.[75] Shah Jahan had wanted to use Mir Jumla to prevent Aurangzeb from controlling Bijapur and not violating the treaty with the King of Bijapur. As Mir Jumla was returning to Agrah, Aurangzeb arrested him and put him in Daulatabad prison while his vast property, artillery and the army were appropriated. By the time he moved north Aurangzeb had clearly resolved his problems in the Dakhyn.

Aurangzeb's Consolidation of Forces

Before the Dharmat battle started, Aurangzeb had activated Shuja against Dara and weakened Dara by depriving him of the help of

Sulaiman Shukuh; caused distrust between Murad and Shuja; helped Murad with money and a promise to make him the king of Dihli; cemented the relationship with Mir Jumla; made marriage alliance of his son with the daughter of the King of Golconda, won over the Court's nobility in the Dakhyn except Mahabat Khan; goaded Murad to conspire with the King of Persia (who did nothing), to create problems in the North so as to divert Dara's forces; to make Murad to adorn the garb of a Muslim religionist for fighting against heretic Dara; rearranged his relations with Bijapur and pacified Shivaji. This was quite a preparation and mainly through deceit under the garb of his own selfless pursuit of an ascetic life. And yet the slogan that he adopted, as mentioned in an earlier chapter, was 'I will lose my own, or take my adversary's head.'[76] The fact of the matter was that he pierced through all his brothers' lives including his own children as subsequent events were to prove.

Immediately, he was all honey and sugar to Murad at Narmada in welcoming him as his King and royalty at Mandu. The two together formed a powerful coalition in contrast to the confusion in the Imperial court, dissipation of Dara's support base with the help of Jai Singh and Shah Shuja and creating confusion at the court by blocking information. The scene at Agrah was one of fear, anxiety and confusion. Shah Jahan started to communicate to both the princes to return to their respective provinces. Aurangzeb responded with silence and chicanery for no news reached Agrah while Murad was told that these may be Dara's stratagems.

Shah Jahan's Advice and Khalilullah's Counterpoint

On hearing the news of the revolt of the two brothers, Shah Jahan wanted to take to the battlefield in the hope that this would dissuade Aurangzeb and Murad may also fall in line. Manucci noted that this may well have happened. He observed,

> 'Shah Jahan told Prince Dara that the best thing was, in any case, for him (the king) to be present in the battle, even in such feeble condition as he was: by his going forth it might happen that the traitors would be held in more subjection.' [77]

Despite Dara's satisfaction with this course of action, Khalilullah Khan advised Dara who acted on the following advice:

> '...it is not right for your highness, whatever happens, to allow the king to be present and to fight this battle, because I give you my word that victory will be with your highness, and if, perchance, the king take part, the name and fame thereof must inevitably be his.'[78]

Dara prevailed upon his father, in accordance with this advice, under a threat of committing suicide in a dramatic manner with a dagger in his presence. The disconsolate old man fell in line and appointed a Rajput and a Muslim as generals to go meet his rebellious sons and give them battle under strict instructions not to kill them but deter them and make them return to their Provinces. Shah Jahan appointed the two generals Chatrasal and Reram Singh Rotella above them. Dara asked Sulaiman to return[79] and gave costly presents to the two generals, Raja Jaswant Singh and Qasim Khan, before they left. The two sides were unequally matched. For the forces of the south were well oiled, strong and clear in their aims, the one from the North was truncated, unsure and irresolute about the goals. The Generals, especially the Rathor chief was a novice in the art of war.[80]

Dharmat Battle

Aurangzeb and Murad linked in the neighborhood of Dharmat about fourteen miles southwest of Ujjien on April 14, 1658. This was the first failure of Jaswant Singh who was supposed to prevent this junction. It was his inexperience.[81] The battle was fought the next day and Jaswant Singh lost. He was out-maneuvered by Aurangzeb who crossed the river to join up with Murad's forces. In confusion Jaswant Singh withdrew a few miles to Ujjen, not listening to a Brahman's advice to retreat to Jodhpur, he advanced a few miles camping opposite to Aurangzeb's camp at Dharmat village. To his chagrin he discovered that the two brothers have joined.

He capitulated and seeking pardon he sent a messenger to Aurangzeb. Aurangzeb refused to parley. Smarting under the fact of fighting royal blood and obliged to carry royal orders at the same time he offered battle in company of Mir Qasim, who was his equal now for he had been made the Governor of Gujarate. Both were respective generals of Rajputs and Moslems and both were not in consonance of a single command structure. The other side was more coordinated and unified. This mismatch resulted in the defeat of the Rajput cavalry against the English and French artillery under Aurangzeb. [82] The battle field was not favourable to the cavalry owing to swamps with rivulets all over.

Rajputs slaughtered and Jaswant Singh's flight

In the face of the artillery fire, Jaswant was on the back foot and paralysed by Aurangzeb's advancing army. Rajput war cry of 'Ram, Ram' by Rajput soldiers and their valour in taking forward suicidal steps was no match to Aurangzeb's forces. The Rajput clannish and not coordinated valour had no support from the troops of Qasim Khan as was to be. The man had a secret understanding with Aurangzeb. Jaswant Singh's central column came under heavy artillery fire. Rajput troops were taking to flee and escape. So did Jaswant Singh, under advice of his men. The escape of the remnant Rajput soldiers was followed by Qasim Khan's troops as well who had just put up a show of fire to cover the hidden powder that finally Aurangzeb helped himself to as was planned with Qasim Khan.

So Hindus moved to Rajputana and the Mughals to Agrah. Six thousand Imperial soldiers turned the battle ground of swamps crimson with their blood that included six brothers of a royal family. But back home greater *ignominy* awaited Jaswant Singh whose wife refused to allow him access to the fort and meet him for he showed lack of courage and valour. He died much later. Qasim Khan had shown his *treachery* for that is how his inaction was to be later understood at Agrah. He was declared to be a traitor. The court that had started to go to Dihli returned to Agrah by April 25, 1658.

The juggernaut from the South was moving onwards and Dara was not left with any choice but to put up a fight. This defeat was a prelude to a greater one after an interlude marked by slow pace of the jauggernaught in order to recover and rejuvenate stamina after the battle. Aurangzeb and Murad were boastful of the victory that they thought made them invincible and could meet the forces of Turkey and Persia, while Dara Shukuh flew in rage and called Jumla's son,

Shaista Khan and Muhammad Amin Khan as traitors intending to kill them and blamed his father for having allowed Mir Jumla to go south and move over his Army to Aurangzeb, who announced that thirty thousand soldiers in Dara's Army were prepared to come to his side.[83] Showing patience Shah Jahan prevailed upon him against any such act.

Again the contours of the battle were similar to the one faced by Sulaiman Shukuh though the results were the opposite. Treachery had the same role. The victors were the Imperial forces in one the other battles and the opposition. The second battle had negated the first battle's gains to the imperial court. The two battles were really small affairs in terms of longevity, forces used and tactics employed though fatalities were high in the second battle. By present standards they must be skirmishes but with disastrous forebodings for the powers that be in the status quo. In terms of ensuing fatalities, it qualified to be a war since fatalities were high even if we concede that there was hardly any evidence of fatalities on the side of the rebellious Princes' army.

Shah Jahan conceded to Dara taking the field as fait accomplish

Every battle/war had its own diplomacy. In this case the letter diplomacy again came to the forefront. When Shah Jahan heard of the Dharmat battle he raised his hands to the sky with eyes looking up and bemoaned after remembering God,

> 'Already I knew the time of my rule was nearing its end, but not that there would fall upon me this calamity, so that, filled with anguish thereby, I cry…O God! Thy will be done' – 'it is my sins that chastise me, and I deserve it all…my God!'[84]

It appeared that he remembered what he did in order to come to power, i.e. assassinating his brothers. Qanungo held the view that Shah Jahan's personality had two sides to him. One was liberal, man of peace, arts and justice. The other side was that of practical man, a bigot lacking in humour.[85] He conspired to come to power with the final stratagem of a coffin. He further held that Dara represented one part of his personality in his learning, arts, and sense of justice and the other was represented by Aurangzeb's craft deployed for usurping power. So significant was this episode of the coffin, Waldemar Hansen titled a whole chapter after it.[86] Qanungo thus described the three father and his two sons

> 'The character of Emperor Shah Jahan partook of a double nature- an actual combination of Muslim orthodoxy and the profane tradition of the age of Akbar. He was Dara and Aurangzeb in one; the latter representing the "other side of the medal."
>
> 'Dara and Aurangzeb inherited respectively the non-essential and the essential elements of Shah Jahan.'

Dara was an idealist while Aurangzeb was practical. Dara was a liberal while Aurangzeb was a bigot. Qanungo admitted of Dara's worldly wisdom and intelligence. Shah Jahan handed his powers to Dara Shukuh who earnestly started to prepare for the next round of battle. He asked for Sulaiman Shukuh to return. Shah Jahan advised him to wait for his son so that he had a better chance to fight.[87] Dara was more eager to fight.

Dara's Departure for Dholpur

Affectionately Shah Jahan bid farewell to his cherished and eldest son, Dara watched by the tearful Begam Saheb, Jahanara, after giving him gifts and blessings with relevant recitations from the Quran and Hindu orthodox faith.[88] While he was doing this he had turned towards Mecca. Manucci detailed that Shah Jahan praised Dara for his sense of loyalty and submission towards his word, decided to spare his father's infirmities in the wake of offering to take the battle himself. Called Dara his worthy son and his other two sons as unworthy of the name.[89] He reached Dholpur, thirty seven miles south of Agrah and about a mile from the left bank of the Chambal River on May 22, 1658. By now Aurangzeb and Murad Baksh had moved up to the prison fort of Gwalior after a month's march where they learnt of the arrival of the Imperial forces at the Chambal River, through their sources.

Forces

Dara could not leave immediately as the Army was not fully ready. So after three days he left on the stallion from the court itself in a magnificent procession for Dholpur with a huge force comprising of more than one hundred thousand horsemen assembled and more than twenty thousand infantry. There were one hundred pieces of artillery, every one carrying shot of from eight to twelve pounds; in addition there was a twenty pounder culverin, and over two hundred European artillery men. There was no shortage of suppliers, sarrafaros (sarraf) who provide cash required by the whole army, many majestic and well-armed elephants, and five hundred camels with a man atop with a swivel-gun, carrying a ball of from three to four ounces, which he loaded and fired without dismounting. In addition there were five hundred elephants with howdah, with two men each with two guns like as on the camels.[90] We noticed earlier that Manucci described Dara in the battle field as a *tower of crystal*. As the forces moved towards the horizon, Dara's father had a last glimpse of his son merging with the horizon. He never was to see him again. Dara had said he would show up only if he succeeded which never happened.

Dara's Dholpur plans and weaknesses

Immediately Dara's plan, who reached Dholpur on 18th May, 1658, was to meet Aurangzeb at the Chambal River in order to deter him from crossing it. He adopted a wait and watch policy for Sulaiman Shukuh. That led to loosing advantage over Aurangzeb's fatigued army in need of rest and recoup. Qanungo described the wasting of time as wrong tactics thus. According to his plan

> 'He sent an advanced division of his army to Dholpur with instructions to guard the ferries of the Chambal and erect batteries and earth-works at strategic points. If he had organised a single flying column under some dashing and active officer like Rustam Khan Bahadur or Rao Satrasal Hada to watch the movements of the enemy along the whole line of the Chambal, no plan of campaign would have been more effective in checking Aurangzeb.'[91]

Reasons for Precipitate Action

Bernier discussed causes of Dara's precipitate action for Dholpur. These were: he was entrusted by Shah Jahan to take ultimate decision and controlled his treasure and royal armies; his brothers were coming with a weak and worn out army; once defeated they would have no way to escape making him absolute lord during the waiting period for Sulaiman his father could enter into dissuading communication with his brothers who would return quietly to their provinces and finally claim singular glory without sharing it with his own son Sulaiman. These factors in his mind made him immune to voice of prudence and friendship.[92]

Failed to understand the Lull

He failed to take advantage of the weaknesses of Aurangzeb's side by moving his forces up and down the bank of the river and waiting for a defensive action. He had not anticipated the trick of Aurangzeb. On the opposite side of the bank Aurangzeb's camp had least activities as observed by Dara's spies, As a result Dara could not gauge the truth before it was too late. These tactics of inactivity were to fool Dara's soldiers. Aurangzeb was helped by three persons to reach Dara's rear guard by crossing an unknown ford of the river a few kilometers away to reach Dara's side from the rear. Waldemar Hansen points to the role of traitors here. He said,

> 'But an obliging local traitor informed Aurangzeb that forty miles east of Dholpur there was a little known crossing only knee-deep; few travellers and no army had ever gone that way, and Dara had neglected to guard it-Aurangzeb, on the testimony of imperial scouts, was still away from the river.[93]

The two men who helped Aurangzeb in his tactics were Ganpat Shinde- a Maratha and Champat Rai Bundela.[94] Shinde advised Aurangzeb to follow the Maratha tactic of having small guerrilla bands to attack the opposition at unexpected points (like from the rear) and quickly run away. The strategy described was **'holding the enemy nose and then kicking him on the back side.'**[95] (Bold letters ours).

The other told him about the Point for crossing-over called Ater. The crossing was difficult owing to the river terrain inhabited by crocodiles who swallowed human beings causing immense damage to the numbers of the Army of Aurangzeb and Murad Baksh. The small rafts helped them in this crossing by saving them from the crocodiles (ghadials).

Dara dithered on Advice

Once Dara realised that his rear was getting vulnerable there was consternation. Now his own officers played mischief. Khalilullah Khan,

Danishmand Khan and an astrologer misguided Dara. They prevented Dara from taking advantage by attacking an exhausted army of Aurangzeb.[96] The last mentioned did so on the ground that the day was not auspicious for him to attack for it would make Aurangzeb the king. He was Aurangzeb's confidant. Dara having now learnt about the movement of Aurangzeb's forces still did not take action for the next three days. Thus allowed his opposition to regroup their forces making them battle ready. He had to fall back in consequence of this. Generally the defensive strategy helped in weakening opposition but it depended on the condition of the army and strategic strength of the receding army to the point where it proposed to give battle. Not in case of Dara's forces. Here Dara's defensive posture strengthened the Opposition rather than weakening them and causing de-moralisation. Instead Dara fell about eight miles east of Agrah at Samugarh. Even before reaching Samugarh his constant companion-treachery kept with him. The tragedy of this non action was all the more since, contrary to the advice he followed, there were two elements suggesting action. One,

> 'Dara was desirous of moving personally in pursuit of him.' [97]

Secondly, Manucci noted, General Hebraim Can (Ibrahim Khan), son of Ali Mardan Khan, advised to send instead, with the greatest expedition, twelve thousand horsemen to fall suddenly upon Aurangzeb and his soldiers, who were much fatigued, very scattered and lying about on the river bank. But Khalilullah Khan intervened against it.[98]

Battlefield Formations at Samugarh

Qanungo detailed, like Manucci, the positioning within the opposing forces. On Dara's side the artillery was on the first line behind which was the infantry with matchlocks supported from their rear camels carrying swivel guns followed by furious elephants followed by five divisions of army arrayed for The van was composed of about ten thousand well appointed Rajputs and Pathans under Rao Satarsal Hada, and Daud Khan. Between the centre and the van stood 10,000 troops and advanced reserve under Kanwar Ram Singh Kachchawa, and Sayyad Bahir Khan. In the centre the Crown prince, mounted on a tall elephant, took post surrounded by 3,000 faithful household troops of his own and at least twice his number of troops of the imperial mansabdars.

Formations and Mughal Soldiery

The three-fold formations were centre, right and left wings. The Mughal Army though of whites was ethnically plural. AS Bernier described it.

'Mogols, that is (according to the present acceptation of the term Mogol) foreigners whose complexions are white, and who profess Mahotamism; such as Persians, Turks, Arabs and Uzbeks.'[99]

Afghans need to be included too along with the Rajputs. The plurality and mercenary character, cemented by the State sovereignty in times of a strong Emperor like Akbar, Jahangir and Shah Jahan but became fissiparous once uncertainty set in the time of ensuing crisis of conflict. The right wing of 15,000 strong army was composed of Central Asians mercenaries under the command of the supple and treacherous Khalilullah; and the left wing was commanded by his younger son, Prince Siphir Shukuh, and Rustan Khan Bahadur Firuz Jang.

Defensive-Offensive (?)

Both sides saw the advantage of a defensive strategy. Yet an artillery exchange from too long a distance ensued starting by Dara's artillery at noon and Aurangzeb's fire ceased after a while sending a wrong signal to Dara as though his forces had been badly hit. This was not to be so. He erroneously went into a general attack with disastrous consequences. Aurangzeb's forces successfully barred but it were the forces of Dara under Rustam Khan that had scattered the forces of Bahadur Khan who was leading the assault from the side of Aurangzeb.

The premature kettle drums of victory were sounded on Dara's side and Dara dashed forward to support his victorious left flank, falling upon Aurangzeb's advanced Reserve under Shaikh Amir who was pressing Rustam Khan's left flank. Dara was able to push Shaikh Amir but could not save Rustam Khan and the flight of his troops under Siphir Shukuh. Dara's invincible courage came to the fore but his force melted and became what Qanungo calls 'predicament of a ship with its broken rudder, since Dara had given up the Centre.'[100] The military action of artillery use was roundly criticised by Manucci thus

> 'During the time we were making this deafening din with our guns, enemy saluted us nothing but with a few bombs in a tail, after the style of rockets.'[101]

Aurangzeb's life in Danger, Khalilullah Khan's Treachery

Most of Dara's actions at this stage were factors contributing to his defeat.[102] Manucci added the real cause. That was the role of Khalilullah Khan. Both Manucci and Francois Bernier referred to the start of this traitor's role. It began with the understanding of Aurangzeb and Khalillulah Khan. Aurangzeb finally sounded the signal shot of his readiness for immediate attack. On receiving the signal Khalilullah came in search of Dara and having found him announced to him greetings on the victory and suggested an advance instead of the use of artillery. Ignoring Rustam Khan's contrary advice to wait, Dara moved forward creating confusion among his troops who plundered, looted and killed their own companions. Yet, Dara came close to the enemy shelling showing exemplary spirit. Musketry were drawn closer in face of enemy barrage of cannons, swivel pieces and musketry. Europeans were able to join. Yet this happened in the surrounding reality of his army's disarray.[103] Yet out of sheer dint of his courage and vigour, wrath and foresight he attacked his opponents.[104]

Held his ground against the reinforced forces of Aurangzeb, under Sher Mir (a Khawafi who died in 1659) in the battle of Ajmer. Dara made the enemy retreat. *Aurangzeb ran great risk of being taken.* He behoved his men to fight and expressed the opinion that he will die at that spot. He ordered to chain the elephants with him as an attestation of his resolve pricking his elephant forward.

Shah Jahan's sin visited Dara

Dara, wanting to pursue Aurangzeb, made a short halt out of fatigue. But the news of his generals and forces poured in. Rustam Khan's formation was in disorder. Chhatar Sal Rae was killed. Despite this he was able to rout the forces of Najabat Khan and Sultan Mahmud who were leading Aurangzeb's forces. Dara proved to be a valiant soldier. It was at this point when Dara was at the cusp of an all-time conclusive victory that the sins of his father appeared in the form of chicanery of Khalilullah Khan. Shah Jahan's sexual bonhomie with Khalilullah Khan's Turkish wife did Dara in. The traitor asked Dara to dismount his elephant since he was victorious and follow the Opposition. This was to lead to an irretrievable loss. Once Dara did it, his troops could not see their prince and concluded erroneously that he had been dead, fled like dark clouds blown by a high wind, seeking safety for their lives in the belief that the enemy was at their throats. Khalilullah transferred his troops and loyalty to Aurangzeb. All this happened in three hours' time.[105] Bernier recorded that Kafi Khan held the view that Dara dismounted the elephant out of need to lee rather than the courage to win the crown.[106]

Hard and Soft Soldier (?)

. All this was achieved without much fighting directly between Dara and Aurangzeb. If at all the fight was between Dara's courage and Aurangzeb motivating his followers and encouraging deceit in Dara's camp, as was done at the battle of Dharmat. The battle began with an artillery bang on the ground and ended with a whimper in the air. The pattern repeated in the tactics involving the terrain, i.e. the crossing of the river and treachery overtaking courage and valour in that move. The former being represented by Aurangzeb and the latter by Dara though all chroniclers observed that Aurangzeb was baked as a man of the camp with vast battle experience while Dara, being a novice, was a gentle man who was used to soft and protected court life.

Other Features of War

The other features, as put by Waldemar Hansen pointed to the differences of the soldiers in terms of Shia-Sunni and Moslem and Rajput men as well as the fact that the moslem khans transgiverated against an ambiguous pattern of kinship and matrimonial alliances-related to religion, or their past personal devotion to a particular prince.[107] Also the technical aspect was that only the soldiers in the front participated and the untrained follow up after the van just caused confusion, loot, plunder, and general hilarious cowardice of butchers and other crafts men who had been hurriedly enlisted. Bernier talked about the army in the following terms thus,

> 'These immense armies frequently perform great feats; but when thrown into confusion it is impossible to restore them to discipline. They resemble an impetuous river which bursts its banks; and whose waters, unrestrained in their course, disperse over the surrounding country, while no means can be devised to arrest them in their career of desolation.'[108]

He further noted that in the fight with bow and arrows and swords at the level of close proximity of the two forces Dara's courage and valour were inspiring after the central array of the enemy forces was breached.[109]

He did not give a uniform account of themselves owing to racial differences, Uzbeks and other Moslems behaved differently or of Aurangzeb's' views and Dara's views on religion. Even though one was a *Qadiri* and the other was a *Naqshabandi* within the Sufi tradition, i.e. *liberal* and *conservative* traditions.

The Europeans could not be ignored. Their role in the Army, as per Manucci was ill conceived, the loyalty of Manucci was recognised and Manucci as an eyewitness, who was committed to Dara as well as part of his artillery said about the artillery firing initially which did not produce any result

> 'I was much amazed at their making us work thus for nothing.'[110]

Jump in Chronology

In the final analysis, Waldemar Hansen observed the war was more like the one at Waterloo-with its treachery, defensive tactics and different results.[111] The war here had a disastrous effect for Dara and India. Dara lost his right to rule and endangered life and India lost for centuries the fight for composite culture. The final stamp came at Ajmer to this defeat through another battle with an interlude of Dara Shukuh's flight. We jump the chronology to discuss the war before we return to deal with the tragic flight, arrest and martyrdom of Dara Shukuh. Before his arrest he fought another action not called a battle, by Bernier.[112] Manucci called it a battle.[113] Waldemar Hansen and Murad Ali Baig called it a battle.[114]

Deorai Clincher

Dara Shukuh left Ahmadabad on 14th February, 1657 for Ajmer which was the heart of Rajputana being equidistant from Jaipur, Udaipur and Jodhpur hoping for help from Jai Singh, Jaswant Singh and Maharaja Raj Singh. They were treacherous and the battle was a decisive defeat for Dara despite his superior battlefield tactics supported by Fayaz Khan and Shah Nawaz Khan who had received him well at Ahmadabad. The ace of treachery was Raja Rup Singh who had sworn his loyalty much earlier to Dara Shukuh by drinking the water with which Nadira Begum, Dara's senior wife, had washed her breasts, as we noted earlier.

Betrayals as Game Plan

Dara reached Ajmer to only find that Jai Singh had bolted from promise and loyalty on the directions or threats of Aurangzeb. Aurangzeb had adopted a policy of carrot for going hostile to Dara and stick of reprisals for supporting him. Dara had begun to move to Ajmer on the false news that Jaswant Singh after the unsuccessful results of the fight with Shah Shuja was returning with Aurangzeb's wealth. Jaswant Singh had promised help but he never arrived at Ajmer. Dara Shukuh had sent his son, Siphir with a letter to Jaswant Singh but to no avail. The real fact was that Aurangzeb had not had any reverses in the fight with Shah Shuja and was coming to Ajmer. Jaswant Singh's role was a part of the game plan to trap Dara. Dara now wrote to Maharaja Raj Singh whom he had shielded from Shah Jahan's attack to find that even he was of no help. Dara moved on to Deorai about four and a half miles from Ajmer. Waldemar Hansen thus commented on the role of the Rajput Rajas,

> 'The Rajputs or Hindu chiefs were politically myopic, and downright blind when it came to identifying with anything beyond his own narrow sphere of interests.'[115]

Deorai Exchange

Dara chose a hilly track of Deorai and the battle there was from 14th to 16th May, 1659. The infantry of Dara was looked after by Shah Nawaz Khan[116] who was at the rear of the horse shoe ridge with the plains in between the two parallel ends. Fayaz Khan and

Sadat Khan looked after the other fronts. The use of fireworks and earthworks made the initial exchange of fire between the two forces to the advantage of Dara Shukuh. Fayaz Khan had used groups of ten soldiers to lay powder and lace the dry grass with it initially. In the frontal exchange Aurangzeb had no success. In one exchange he had to be brought backwards for his life was in danger according to his soldiers while Dara's supporters chanted 'Dara…' Dara…' and 'Dara'.

Raja Rup Singh's Betrayal

That night Aurangzeb called a meeting of his Generals. Raja Rup Singh suggested to him to go backside of the ridge for there was a way up from there and then attack Dara. The strategy was based on Raja Rup Singh's Jammu mountaineer soldiers' experience. Aurangzeb's forces moved up the hill from the rear and a cannon ball hit Shah Nawaz Khan's head off. Soon, Dilir Khan, Shaista Khan, Mumtaz Mahal's brother and Jai Singh came in to fight Dara. Being in the centre, Dara was witnessing the collapse. He had no choice but to flee with Siphir. By one account he left his haram unprotected to be later joined with him with the efforts of loyal eunuchs.[117] Other accounts do not portray such a heartless picture of Dara. It led to dregs of flight the closing in on a beast at bay.[118]

Features of Battles

The features of these battles were that kinship was as meaningless as loyalty was; religious divide did not colour it as an ideological battle; there was no cohesive Army in crisis situations; there was no saga of Rajput sense of loyalty or honour among the Generals; the Europeans had marginal role to play in the victory or in defeat; The Mogol-Rajput alliance changed as lightly in the direction of the tilt in the balance of forces and power; Rajput commitment was paper thin; there were signs of emerging / nascent Indian hood for India born Mughals, remained loyal to the country as is most poignantly evident by Nadira Banu's desire to be buried in India and Dara Shukuh not leaving the country despite his going up and down the country twice in flight. The entire career of the Mughals was spent in expanding the Empire and uniting India and protecting it from the Mongols, Persians and Europeans. Akbar's India was as large as that of Ashoka's. The territoriality gave central region pivotal importance to India and it's nascent vision of compositeness in style of living, thinking, adoption of customs and common toil to produce India's wealth and it was the warlike history that became the Mughal and the Hindu purdah for this as it did on the feminine faces of the two communities who were finding coexistence with Sikhism and Christianity.

End Notes

1. Kalinga Ranjan Qanungo considered him a perfect balance between the natures of Dara and Aurangzeb and more like his grandfather, Jahangir. Qanungo, op. cit.
2. Bairam Khan, a religious liberal. Iqtidar Alam Khan, 'Akbar's Personality Traits and World Outlook-A critical Reappraisal, In Irfan Khan, edited by, Akbar and His India, op. cit. p. 79.
3. He was Shah·Jahan's father-in-law-Asaf Khan.
4. Jahangir details Shah Jahan's rebellious behaviour in 1623. Jahangir, op. cit, vol. II, pp. 253-281.
5. There is not much evidence about the role of the older ladies in this conflict. So a comparison with the earlier generation could hardly be made. In fact the times of **Intemperance** were increasing. The following examples suffice to indicate the intemperance. Nur Jahan was known to be a game changer. Men were tipplers since Babur made efforts to leave the intake of intoxicants, Humayun (opium), Jahangir (opium plus) and Shah Jahan, Shah Shuja and Murad Baksh with the exception of Dara and Aurangzeb, it appears. In later period they were also debauches. Shah Jahan during his last days invited strangury owing to the intake of potency medicines in order to lay with girls much younger and lower in the social scale. On Babur and Jahangir see their Memoirs. On Humayun see the Memoir of Gul-Badan Begam. On Shah Jahan all accounts of his especially the ones by Manucci and Bernier.
6. At the birth of Aurangzeb Jahangir noted 'As my son Shah Jahan had not made a birthday entertainment for his son (Aurangzeb), he petitioned at Ujjain, which is the place of his jagir, that the Thursday entertainment of the 30th should be held at his abode. Of necessity, having consented to the carrying out of his wish, the day was passed in enjoyment at his quarters... My son, Shah Jahan brought a tray of jewels, and *jeweled* ornaments, and fifty elephants, thirty male and twenty female, asked me for a name for him. Please God it will be given him in a favourable hour....The value of the offerings that were accepted will be Rs 200,000.' Jahangir, op. cit. Vol. II, p. 50.
7. Niccolao Manucci's description of Dara Shukuh at the head of the Army on the battlefield at Samugarh, op. cit.
8. Waldemar Hansen, The Peacock Throne, Motilal Banarsi Das, New Dihli, 1972, p. 492.

9. Since the time of Iyaltimish Indian rulers kept away from conflict with them and therefore allowed them to spoil the land on the boundaries.
10. Waldemar Hansen noted the weakness of the Mughal Army in contrast to the Persian Army that plagued both Aurangzeb and Dara. *Ibid.* p. 159. Stephen Blake Made a similar point.
11. Swords, lances, daggers, scimitars, short swords, also with curved blades, long straight swords fashioned with inferior and superior metals of the same kind, battle axes, bayonets, javelines and long heavy lances and long distance bows and arrows. It had sources in Persian military thinking that inturn was influenced by the Turkish Military.
12. Kalinga Ranjan Qanungo, op. cit. p. 29.
13. Muhammad Kazim, Alamgir-Nama, Elliot and Dawson, History of India By Its Own historians,, Vol. VII, p. 179.
14. Kafi Khan, Muntakhabul Lurab, *ibid*, p. 215.
15. Amal I Salih, Badshah-Nama, *ibid.* p. 136.
16. Waldemar Hansen, op. cit. p. 145.
17. *Ibid.* pp. 184-185. The description of Dara Shukuh's dress and appearance in the court as Shah Buland Iqbal is based on Inayat Khan's record in his chronicle op. cit. p. 112.
18. Kalinga Ranjan Qanungo, op. cit, 23-29.
19. Jahangir listed the teachers of Shah Shuja and called him the eye of the Sultanate in his Memoirs. Op. cit. p. 82.
20. No Shia (Sufi) or Sunni conflict played out with them.
21. Kalinga Ranjan Qanungo, op.cit. pp. 204-206.
22. Francois Bernier, op. cit. p. 10.
23. Niccolao Manucci, op. cit. p. 182.
24. Dihli, Agrah, Lahor, Kashmir, Dakhyn, Khandesh and Birar, Malwa, Gujarate, Bihar, Oudh, Allahabad, Ajmir (spelt as Ajmere later), Sindh and Bengal. The revenues of Khandesh and Birar, Dihli, Agrah had higher revenues in comparison to the other provinces. Muhammad Sharif Hanafi, Majlisu-S Salatin, Hafeez Press, Lahore, pp.145-146.
25. Francois Bernier, op. cit. p. 15.
26. Kalinga Ranjan Qanungo, op. cit. pp. 208-210.
27. On some related edicts See Irfan Habib, edited, *Akbar and His Times*, op. cit, pp. 266-288.
28. Niccolao Manucci, op. cit. pp. 186-87.
29. The first mansab mentioned was Mirza Shahrukh with 5,000 zat i.e. salary and 2000 sawars. Mansabs above 5000 were reserved for the princes. The zat and the sawaar rank indicated their duties to be performed. Jagirs were transferable and no mansabdar held a jagir. Wealth concentrated among these two categories were given from the State Treasury from which the Mansabs also borrowed for their expeditions. S. A. A. Rizvi, op. cit, pp. 175-176.

30. Shining now in the British Crown.
31. Satish Chandra, op. cit. pp. 491-492.
32. Waldemar Hansen, op. cit. pp.184-86.
33. Ellison Banks Findly, op. cit., p. 46.
34. *Ibid*, p. 48.
35. Waldemar Hansen, op. cit. p. 190. This issue was raised much later in the twentieth century during the Prime Ministership of and about Pandit Jawaharlal Nehru.
36. Francois Bernier, op. cit, p. 8.
37. His father gave him little credit for all his show of being a religious man. Niccolao Manucci, op. cit. p. 180.
38. Niccolao Manucci, *ibid*. p. 222.
39. Francois Bernier, op. cit. p. 67.
40. *Ibid*. p. 101.
41. Both Bernier and Manucci agreed on most of her characteristics: good looks, given to pleasant behaviour, intelligence, vivacious, loving music, dancing and drink, interested in architecture as she collaborated with her father's grand architectural marvels of Taj Mahal, Red Fort in Dihli, Jama Masjid, and laying out of Chandni Chowk. Both note her closeness to Dara for he had promised her marriage after he became the emperor and her love and care of Shah Jahan during his reign and when in prison. Where they differed was on the issue of her relationship with her father. Manucci disagreed with Bernier who held that the father and daughter had illicit relations. She was a rich lady called Begam Saheb. She had intelligently and discreetly handled state affairs and her power in the Court was immense as was her salary. She again rose to power during the reign of Aurangzeb after the decline of Raushanara. Niccolao Manucci, op. cit. pp. 210-213; Francois Bernier, op. cit. pp. 11-13.
42. Both Manucci and Bernier agree that she was less beautiful, less witted with lesser salary in comparison to her elder sister, keen observer about whatever was happening in the haram and the court, had less political power, announced her hostility to Dara and Jahanara, and conveyed to Aurangzeb intelligence about the politics at the court and in the haram. She rose in power under Aurangzeb's initial period but fell owing to her own follies. Niccolao Manucci, *ibid*. p.230. Francois Bernier, loc. cit
43. Abdu-l Hamid Lahori, op. cit. p. 3
44. Kalinga Ranjan Qanungo, op. cit. pp. 175-183.
45. Inayat Khan, op. cit. pp. 115.
46. His titles show his rising graph: Muazz'am Khan, Khan Khanan Sipah Salar.
47. Details in Francois Bernier, op. cit. pp. 16-17.

48. Inayat Khan, op. cit. p. 103.
49. Abdu-L Hamid Lahori, op. cit. p. 39.
50. Saqi Mustad khan, Masir-i-Alamgir, Bengal Asiatic Society, Calcutta, 1947. p. 24.
51. Abu-l Hamid Lahori, *ibid*, p. 69.
52. Inayat Khan, op. cit. pp. 102-110.
53. Kalinga Ranjan Qanungo, op. cit. pp. 52-57.
54. *Ibid*. p. 59.
55. *Ibid*. p.75-76.
56. *Ibid*. pp. 86-95.
57. Niccolao Manucci, pp. 227.
58. *Ibid*. pp. 223-232, Francois Bernier, op. cit. pp. 16-23.
59. op. cit. p. 92.
60. Kalinga Ranjan Qanungo, op. cit. p. 190.
61. Shuja's daughter, Gul Rukh Banu was married to Aurangzeb's eldest son Sultan Muhammad. Shah Jahan had suspected this alliance as a move against himself. Waldemar Hansen, op. cit. pp. 211-214.
62. Niccolao Manucci, op. cit. p. 219.
63. Francois Bernier, op. cit. p. 32.
64. He was not able to capture the fortress where the wealth of the imperial levy on the merchants was kept. Only when the Dutch artillery men helped him to mine a wall of the fortress was he able to get to his desired wealth. Ibid. p. 219.
65. Both Murad and Aurangzeb were married to the daughters of Shah Nawaz Khan, an able and experienced officer helping Murad and who had been a governor of Ahmadabad. His daughters Dilras Bano and Sakina Bano were married to Aurangzeb and Murad, respectively. Dilras Bano was Aurangzeb's senior wife. Sakina was Shah Nawaz Khan's apple of the eye. Murad Ali Baig, op. cit. p. 212. The death of Dilras Bano took place as Aurangzeb was moving towards Dharmatpur for his first battle for the Crown. Shah Nawaz Khan subsequently helped Dara Shukuh during his flight and the battle at Deorai.
66. Qanungo, op. cit. p. 219.
67. Raja Jai Singh was committed to Shah Jahan but had a grouse against Dara, who had called him a musician in the 'darbar' (court in session). Jai Singh felt humiliated and carried the grudge to that day.
68. Waldemar Hansen, op. cit., pp. 212-214.
69. Bernier said 'It is certain that if Jesseingue…had not purposely held back, the rout of the enemy would have been complete, and their commander probably made prisoner. But the Raja…afforded Sultan Shujah the means to escape.' Francois Bernier, op. cit. pp. 36-37.

70. Niccolao Manucci, op. cit. p. 236.
71. Mohammad Kazim, op. cit., p.156. It needs to be noted that Bernier was close to Danishmand Khan who was pro-Aurangzeb. Manucci depended on his account too. Kazim was pro-Aurangzeb too. There is no evidence on Dara Shukuh from a regular chronicler since he did not become a ruler. The charge against Dara seems to be biased to say the least. The other charges like he captured his father, kept everyone in the dark and hid his illness to arrogate his father's powers have not been accurately founded. On this account Bernier and Manucci's accounts differ as also the accounts of Bernier and Inayat Khan.
72. Niccolao Manucci, op. cit. p. 243.
73. Kalinga Ranjan Qanungo, op. cit. p. 219.
74. Manucci said 'In this way the generals were prevented from receiving their answer within the appointed time, and all of them transferred themselves to the side of Aurangzeb.The latter lost no time in completing his preparations, writing to his friends whatever suited himself.' Niccolao Manucci, op. cit. p. 241.
75. He wrote to Mir Jumla thus 'The desires of my well-wishers can be realised only when…Shah Jahan's death is verified….But I gather from my court agent's letter that it is impossible for the Emperor to recover from this disease….If in such circumstances I delay in equipping my army…and Dara becomes aware of my condition, it will be impossible for me to attract other worldlings and seekers of rank.' Quoted in Waldemar Hansen, op. cit. p. 224.
76. op. cit. p. 242.
77. Niccolao Manucci, op. cit. 245.
78. loc cit.
79. This could not happen.
80. Kalinga Ranjan Qanungo, op. cit. p. 242.
81. Waldemar Hansen, op. cit. p. 230
82. *Ibid*, p. 231.
83. Niccolao Manucci, op. cit. pp. 250-52.
84. Niccolao Manucci, op. cit. p. 251.
85. Kalinga Ranjan Qanungo, op. cit. p. 379.
86. Waldemar Hansen, op. cit. p. 67-92.
87. Francois Bernier, op. cit. p. 34.
88. Kalinga Ranjan Qanungo, op. cit. p. 247.
89. Niccolao Manucci, op. cit. p. 253.
90. *Ibid*. p. 254.
91. Kalinga Ranjan Qanungo, op. cit., p. 246.

92. Francois Bernier, op. cit. pp. 45-46.
93. Waldemar Hansen, op. cit. p. 242.
94. Murad Ali Beg, op. cit. pp. 228, The last mentioned had nursed a grudge against Dara owing to the insult caused to his father Jhaujhar Singh of Orchha.
95. *Ibid*, pp. 227-228.
96. *Ibid*. p. 230.
97. Niccolao Manucci, op. cit. p. 259.
98. loc. cit.
99. Francois Bernier, op. cit. p. 48.
100. Kalinga Ranjan Qanungo, op. cit. p. 253.
101. Niccolao Manucci, op. cit. p. 264.
102. Kalinga Ranjan Qanungo Op. cit. 253.
103. Niccolao Manucci, op. cit. p. 266.
104. loc. cit.
105. op. cit. p. 69.
106. Francois Bernier, op. cit. p. 54.
107. Waldemar Hansen, op. cit. p. 245.
108. Francois Bernier, op. cit. p. 56.
109. *ibid*. p. 50.
110. Niccolao Manucci, op. cit. p. 264.
111. Waldemar Hansen, p. 256.
112. Francois Bernier, op. cit, p. 88.
113. Niccolao Manucci, op. cit. p. 324.
114. Waldemar Hansen, op. cit. PP. 345, Murad Ali Baig does not use the word battle but in describing the strategy of both sides in the hilly terrain with frontal and rear actions in battle. op. cit, pp. 276-278.
115. Waldemar, op. cit. p. 344.
116. Shah Nawaz Khan was Janus faced man who remained with Dara but regularly informed Aurangzeb about his manoeuvres according to Waldemar Hansen. Qanungo dispute this for Shah Nawaz Khan had whole heartedly stood by Dara till me was blown away by a cannon ball of Aurangzeb's Army. It is said that some of his own men took the revenge since he had shifted sides and gone over to Dara. Kalinga Ranjan Qanungo, op. cit. p. 291.
117. Francois Bernier recorded that Dara left his baggage behind. p. 88.
118. Waldemar Hansen, op. cit, p. 348.

Chapter - 5

Hare and the Hound

Dara's flight from Samugarh and Aurangzeb's spider-like chase was a story of the former's sad and tragic journey to captivity. Defeated at Samugarh, crestfallen Dara, started his retreat with diligence[1] and in the company of a handful of followers and family towards Agrah he reached his mansion by nine pm in a psychological state of inability to face his father, confused and despondent.[2] Three Kos (1.6 miles per kos) from the battle field Dara laid prostrate in mind and body waiting for fate to take over.[3] In that dazed and sorry state he paid no heed to the approaching sound of the kettle drums of the victors. He had to be moved by his handful of followers into action towards Agrah.

Emotion and Refusal

The accounts of both Manucci and Bernier are not very different at this point. The father and son could not meet despite much consoling emotion exchanged between Dara, Shah Jahan and Jahanara. Shah Jahan could not meet him for Dara had remembered his words at the time of leaving for the battle. Shah Jahan had observed then

> '...but remember this...my injunction...if the battle be lost have care how you come again in my presence.'[4]

Dara Shukuh responded to his father's wish to meet him thus

> 'Give up your wish to see my abashed face again. Only I beg your Majesty's benediction of farewell on this distracted and half-dead man in the long journey that he has before him.'[5]

Advice

Shah Jahan consoled him throw a messenger, Fahim Khan and Jahanara sent valuable jewels for him. Further to help him in his onward journey to Dihli, Shah Jahan sent animals laden with valuables, soldiers, animals and elephants with the advice: he should go to Dihli and there remain at a place where he can receive letters; that the Dihli Governor would receive him well, that he could have horses there, have access to the treasure and horses in the stable. This was a very tangible help that Aurangzeb later on in one of his missive accused his father of.

Betrayed

Aurangzeb was quick to win over the Governor of Dihli and laced the route to and from Agrah with his soldiers under Bahadur Khan.[6] As a result early travelers could move to catch up with Dara who had moved on from Dihli but others, including Europeans-Manucci included-were not able to go over for they were plundered and looted. Manucci was spared by chance through the help of a captain on horseback who accompanied Manucci back to his house. As a result he could be a witness to the next few days' happenings. These began with Aurangzeb's and Murad Baksh's entry leading up to Aurangzeb's control of the city, the fort and the confinement of Shah Jahan, Jahanara and the slave women.[7]

Aurangzeb after entering Agrah camped at Nur Manzil that became part of Agrah cantonment later on. On his arrival a charade of diplomatic finesses began between father and son (Aurangzeb) for a meeting that did not take place for each other's game of machinations had the field day. They said sweet words but conspired to kill/arrest/inhibit each other. Aurangzeb instead of appearing before the court sent first his trusted eunuch and then Sultan Muhammad, his son. Similarly Shah Jahan sent letters of affection to Aurangzeb[8] who was busy enticing the court nobles, made his son Sultan Muhammad the Kotwal of Dihli[9] and spread his forces in the city so as to negate any contingent support to Shah Jahan. Then he posted his forces in front of the fort near the Taj Mahal. Shah Jahan had similarly planned to get Aurangzeb killed or arrested with the help of his Tartar, Qalmaq and Uzbek women who manned the entry to the fortress.[10]

Sultan Muhammad takes the keys

Aurangzeb never went inside the fort though he spread many rumours about his wish to enter the fort to meet his father. Every time he expressed his wish of entering the fort his advisers negated it. He sent his trusted emissary for diplomatic finesse instead. That was followed by the sending his son, Sultan Muhammad inside the fort to tactfully control the fort by eliminating the guards and neutralising those inside. Immediately on entry his son took over the entry points by killing the guards, met his grandfather and did not accede to Shah Jahan's offer of the Crown to him. He asked for the keys of all the entry points from Shah Jahan who was now alone with Jahanara and Asad Khan. In contrast when Aurangzeb had entered the city most of Shah Jahan's nobility went out to receive him accept Danishmand Khan[11] and Mukkaram Khan. In the stampede to join Aurangzeb were Agrah's chief Moslem justice, Sayyid Hidayatatullah Khan and an old Court chamberlain, Fazil Khan.[12]

Shah Jahan's Ineffectual Retaliation and slump

Having realised his difficult position, the Emperor moved through the fort asking his soldiers to fire at the enemy but without much ado. The jauggernaught dug its feet opposite the Fort, near the Taj. This happened for three days. After this a European artillery man escaped the Fort as a result of the bribe by Aurangzeb. This led to the general demoralisation, demobilisation and flight of the forces of Shah Jahan followed by the treachery of Sultan Muhammad. Aurangzeb then sent a message to his father which was to the effect of denying liberty to the Emperor, as put by Manucci,

> 'He sent word to his father that he should take his ease in his harem, that he was no longer in a state to rule, that he should enjoy himself with his ladies and abandon all anxiety. When Aurangzeb effected this project Shah Jahan was sixty-one years of age, and had reigned thirty two years and three months'[13]

Confinement and new plan of Shah Jahan

Aurangzeb never met his father, before or after his fall and under Aurangzeb's eunuch, Itibar Khan, the Emperor, Jahanara Begum and their slaves were walled up in the haram with the exception of

Raushanara Begum who was allowed to leave the Fort. Two days later Jahanara met up with Aurangzeb with another plan of Shah Jahan that offered to make Aurangzeb receiving the whole country with only Bengal going to Shuja, Gujarat to Murad, Muhammad to get Dakhyn and Dara to get Punjab. Aurangzeb summarily rejected the plan by saying,

> 'Dara is an infidel to Islam and a friend of the Hindus. He must be extirpated for the sake of the true faith and the peace of the realm. I cannot visit the emperor before concluding this business.'[14]

Aurangzeb's Justification

Soon after Aurangzeb accused his father of secretly helping Dara at Agrah to put up a fight once he learnt from Shaistan Khan that Shah Jahan aimed to kill him as he was moving to go to the King on the suggestion of Jahanara. It appeared that Aurangzeb was dissimulating to put the blame on Shah Jahan and cover his own deeds of deception in front of the common people of Agrah who in any case were out to welcome him. In another letter he had blamed Dara for Aurangzeb's disobedience after the battle of Samugarh.

Strategic issues (I and II)

Qanungo and Waldemar Hansen raise two strategic questions-one each for Dara and Aurangzeb. Qanungo wondered as to the wisdom of Dara to recall his son Sulaiman[15] to Lahor rather than send him to Shah Shuja in his support for adding to the problems of Aurangzeb who had a restless Murad Baksh and problems in Golconda and Bijapur and ensuing revolt of Shah Shuja. This may have helped him but Dara only reacted impulsively on the basis of his immediate condition. He lacked boldness of diplomacy and political foresight. [16]

Secondly, Hansen raised the issue of why was Dara allowed by Aurangzeb to flee and not finish him there despite following him. He excused Aurangzeb by holding that Aurangzeb was more interested in finishing off the incumbent in Office after which it would be not difficult to deal with Dara. And his immediate murder would have alienated both the nobles and Shah Jahan. Perhaps, the author maintained that Aurangzeb was looking for some shred of proof that Shah Jahan loved him.[17] The author did not call this naiveté on the part of a man of the status of being a grandfather as also lacking in strategic foresight of avoiding the strain of traveling up and down the country twice to nab Dara Shukuh. Both men in strategic thought did not seem to be very different despite the fact that Dara seemed to have villainous individuals with him while Aurangzeb had all the Aces and allies, even if a little mulish by way of his younger brother.

Aurangzeb's possible reasons

There could be *two* possible reasons for the delay in getting at Dara. First, Aurangzeb had to prove to one and all that Shah Jahan was conspiring against him so that the people of Agrah were not left with any sympathy for the Emperor who had justly ruled over them, promoted many from indigence to prominence and contributed to the expansion of the country. The events involving the forgery of Itibar Khan, his eunuch, finally put Shah Jahan in confinement and snapped all his links with the world outside. Aurangzeb used the same forged letters as an alibi for his actions. This way he wanted to show to the world outside that he was doing according to their bidding and not visiting his father till he crushed the power and ill designs of Dara.[18]

The second reason was as sinister and significant. He had too much baggage in his train. He had to do away with Murad Baksh who was a drunken nuisance by the time he seriously restarted his pursuit of Dara. Once he decided not to meet his imprisoned father and appointing Shaistan Khan the Governor of Agrah, he started towards Dihli with a stop at Matora (Mathura today). His more disciplined army with its blanket of deceitful silence and murmurs marched ahead of Murad Baksh's army which had generally a musical and drunken gaiety and the spirited atmosphere for Murad Baksh had been opiated by the farces of Aurangzeb of calling him the new emperor. He did not even leave any of his soldiers back at Agrah[19] and so never realised that he may have lost everything related to Agrah.

Operation Murad Baksh near Mathura

Detailed account of Murad Baksh's imprisonment need not detain us. Aurangzeb staged the theatre of the absurd for Murad Baksh, i. e. funny outside and tragic from within. Despite all his counsels Murad Baksh walked into Aurangzeb's trap which reduced him thereafter to a drunken state and fettered at Mathura. Thereon he was sent from there in a covered litter to the fort Salemgarh (spelt also as Salimgarh) in the middle of the Jamuna opposite the Red Fort in Dihli and finally to the Mughal prison house, the fort of Gwalior, where he breathed his last after three and a half years of his imprisonment on December 4, 1661.[20]

Dara at Lahor (now Lahore)

Being on the run was no fun for he was in constant fear, uncertainty, and hunger and on the bed of stones and treachery even though in Lahor he felt for a brief period elation at the thought of being able to offer to Aurangzeb some resistance. This passing hope was based on the military strength of Mongols, Pathans and Sayyids in his Army supported by the Rajput cavalry and 10, 000 infantry extraordinary signs of loyalty much awaited Rajrup Singh never came as was expected of him. Aurangzeb's intervention prevented it. Same Rajrup Singh had again ditched Dara at the battle of Deorai by suggesting to Aurangzeb to attack Dara's rear, as we noticed in the last chapter.[21] If it could be called a balance to all this treachery it was provided by Daud Khan's unswerving loyalty[22] and Manucci's honesty and dedication to Dara.

Hamlet's dilemma-Dara's style

The military condition, possession and activities of Dara in Lahor are provided by Qanungo on the basis of Masum, who was Shah Shuja's Chronicler thus,

> 'The prince began to waver in mind to be or not to be at Lahor; now he would think that he should strengthen the city and the citadel of Lahor, summon the nobles of the neighbouring districts to his aid, and make a last and determined effort; now he would think thus: "As no ray of hope appears in any direction (lit. no scent of good from any quarter reaches my nostrils) it is better that this half dead self-which has come out safe from the battle should betake itself to such a place where with my own eyes I may not witness the slaughter of wives and children.'[23]

The common populace failed him too despite being the recipients of his largesse to pray for his success.[24]

Half-hearted Measures at Beas and Satlej (Satluj) Rivers

On the way to Lahor, Daud Khan had been posted at the ferry of Talwan with instructions to hold the line of the Satlej against the enemy. He also dispatched Izzat Khan as Daud's reinforcement and guard the ferry at Rupar on the Satlej. We already noticed Raja Rup Singh's episode of false loyalty.

Daud Khan advised Dara to send Siphir along with him with a force to prevent Aurangzeb from crossing Beas by being present at Sultanpur near Beas River. Dara procrastinated on account of Nadira's emotional outburst born of fear of losing her youngest son. By the time he sent his son to join up with Daud Khan it was too late.

Daud failed to hold on since Aurangzeb's captain, Bahadur Singh crossed the river in a month's time followed by Khalilullah Khan. Daud Khan's troops had to fall back upon Govindwal on the bank of the Beas where Siphir Shukuh joined him.

In the meantime Aurangzeb himself reached Rupar on August 14, 1658. On the news of Daud's falling back he sent Mirza Raja Jai Singh to reinforce Khalilullah Khan who formed the junction with Khalilullah Khan's forces at Garh Shankar, 32 miles west of Rupar. Here they heard of the news of Dara's flight to Multan after recalling Siphir and asking Daud to hold on to the line of the river which was the only barrier between him and Aurangzeb.

Multan or Kabul?

Dara wished to move to Kabul in the belief that Mahabat Khan, the Governor there would welcome and help him. Instead he moved to Sindh. Dara could have moved to Kabul and from there to Persia as Humayun, his great-great grandfather, had done and come back with their help. Manucci pointed to the unreliability of Mahabat Khan who had been influenced by Aurangzeb though Bernier was positive about this possibility.[25] He decided to move, out of depression and failure to fight.

Bhakkar onwards

Multan[26] turned out to be his next destination and his journey was much reassuring for he had taken with him treasures that attracted numerous soldiers and 14,000 infantry on 5th September, 1658. Desertions began after this resulting in half the number by the time he reached *Bhakkar within the mighty River Indus*, halting there for five days marked by depositing his treasure, many ladies of the haram, and his heavy pieces of artillery with Europeans at the head of whom was Manucci. Rest, including Daud Khan returned to their jagirs. Qanungo detailed an exchange of communication about the possibility of the Persian help but to no avail.[27]

Aurangzeb left to deal with Shah Shuja

Soon it was known that Aurangzeb had arrived at Multan on the 25th and then turned back towards Agrah owing to the news of Shah Shuja's advance towards Agrah. Waldemar Hansen characterises this return thus,

> 'But within five days, the obsessed new emperor of Hindustan would have to relinquish his role of personal bloodhound and leave pursuit of the fugitive to divisional commanders.'[28]

He left behind a force under Saf-Shikan Khan and Shaikh Mir with instructions to expel the fugitive from Uchch.[29] With the two Generals on hot pursuit on the right bank of the river, Dara had difficulty in cruising through the waters of the river from Bhakkar till Thata. Qanungo described its dangerous flavour thus

> 'The most critical stage of the pursuit was the passage of Dara's boats under the gun fire of the fort of Sehwan, and the escape of Dara's troops through the narrow defile near that fort (2nd November, 1658).'[30]

Dara with Rao of Cutch

Thereafter Dara gave a narrow slip to Saf-shikan by crossing the river Indus on 16th November, and after that the pursuers lost him despite their crossing the river as well. Dara then crossed the inhospitable salt region of Rann of Cutch (Rann of Kutch) to the hospitality of the Rao of Cutch who married his daughter to Siphir Shukuh. Relief of sorts may have smoothened Dara's nerves but for a short while.

Dara the Gambler

Gaining fortune of some consequence he tried his luck again and reached Ahmedabad. This was a place where the Governor Shah Nawaz Khan (we noticed earlier he was father-in-law of Murad Baksh and Aurangzeb)[31] welcomed him and learnt of Dara's plan for another confrontation.[32] We noticed that this was a failed confrontation in the last chapter. However, he reached that place again as a result of the trap for him by Aurangzeb[33] through Jaswant Singh who dissuaded Raja Jai Singh to help Dara. While in Ahmadabad, Shah Nawaz Khan helped Dara to take back the port of Surat from Aurangzeb's man named Sadiq Muhammad Khan. He toyed with the idea of enlisting the support of the rulers of Bijapur and Golconda but finally moved towards Ajmer.[34] Then to Deorai semi battle and the next phase of his heart rending flight began.

Flight from Deorai

First to Mairta in Jodhpur where he halted on the night of March 14, 1659 then to Gujarat by way of Par and Margaon travelling thirty miles a day pursued by Jai Singh and Bahadur Khan with the order to capture (dead or alive) the fugitive with their superior force of thirty thousand soldiers.[35] Manucci added that the escape was very desperate since Dara was unable to carry his entourage of the haram with him that joined him later on with the help of loyal eunuch though on the way koullys, i.e. robbers who overpopulated that region, including his friends Barqandaz Khan and Mushkin, looted his treasures. The former looted his horses to gift to Aurangzeb and the cutter looted his two mules laden with gold coins to gratify Aurangzeb.[36]

Traversing the desert land and plains of Sindh in the condition of thirst, hunger and extreme heat, he reached the land of Cutch to be received well. Nowhere could he rest owing to dogged pursuit by Aurangzeb's forces. Jai Singh gave him an opening to go to a foreign land to no avail.[37] He managed to cross the river with rafts made of wood of neighbourhood houses and trees for lack of boats and support from the local people. Owing to the presence of Aurangzeb's Generals- Bahadur Khan and Khalilullah Khan- he could not move to Persia nor were his women willing to leave their own land. In this situation he decided to move to Jiwan Khan who was given the title of Malik Khan, whom Dara had helped thrice by protecting him from the wrath of Shah Jahan earlier.

Jiwan Khan

He was an Afghan and by and large had retained the psyche that they were inheritors of the legacy of Sher Shah Suri, courageous with capacity to be brave retaining tinge of hostility for the Mughals. He controlled the territories that were on the borders of Kandahar and out of consideration for Dara he came out to receive him. A man of mood swings in his character, he played the chameleon-now decent and then deceptive, now welcoming and then hostile, now warm enough for the mourning period of the Nadira Begam's death[38] and then getting hostile towards Dara and got him arrested. He facilitated Dara to go to Dadhar so as to escape to Persia via Kandahar and then getting him arrested at Dadhar by his men who brought the father and the son-Dara and Siphir-back to the fortress. Jiwan Khan showed swings of mood or sentiment but finally his Afghan anger got the better of him. Tavernier noted that it was at this point of time Dara expressed himself thus

> 'Finish! Finish! Ungrateful and infamous wretch that thou act, finish that which thou has commenced; we are the victims of evil fortune and unjust passion of Aurangzeb.'[39]

Further he said that he was being given this treatment owing to his help to Jiwan earlier and reminded him that the hands of a man of royal blood were not be tied at his back. On hearing this Jiwan separated Siphir from his father and placed guards over Dara Shukuh and his son and sent a message expressly to Jai Singh[40] and Bahadur Khan to whom Dara Shukuh surrendered.

Journey in Disgrace

It took a month for Dara to be brought to Dihli in disgrace from June 16, 1658 to August 23, 1658. Accompanying him were Siphir Shukuh, and his two daughters. After two days Aurangzeb enquired about the prisoner and then ordered the hunch back Nazare Beg to parade the captive in dirty and coarse clothes in the streets of Dihli through Chandini Chowk, Sadullah Khan Market and under the Dihli citadel in an open *howdah* over a dirty and a filthy elephant. Apart from his clothes he wore a turban that was an affront and a wrap of poor look appearing to be a Kashmiri, the hunch back was given the opportunity to stand behind a dejected Dara Shukuh with an unsheathed sword. Dara never raised his head through the procession except once when a beggar demanded alms and Dara lifted his head and on hearing the beggar say that he had always received something whenever Dara passed that way. He gave away his warp to him. Qanungo described him a crushed twig.[41]

Common people support

Bernier noted the repugnance of the common people thus

> '...the crowd was immense...people weeping and lamenting... wailing... but no effort to save him took place.'[42]

This was a fair assessment of the passivity of the people of India though there have been accounts of people revolting during the time of Akbar as we noticed in chapter one.

Dara and Raziya

In the thirteenth century during the danger of assassination of Raziya Sultan people had come out to protest against her being victimised by her mother and brother.[43] Like Raziya, Dara was also popular with the people. Like Dara, Raziya was also a liberal in her own time and an educationist with Dara developing a vision of composite culture and Raziya introducing inter-racialism in the then Iyaltimish's nobility and being liberal towards her concerns for the people and equality of women. Like him she enjoyed great support of her father who wanted her to be the Sultan like Dara was supported by Shah Jahan. Both faced challenges to their proposed enthronement by the siblings. In Dara's case it led to battle, flight, captivity and martyrdom. In Raziya's case to a conspiracy and first to deny the Crown, then to kill and finally to oust her from the throne. Like Dara she collected new forces in company of her provincial jailor husband at Bhatinda and gave battle at Kaithal and finally martyrdom in the fields of Kaithal by Sunni and Hindu robbers. On assuming power, with the help of the people of Dihli she declared herself a Sultan, started to wear the male tunic and gave up the veil. Like him she was also considered a person against the Islamic scriptures that annoyed their respective nobility. She held her durbars in the open with the people.[44]

She suffered sectarian strife-Shia-Sunni as did Dara though both were of the same persuasion as the others were. Both paid with their lives for making India plural in the making of inter-racial and inter-religious social structure.

Khawasapura

Dara was put up in the Khwasapura mansion under the charge of Shafi Khan and his strong force of guards.

Alarmed

Aurangzeb was alarmed at the reaction of the people and fearing this reaction Aurangzeb held a discussion in the Diwan-i-Khas as to the future of Dara. The nobles were divided. One section, like Danishmand Khan, wanted him to be imprisoned and sent to the fortress of Gwalior while as the other faction led by Raushanara Begam joined by Khalilullah Khan and Shaista Khan and Taqurrak Khan, a wretched parasite recently raised to the rank of Omrah and a former physician, Halein Daud held inflexibly to the view that he should be killed.'[45]

Ulamas issued a fatwa (religious order) saying

> 'The pillars of canonical laws and Faith apprehended many kinds of disturbance from his life. So the Emperor, both out of necessity to protect the Faith and Holy Law, and also for reasons of State, considered it unlawful to allow Dara to remain alive any longer as a destroyer of public peace;[46]

Malik Jiwan and popular Revolt

Aurangzeb on the following day felicitated Jiwan Khan who desired to leave the city and in the process faced the ridicule of the people, whose revolt through pelting of stones was the incident that the Kotwal of the city had to intervene to save the situation from getting worce.

Evening of life

That very evening Nazare Beg and his men entered the room of the captives. At this time Dara and Siphir were sitting with their toes on the back side, like in the yoga as the people were wont to do.

Their knees were touching each other. On seeing these men Dara queried if they had come to slay them. They answered that they had no idea. They had come to separate his son from him and put him in a separate place in custody. Nazare Beg ordered the son to get up but he was clutching his father's knees. Dara asked them to convey his message to his brother to spare his son. He was given a rude answer that they were not his messengers.

At this stage Dara took out a small knife from his pillow to strike at the man but in vain since he was overpowered and Dara could hear the shrieks of his son coming from the other room till he passed out.

Dara and Aurangzeb exchange

Jadunath Sarkar referred to this exchange between the two thus,

> 'Dara learnt of his fate and made a last appeal to Aurangzeb's pity. He wrote, My Lord Brother and Emperor! The desire of kingship is not at all left in my mind. Be (it) blessed to you and your sons. The plan of slaying me which you are cherishing in your heart is unjust. If you only grant me a house fit for (my) residence and one young handmaid out of my own handmaids to wait on me, I shall employ myself in praying for your (good) in the retired life of a pardoned man.'[47]

Aurangzeb noted on the side of the letter 'You first acted as a usurper, and you were a mischief maker.'[48]

Manucci narrated practically the last exchange between the two brothers thus,

> 'Before issuing sentence of death against Dara, Aurangzeb sent to ask him, if Fortune had been as favourable to him as it had been adverse, and he had held him (Aurangzeb) a prisoner, what would he have done? Knowing that in no way would Aurangzeb spare his life, and that the question was meant as a mere scoffing, Dara replied boldly and resolutely, like a prince and high-hearted leader, that if such had been the case the four principal gates of Dihli would have yielded the answer to his question, where upon have been exposed the four quarters of his body.'[49]

A furious Aurangzeb at this contumacy and license of speech ordered the beheading and chose the hunch back Nazare Beg who did it at Khirzabad. When he was being beheaded Masum reported that Dara recited the traditional kalima-i-shahadat, i.e. traditional confession of Muslim faith.[50]

Ascertain

In order to be sure that the head brought to him was Dara's, Aurangzeb got it cleaned, washed and ordered it to be brought to him in the garden. After ascertaining it he ordered it to be sent to his father in a box.[51] Here again accounts differ-some say he never saw Dara's head which was offered by Itibar Khan when Shah Jahan sat for dinner. Before seeing this Shah Jahan's remarks showed that he was not prepared for this shock. He said

> 'It is atleast a consolation for an unhappy father to find that the usurper has not wholly forgotten me,' but when the packet was opened, and he beheld 'the head of the son as tenderly beloved, the old man fell into a swoon.' [52]

Other accounts show that his body and head were sewn and put up on an elephant to be paraded in Dihli while being taken to the Humayun's tomb to be ingloriously interned without washing it or offering any prayers. Siphir Shukuh[53] was sent to Gwalior and his daughter to Shah Jahan, who later married Aurangzeb's son.

Captive (Local) and Martyr (Universal)

Dara Shukuh was narrowly dated in his times and universal in his views. The feudal/medieval times of seventeenth century with the legacy of Akbar's India made Dara a Man of Akhlalq. He remained within the confines of the ideology of his times. Of the feudal times Bernal said,

> 'Mathematics made no serious advance till Renaissance. In mechanics, the work on levers produced no effect on actual mechanics. In astronomy Ptolemy's system remained, the medieval astronomers showed some improvements in details in astronomical calculations, to trigonometry, and popularised the cross staff a kind of primitive saxton, serving early navigators voyages of the

15th and the 16th centuries. But there was no radical revision of astronomy, and professional astronomers continued to follow Ptolmey till well into the seventeenth century. The ethereal-cosmological scheme of Aristotle and Alexandrian astronomers had become rigid, theological-physical world, a world of spheres or orbits-the spheres of the moon and the sun; the spheres of the planets; above all the great sphere of the fixed stars beyond which lay heaven; and, as theologically necessary counterweight, the underworld, the circles and pits of hell so grimly described in Dante's Inferno. The world was ordained as one of rank and place. It was a compromise between the Aristotle and the picture of a permanent world and the Jewish and Christian pictures of the world created by one act, only to be destroyed by another.'[54]

In this the culture areas of scientific knowledge that Rehman talked about, as we noted in Chapter One, show how the Islamic world remained within the medieval world's general framework of intellectual traditions where science or its understandings were the end and not a new beginning. Akbar's world was clearly familiar with astronomy, ship building and the wheel as part of the intellectual movement that inherited Aristotle and Avicenna.

Dara's world view added the Islamic dimension to it with the idea of the Upanishads being mentioned in the Quran. This then was part of the universal particularity of its time. His entire descriptions of different spheres in the process of finding Him through mysticism was marked by his times. Dara's Shukuh's interest in astronomy was made evident by the fact that he got a building constructed for the purpose in Kashmir among many other buildings even though he was never a ruler.

Split of an Acorn

The ideology of the Mughal State that was split between the Orthodox Ulana and the Sufi within Islam was making strides not towards the idea of evolution from creation. It still was opposed to the position of some who were of the view that Gabriel (Jibral) was within Prophet Muhammad- a position taken by Sheikh Muhibb-ullah, whom Dara supported and had a dialogue with and the Free Thinker, Sarmad who was Dara's friend, were mistreated as heretics and against the medieval idea of God,[55] representing creation.

Despite all his intellectual ferment Dara remained within the then State-ology and its contentious parameters. The idea of evolution had settled only in the eighteenth century and so there was no one then who could talk about it notwithstanding the existence of celebrated scientist that Akbar's India had a Persian Indian-namely, Shah Fatullah Khan a polymath, a scholar, jurist, finance minister, mechanical engineer and mathematician.

Visionary Mystic

As for the future of the country and its people Dara Shukuh became a visionary mystic of the split. He espoused the cause of the land and its people who were divided by many tectonic fault lines of religion, races and way of living despite the cohabitation of the masses coexisting in different cultural neighborhoods in the villages, qasbas and the mohallas in the city. The love of the land of this Royalty was the position of the rulers for five successive generations till Aurangzeb and the royal women who desired to be buried in their country[56] despite the commonality of the Islamic world.

Now there was the Islamic India with accommodation of heterogeneity in the territoriality of the State which was being expanded. Unfortunately this was a weak political process and was traumatised much later in the middle of the twentieth century. In building an India that moved beyond the limits of Indo-Islamic identity from within, Dara Shukuh's work as a man of the pen showed his vision as much as events during his life showed his indiscretions.[57] During his flight there was evident his was gullibility and respect for the sentiment of his wife for the land of their birth.[58] The population was dispersed among *mohallas* joined by *qasbas*[59] to villages.

A loving husband if the album of paintings and his calligraphy therein he prepared is any proof and the construction of her tomb in Lahor, cherished his children, the way he pinned his hopes on Sulaiman Shukuh during the war of succession and the manner of his wailing at the time of separation from Siphir in captivity, a loving brother to Jahanara for whom he wanted to reform the Mughal practice of not allowing Mughal girls to marry, a caring interlocutor with his father for the cause of the people facing the wrath of the Emperor, his own third brother, Aurangzeb, the various Rajput and Afghan men in the power structure, and protection of the temples of the Hindus.

He remained a committed intellectual to the cause of unifying diversity a process that was already afoot since the days of Amir Khusrau, Kabir and Guru Nanak and generally the Sufis and Sarmad the free thinker who was his contemporary but not yet firmly rooted in the soil of people's minds. Govind Singh's Zafarnama written much later pointed out to Aurangzeb how his good intentions were being undone by his administrators and wanted him to stop that breakup of the monarchy from the Sikhs.[60] Dara was for comingling and fought that battle to include the Jesuits who were promised a church in Agrah once he became the ruler that never happened.

The idea of unity in diversity and its follow up came later in the Twentieth Century. Like his great-grand-father, Akbar, he was far ahead of his times. His album for Nadira Begam among other things shows his intrest in Hindu philosophy since the age of fourteen.

Chained by the ideology and power politics of his times, in which treachery in royal blood-bath played a major role, he was unable to translate his ideas into policies or practices to shape the process of accommodating diversity as part of rejection of Din Dari and accepting Jahan-Dari of the period of the Sultanate, i.e. *Suhl-I-Kul* of the period from latter half of Akbar's reign till his end.[61]

Notes

1. Francois Bernier, op. cit, p. 57.
2. Niccolao Manucci, op. cit. p. 274.
3. Kalinga Ranjan Qanungo, op. cit. p. 260.
4. Francois Bernier, loc. cit.
5. Kalinga Ranjan Qanungo, op. cit. p. 261.
6. Niccolao Manucci, op. cit. p. 276.
7. Both Manucci and Bernier record the same substance of this phase.
8. Khalilullah Khan explained to Aurangzeb that the Emperor planned to kill him and till Shah Jahan was free there was danger to Aurangzeb's life. Waldemar Hansen, op. cit. p. 261.
9. Niccolao Manucci, op. cit. p. 279.
10. loc.cit.

11. Danishmand Khan, a Persian scholar, came to India to practice medicine, taken into Shah Jahan's service in 1650 and within seven years had risen to the position of Mir Bakshi, with the rank of 3,000 (800 horses). He died on July 28, 1670. He was Bernier's patron. Mukarram was a physician to Shah Jahan at Agrah and died early on 15th August, 1662. He resigned his offices in the first year of Aurangzeb's reign and had come from Iran in the seventeenth year of Shah Jahan's reign. Niccolao Manucci, op. cit, p. 279.
12. Waldemar Hansen, op. cit. p. 261.
13. Niccolao Manucci, op. cit pp. 280-281. Shah Jahan ruled from February 28, 1628- June 18, 1658.
14. Quoted in Waldemar Hansen, op. cit. p. 266.
15. Sulaiman Shukuh's journey was chequered. He won against Shuja; could not join his father at Lahor. Considered dead. He had moved to Srinagar and was treacherously made captive while fleeing to Tibet, Medini Singh, son of Jai Singh arrested him fettered his feet and handcuffed his hands, was taken to Salimgarh, then sent to the fort of Gwalior and was administered opium water like his uncle Murad Baksh was. At Salimgarh he was in company of Sultan Muhammad who had revolted against his father and had joined up Shah Shuja. Both cousins were together in Salimgarh. Sulaiman requested his uncle not to give him slow poison by giving him liquid opium but to kill him with immediate effect. This pleading was in vain. Even his children were not treated with any kindness. He was only twenty six years old at the time of his arrest. His cousin Sultan Muhammad was twenty four. Sulaiman's daughter later married Aurangzeb's son Mohammed Akbar.
16. Kalinga Ranjan Qanungo, op. cit. p. 262.
17. Waldemar Hansen, op. cit. p. 263.
18. Niccolao Manucci, op. cit. 282-285.
19. Manucci wrote 'Not perceiving the finessing and wiliness of Aurangzeb, he relied on the promises and oaths of fidelity which had been made to him upon...(The Quran). He neglected to listen to these faithful men, and allowed himself to be played with by that fabricator and deceiver.' *Ibid.* p. 285.
20. Mannuci's account is more detailed than Bernier's. Waldemar gives some details. Qanungo makes hardly any mention of all this.
21. Niccolao Manucci, op. cit. p. 295; Qanungo, op. cit. p. 265.
22. Manucci and Qanungo did not agree on the point of Daud's loyalty. The former mentioned about his being enticed into desertion of Dara and joining the forces of Aurangzeb but in Qanungo's opinion Manucci writing much later must have done so owing to faded memory and must have added fiction to facts. Niccolao Manucci, *ibid.* p. 297; Kalinga Ranjan Qanungo, *ibid.* p. 270.
23. Quoted in Kalinga Ranjan Qanungo, *ibid.* p. 267.

24. Niccolao Manucci, op. cit. p. 297; Francois Bernier, op. cit. p. 71.
25. An ancient city was a centre of merchandise and spices and drugs of India before the Portuguese advent. Niccolao Manucci, op. cit. p. 300.
26. Kalinga Ranjan Qanungo, op. cit. p. 273.
27. Waldemar Hansen, op. cit. p. 302.
28. loc. Cit.
29. Kalinga Ranjan Qanungo, *ibid.* p. 274.
30. Aurangzeb had no regard for kinship in his pursuit of power and so the Governor was killed at Deorai by his troops. By this time his wife d/o Shah Nawaz Khan, Dilras Begum was also deceased. Bernier called him a double faced traitor though Qanungo disputed this assessment of Shah Nawaz Khan. Qanungo, op. cit. p. 291.
31. Aurangzeb's design to trap Dara was to ask his son, Alam Shah to suggest to Dara to join him to fight Aurangzeb. The stratagem did not merit Dara's deep consideration and was rejected as another deceit. Niccolao Manucci, op. cit. p. 308.
32. Aurangzeb had a deeper reason to deflect Jaswant Singh from Agrah out of fear that Jaswant Singh might act against him at Agrah and release Shah Jahan for he was under an almost correct impression that Aurangzeb had lost to Shah Shuja. This was true though Aurangzeb employed the same tactic to win almost a lost battle by the stratagem that he had employed to defeat Dara at Samugarh. This time he used Allawardi Khan to mislead Shah Shuja who finally killed the man for his treachery that Dara could not do owing to the fact that Khalilullah Khan had immediately run to join the forces of Aurangzeb while Allahwardi Khan remained near Shuja's forces spreading the canard of his defeat.
33. Kalinga Ranjan Qanungo, op. cit. p. 276.
34. *Ibid.* p. 295.
35. Niccolao Manucci, op. cit. p. 327.
36. *Ibid.* 329.
37. The accounts of Bernier and Manucci coincide on her death in the fortress. Did she die in the fortress or on the way to Dadhar? Qanungo believed that her death took place on the way to Dadhar. The reason for her death was dysentery. Bernier had also attended to her earlier while she developed a wound in her leg since he was then with Dara's entourage. Dara was mourning in ordinary white clothes for some days and decided to send her to Lahor to be buried near Mian Mir's grave in deference to her desire. Tavernier noted Dara's condition thus,

    'The Prince was so affected by this news that he fell as though he was dead, and when, by the assistance of those who were with him, he came to himself, in excess of his grief he rent his garments; this is a custom of great antiquity in the East, as David rent his at the news of the death of Absalom, his son.'

Jean-Baptiste Tavernier, Travels in India, Vol. I, Oriental Books Reprint Corporation New Dihli, 1977. p. 280.

38. Quoted in Waldemar Hansen, op. cit. p. 363.
39. Tavernier mistakenly mentioned Jaswant Singh as the person to whom the message was sent. Jean Baptiste Tavernier, op. cit. p. 281.
40. Kalinga Ranjan Qanungo op. cit., p. 310.
41. Francois Bernier, op. cit. p. 312.
42. Minhaz, Tabakat- I - Nasiri, op. cit. p. 636; Rakesh Gupta, Raziya Sultan, Shubhi, Gurgaon, 2011. The chronicler of her times states, 'Raziyyat Sultan –May her soul rest in peace –was a great sovereign, and sagacious, just, beneficent, the patron of the learned, a dispenser of justice, the cherisher of her subjects, and of war like talent.'
43. *ibid*. p. 643.
44. Francois Bernier, op. cit. pp. 99-100.
45. Kalinga Ranjan Qanungo, op. cit. p. 314.
46. Jadunath Sarkar, Op. cit. p. 338. Refers to Kafi Khan.
47. loc. cit. Refers to a British Museum Manuscript.
48. Niccolao Manucci, op. cit, p. 339.
49. Quoted in Qanungo, op. cit, 319.
50. According to other Indian accounts he did not see Dara's severed head.
51. Francois Bernier, op. cit. p.103
52. Aurangzeb married Siphir to his daughter much later after he was brought to Aurangzeb's haram.
53. J. D. Bernal, *Science in History, Vol. 1,* Penguin, 1969, pp. 304-305.
54. Kalinga Ranjan Qanungo, op. cit. pp. 357-360.
55. Amir Khusrau, idea of Watan coincided with rise of the artisan class that grew up in the cities, the rise of Bhakti movement and Sikhism seeking human equality opposing caste hierarchy and fundamental unity of all religions. Satish Chandra, 'Secularism and Composite Culture in a Pluralistic Society', Bipan Chandra Sucheta Mahajan, Composite Culture in a Multicultural Society, Kindle, loc. 3172.
56. Mulla Shah was credited for pointing out this criticism of him. *Ibid*. p. 357.
57. The land of their birth had covered the flux of exclusivity and inclusivity of the Bharat Varsha since the coming of the Arya and the distinction made between the Dharma and the Rajdharma or, later Ashok's protection of heterogeneity. B. D. Chattopadhyay, 'Accommodation and Negotiation in a Culture of Exclusiveness: Some Early Perspectives' in Bipan Chandra and Sucheta Mahajan, op. cit. loc. 2943.
58. Qasbas had come into existence with the settlements of Afghans in the regions that were adjacent to both the cities and the villages.

59. Govind Singh's poetic vision pleaded with Aurangzeb to be just and not be strife ridden. The tone and tenure of the text is placating inoffensive and friendly.
60. Dara, once of age, persuaded his father not to destroy temples and in his own right recognised equal religious rights.

Bibliography

Memoirs

1. Babur Nama, *Journal of Emperor Babur*, transl. Annette Susan Beveridge, abridged, edited and introduced, Dilip Hiro, Penguin Books, New Dihli, 2006
2. Gul-Badan Begum, *The History of Humayun* (Humayun-Nama), transl. and introduction, Annette S. Beveridge, M. R. A. S., IDARAH-I-I DELLI, Dihli, n .d.
3. The *Tuzuk-i-Jahangiri, or Memoirs of Jahangir*, transl. Alexander Rogers and edited, Henry Beveridge, Vols. 1 & 2, Low Price Publications, Dihli, 2006.

Chroniclers

Ziaud Din Barni, *Tarikh-I Firoz Shahi*.

Ibn Batuta, *Travels In Asia and Africa, 1325-1354,* Routledge & Kegan Paul, London, 1983.

Francois Bernier, *Travels in the Empire, A. D. 1656-1668,* A Revised and Improved Edition based upon Irving Brock's Translation by Archibald Constable, S. Chand & Company, (Pvt.) LTD. New Dihli, 1972.

Abu'l-Fazl, *The History of Akbar*, edited and Translated by Wheeler M. Thackston, Vol. I, Murty Classical Library of India, Harvard University Press, 2015.

Blochman, Ain-i-Akbari Vol. I & II, Ebooks, Kindle.

Mahommed Kasim Ferishta, *History of The Rise Of The Mahomedan Power In India, till the Year 1612,* John, Brigs, M. R. A. S., Editions Indian, Calcutta, Vol. III, 1966.

Mehammad Sharif Hanafi, *Majlisu-s Salatin*, Hafeez Press Lahore, New Dihli.

R. C. Jauhari, *Medieval India in Transition, Tarikh-i-Firoz Shahi*, Sundeep Prakashan, 2001.

Muhammad Salih Kamba, *Amal-i-Salih*, Hafeez Press Lahore, New Dihli.

Inayat Khan, *Shah Jahan-Nama*, Hafeez Press Lahore, ND.

Muhammad Sadik Khan, *Shah Jahan-Nama*, Hafeez Press, Lahore, ND.

Muhammad Amin Kazwini, *Padshah-Nama*, Hafeez Press, Lahore, ND Saqi Mustad Khan, *Masir-i= Alamgiri: A History of the Emperor Aurangzeb –Alamgir (1658-1707 A. D.),* transl. Sir Jadunath Sarkar, Calcutta, 1947.

Abdul Hamid Lahori, *Badshah–Nama*, Hafeez press, Lahore, ND.

Rai Bharat Mal, *Lubbu-t Tawarikh-I Hind*, Hafeez Press, Lahore, ND.

Niccolao Manucci, *Storia Do Mogor*, transl. and introduced, William Irvine, Vol. I, Editions Indian, Calcutta, 1965.

Hasan Nizami, Taju-Lma-Asir, Elliot and Dawson, *History of India, Vol. II,* Cosmopolitan Publishers, Aligarh.

Jean-Baptiste Tavernier, *Travels In India, Second edition, Vol. I,* Orient Books Reprint Corporation, New Dihli, 1977.

Maulana, Minhajuddin, Abu-Umar-i-Usmani, Tabakat-I-Nasiri, *A General History of The Dynasties of Asia, from A. H. 194 (810 A. D.) to A. H. 658 (1260 A. D.)* transl. Major H. G. Raverty, Vol. I, Oriental Books Reprint, New Dihli, 1970.

Secondary Sources

Jacob Abbot, *Queen Elizabeth*, Illustrated, E Books, Kindle.

Muzzafar Alam, *The Languages of Political Islam in India, 1200-1800*, Permanent Black, Ranikhet, 2004.

K. M. Ashraf, *Life and Conditions of People of Hindustan*, Munshiram Manoharlal, New Dihli, 1970.

Murad Ali Baig, *Ocean of Cobras, The epic battle for the soul of India between Dara Shikoh and Aurangzeb*, Tara, India Research Press, New Dihli, 2015.

J. D. Bernal, *Science in History*, Penguin, 4 Volumes, 1969.

Stephan P. Blake, Shahjahanabad, *The Sovereign City of Mughal India*, 1639-1739, Cambridge South Asian Studies, April, 2002.

Annie Besant, *Mysticism*, Ebooks, Kindle edition, 2010.

Marc Bloch, *Feudal Society*, transl. From French by L. A. Manyon, Foreword by Geoffrey Mozilla, Routledge Classics, Ebooks, Kindle.

Jonathan Clements, *Confucius, A Biography,* Indus Source Books, Mumbai, 2008.

Jatindara Bimal Chaudhari, *The Samudra Samagam of Muhammad Dara Shukoh, Vol. II,* critically edited, Calcutta, 1954.

Dr Roma Chaudhari, *A Critical Study of Dara Shikoh's "Samudra Samagam", Vol. I,* Calcutta 1954.

Satish Chandra, *Essays On Medieval Indian History,* Oxford University Press, New Dihli, 2003.

Bipan Chandra and Sucheta Mahajan, edited, *Composite Culture in a Multicultural Society,* Pearson, Longman, 2007.

Carl W. Ernst, Ph.D., *The Shambala Guide to Sufism,* Shambala, South Asian Editions, Massachusetts, 1997.uste

Ellison Banks Findly, *Nur Jahan, Empress Of Mughal India*, Oxford University Press, New Dihli 1993.

Michael Foucault, *Power And Knowledge, Selected Interviews and Other Writings,* Colin Gordon, transl. by Colin Gordon, Leo Marshal, John Mepham, Kate Soper, Pantheon Books, The Harvester Press, USA, 1980.

Michael Foucault, *Reader,* Paul Rabinow, Edited By, Penguin Books, 1984.

Gopal Gandhi, *Dara Shukoh, A Play*, Tranquer, 2010 (fiction).

Rakesh Gupta, *Sultan Raziya*, Shubhi, Gurgaon, 2010 (fiction).

Ruchir Gupta, *The Mistress of the Throne*, Shristi, New Dihli, 2014 (fiction).

John Guy, *The True Life of Mary Stuart, Queen of Scots,* A Mariner Book, Houghton, Mifflin Company, Boston, New York, 2004.

David Gilmartin and Bruce B. Lawrence, edited, *Beyond Turkey and Hindu–Rethinking Religious Identities in Islamicate South Asia*, University Press of Florida, Gainesville, 2000.

Montserrat Guibernau and John Rex, edited, *The Ethnicity Reader, Nationalism, Multiculturalism and Migration,* Polity Press, 1997.

Bikrama Jit Hasrat, *Dara Shikoh–Life and Works*, Banarsidas Manoharlal, New Dihli, 2013.

Christopher Hill, *God's Englishman–Oliver Cromwell and the English Revolution,* paperback, 1990.

Irfan Habib, ed, *Akbar and His India*, Oxford Paperbacks, New Dihli 2014.

- ed, *Essays in Indian History–Towards A Marxist Perception*, Tulika Publishers, New Dihli, 1995.

Thomas Hobbes, *Leviathan.* Cambridge University Press, Landon, 2005.

Scott Kugle, editor, transl. Carl Ernst, *Sufi Meditation and Contemplation*, Suluk Press, Omega Publications, New York, 2012.

Herman Kulke, edited, *The State in India, 1000-1700*. Oxford Press, 1997.

John Locke, *Two Treatise on Civil Government*, Cambridge University Press, Landon, 1998.

Col. Malleson, *Akbar and the Making of the Mughal Empire*, Oxford, Clarendon Press, 1896, kindle edition.

M. Mahfuz-Ul-Haq, M. A., transl. Notes, edited, Variations, *Mama-UL-Bahrain or The Mingling of The Two Oceans,* The Asiatic Society, Calcutta, reprint, 1982.

Mushir Ul Haq, *Muslim Politics in Modern India,* Meenakshi Prakashan, Meerut, 1970.

Meenakshi Khanna, Edited By, *Cultural History of Medieval India*, Social Science Press, New Dihli, 2012.

Mahmood Mamdani, *Good Muslim, Bad Muslim*, Permanent Black, Dihli, 2004.

Karl Marx, *Pre-Capitalist Socio-Economic Formations, A Collection*, Progress Publishers, Moscow, 1979.

Joseph W. Meri, *Medieval Islamic Civilisation: An Encyclopaedia, Vol. I*, internet Archive, Routledge Taylor and Francis Group, Oxon, 2006.

Harbans Mukhia, *The Mughals of India,* Blackwell Publishing, Malden, Oxford, Victoria, 2004.

Hamida Khatoon Naqvi, *Agricultural and Urban Dynamism Under the Sultans of Dihli, 1206-1555,* Munshiram Manoharlal Publishers Pvt. Ltd, 1986.

Khaliq Ahmed Nizami, *Some aspects of Religion and Politics in India during the Thirteenth Century,* Idarahi-I-Adabiyat-I-Dehli, 2009.

Karl Popper, *Open Society and Its Enemies*, Routledge, New Dihli. 2006.

Kalinga Ranjan Qanungo, *Dara Shikoh, Vol. I, Biography*, Calcutta, 1952.

A. Rahman & M. A. Alvi, *et. al*, *Science and Technology in Medieval India, A Bibliography*, ND, 1982.

M. A. Alvin & A. Rahman, Shah Fathullah *Shirazi, a 16th century Indian Scientist,* ND, 1976.

A. Rahman, *History of Indian Science, Technology and Culture,* Oxford, 1966.

S A A Rizvi, *The Wonder That Was India, Vol. II, 1200-1700,* Picador, 2007.

J.J. Rousseau, *Social Contract*, Penguin, London, 2006.

Dr. Edward C. Sachau, *Alberuni's India*, Rupa, New Dihli, 2002.

Sir Jadunath Sarkar, *History Of Aurangzeb, Vol. I-II,* Orient Longman. New Dihli.

Guru Govind Singh, *Zafarnama,* transl. Navtej Sarna, Penguin Books, India, 2001.

B. V. Subbaroyappa, *et. al, A Concise History of Science in India,* ND, 1971.

Hassan Lufti Shushud, *Masters of Wisdom of Central Asia: Teachings from The Sufi Path of Liberation, Inner Traditions,* Rochester, Vermont, Toronto, Canada, Kindle edition, 2014.

Paul Smith, Translations and Introduction, *Dara Shikoh–Life and Poems*, New humanity Books, Book Heaven, Victoria, Australia, 2014.

M. Waseem, transl. and edited, *On Becoming an Indian Muslim–French Essays on Aspects of Syncretism,* Oxford University Press, ND, 2003.

NB: spellings of Dara Shukuh vary as per the text listed.

Index

A

Abbey of St. Victor in Paris 71
Abdul Hamid Lahori 35
Abdur Rashid Dialemi 85
Abraham 48
Abu Abd al-Rahman al-Sulami 106
Abu Fazl 66
Abu Hamid Ghazali 107
Abul Fazl 41, 42, 66, 72, 73, 75, 81, 83, 84, 92, 132, 154, 155
Abul Fazl Faizi 73, 80
Abul Qasim al-Qushairi 107
Accountancy 82
Administration 28
Admiral Drake 25
Afdal-ud-Din Sarkhush 122
Afghan 39, 163, 198, 205
Afghan rebels 44
Afghan tribes 157
Afghanistan 139, 160, 161
Afghans 38, 54, 157, 165, 176
Africa 108
Aftab 73
Agrah 17, 38, 39, 78, 91, 92, 144, 145, 159, 163, 164, 166, 167, 170, 189, 190, 193, 196, 205
Agricultural communities 80
Agricultural poor 31
Agriculture 26
Ahmadabad 20, 180, 197
Ahmednagar 159
Ain-I-Akbari 30, 41
Aisan Daulat Begum 91
Ajmer 39, 47, 71, 77, 78, 112, 180, 197
Akbar 18, 20, 24, 25, 26, 42, 44, 50, 51, 67, 68, 70, 71, 73, 74, 77, 78, 79, 83, 92, 93, 110, 111, 132, 154, 155, 172, 176, 205
Akbar's 16, 41, 45, 53, 54, 66, 72, 75, 81, 82, 84, 92, 94, 97, 104, 148, 156, 202, 203, 204, 205
Akbar's Farman 40
Akbar's India 181
Akbar's ship 21
Akbar's State 26
Akhlalq 65, 81, 97, 202
Akhun Mullah Shah 117
Al Ghazali's 83
Al Mansur 129
Al-Ghawth al-Azam 115
Alanqoa 43
Alberuni 129
Alexandrian 203
Alfred Thayer Mahan 36
Ali Hussein 129
Ali Mardan Khan 156, 175
Ali Naqi 162
Allah, Most high has given 115
Allahabad 38, 39, 144
Allaudin 19, 41, 50, 52, 82
Allegory 86
Alms Bowl 108
Amal i Salih 143
Amal-u-nisa 96

Amalendu De 133
American Jew 127
Americas 22
Amir Jumla 158
Amir Khusrau 82, 97, 104, 130, 205
Amir Timur 40
Amiru-I-Umara 92
Anarkali 68
Angelic 105
Annette S. Beveridge 37, 68, 91
Annie Besant's 107
Ansari 106
Aphorisms of saints 127
Arab 84
Arab Muslim 129
Arab world 84
Arab-Turkic 103
Arabia 108
Arabic 105, 110, 129
Arabic –Persian divides 34
Arabic languages 119
Arabic manual 112
Arabic science 84
Arabic set meters 89
Arabic tajawwuf 106
Arabs 47, 176
Araish Khan 37
Aristotelian ideas 84
Aristotle 72, 86, 87, 203
Arjun Singh 155
Army 39, 163, 171, 172
Asaf Beg 67
Asaf Khan 65, 68, 145, 150, 152, 191
Ashoka's 181
Ashoka's empire 26
Ashraf 50, 52, 82
Asian 76
Asians 176
Asiatic 18
Asiatic Mode of Production 15, 17, 19, 31
Asiatic Society 133
Askari 91
Astrology 45, 74, 84, 97
Astronomy 45, 74, 80, 84
Athar Ali 41, 83
Aurangzeb 26, 31, 55, 67, 74, 78, 80, 81, 84, 95, 97, 116, 139, 141, 143, 144, 145, 147, 148, 149, 150, 154, 155, 156, 157, 158, 159, 160, 161, 164, 165, 166, 167, 168, 169, 170, 171, 172, 173, 175, 178, 180, 181, 190, 191, 192, 193, 194, 195, 196, 198, 200, 201, 202, 204, 205
Aurangzeb's 55, 76, 79, 93, 142, 153, 157, 162, 174, 176, 179, 189
Austin's legal 45
Avicenna 42, 76, 97, 203
Awadh 38, 39
Awariful-Ma'rif 112
Azerbaijan 108

B

Baba Khurram 65
Baba Lal 131
Baburs-Humayun 91
Babur 18, 25, 38, 50, 55, 67, 68, 77, 78, 83
Babur, Gul Badan Begam 81
Babur's 91
Baha al-Din Naqshabandi 114
Bahadur Khan 176, 190, 197, 198
Bahadur Shah Zafar 84, 122
Bahadur Singh 195
Bahaudin Zakarriya 112
Bahraich 46
Bahram Khan 38
Balban 19
Balkh and Badakshan 142
Banaras 163, 164

Banias 23
Banjaras 23
Banking systems 23
Baqi Beg 144
Baqqals 23
Barbul Mirza 66
Barni 40, 52
Barqandaz Khan 197
Barzakh 70, 75
Battle of Plassey 18
Battles of Panipat 36
Bazaars 20, 110
Beas 195
Begampet 159
Beloved Prophet 115
Benares 46, 155
Bengal 30, 38, 112, 155, 162, 164, 166, 192
Bengalis 112
Bernal 202
Bernier 74, 84, 147, 148, 158, 159, 177, 178, 189, 199
Beveridge 43
Bhagvadgita 129, 131
Bhakkar 32, 195, 196
Bhakti 104
Bhakti movement 103
Bhatinda 199
Bhim Narain 155
Bi-daulat 55, 78, 141
Bibi Jamal Khatun 125
Bider 159
Bihar 38, 161
Bijapur 149, 155, 159, 168, 192, 197
Bijapur and Golconda 104
Bikrama Jit Hasrat 122
Blake 25, 45
Bloch 70
Brahmans 50, 104
Brahmo Samaj 130
British 20, 22, 84
British Empire 26
British India 25
British library 68
British Monarchy 18
British Museum 96
British painters 110
British Parliament 25
British sea power 35
Broach 20
Buddhism 45, 107, 110
Buddhists 48
Bureaucracy 22
Burke 109
Burma 165
Burton Stein 29
Bust 34, 147

C

Caliph 33
Caliph III 48
Caliph Recognition 33
Caliphs 48, 89, 104
Calligraphy 82, 104, 204
Cambay 20, 21
Cash crops 26
Caste system 46
Cato 87
Centaur 65
Central Asia 106, 108
Central Asian 40
Central Asian Muslims 115
Centre 47
Chaghatai Turkish 50
Chambal 173
Chambal River 172, 173
Champanir 166
Champat Rai Bundela 174
Chandini Chowk 198
Chandra 41, 54, 149

Chandra Bhan 117
Chandrabhan Brahman 131
Chandravanshis 46
Charles VI of France 24
Chatrasal 169
Chattel slavery 27
Chhatar Sal Rae was killed 177
Chief Wazir 158
Chillah i makus 113
China 23
Chinese Empire 38
Chisti 46, 71, 105, 108
Chisti Silsila 103
Chisti's Centre 77
Chistiyya 112, 113
Chistiyya sect 123
Chistiyya silsila 113
Christian 203
Christian meaning to classical myth 88
Christian mystics 85, 109
Christian priests 111
Christianity 72, 77, 107, 109, 182
Christians 35, 110, 111, 153
Chunar 76
Church 94
Cities 45
Civil society 28
Classicist 87
Clausewitz 141
Cobra 164
Colin Davis 46
Common penny 48
Comparative Religion 130
Compass of Truth 75, 117
Composite Culture 130
Confucian Mandarins 124
Cosmopolitan Religion 130
Cosmopolitanism 88
Court 22
Creator 72, 92
credit system 26
Crown 199

D

Dadhar 198
Dakhyn 26, 30, 38, 39, 54, 94, 146, 154, 157, 158, 159, 162, 165, 166, 167, 168, 192
Daman 20
Danda 28
Danial 25
Danishmand Khan 143, 175, 191, 200
Dante's 203
Dara 56, 73, 75, 77, 78, 79, 80, 88, 93, 96, 97, 111, 145, 149, 154, 158, 161, 164, 172, 175, 177, 194, 195-205
Dara and Aurangzeb 140
Dara Shikoh 117
Dara Shikoh's 142
Dara Shukuh 26, 32, 34, 65, 67, 69, 71, 103, 108, 131, 139, 141, 144, 149, 155, 157, 159, 160, 165, 167, 170, 180, 181, 193
Dara Shukuh's 130
Dara's 67, 90, 92, 94, 95, 111, 147, 162, 163, 171, 173, 179, 189
Daryai's 79
Data Ganj Baksh 107
Daud Khan 194, 196
Daulatabad 167
Davatalla 112
Deep Dal 79
Dihli 23, 38, 82, 144, 145, 166, 168, 190, 193, 198, 199, 202
Dihli Sultanate 18, 29, 33, 41, 46, 47, 50, 91, 140
Dihli Sultans 33
Deorai 180, 197
Depali 79
Descartes 90

Dharma 28
Dharmat 164, 166, 167, 169, 178
Dhikr 125
Dholpur 172, 173, 174
Dhun-Nun-al-Misri 117
Dildar Begam 68
Dilip Hiro 91
Dilir Khan 163, 181
Dilras Bano 167
Din Dari 205
Din-i-Illahi 94
Discovery of America 84
Diu 21
Divine communion 128
Divine lineage 43
Divine royalty 42
Divinity 97
Diwan-i-Khas 200
Dobun Bayan 43
Durkheim 48
Dutch 152

E

East 20
East Africa 23
East India Company 26
Edmund Burke 75, 105
Edward VI 26
Egyptian 129
Eldorado of Dihli 23
Elizabeth 25, 26
Elizabeth's Navy 20
Elphinstone 24
Emperor 21, 51
Emperors 40
Emperor's Court 22
England 19, 20, 42, 56
English 22, 152, 170
English Monarchy 26
English sea power 39
Epic 89
Etymology 86
Euclidean 84
Europe 77
European 18, 76, 191
European artillery 32
European authorities 24
European idea 45
European physicians 84
European powers 33
European Rivalry 34
European ships 35
Europeans 23, 35, 152, 154, 179, 181, 190

F

Fahim Khan 190
Fakhr-i-Muddabir 41
Faqir 128, 146
Fargana valley 29
Farman 20, 28
Farr i izzidi 42
Faruq Mirza 66
Fasting and prayer 105
Fatehpur Sikri 32
Fathur Rabbani's Silsilas 105
Fatwa-I Jahandari 40
Fatwas 28
Faujdar 54
Fayaz Khan 180, 181
Fazil Khan 191
Fazl 50
Feudalism 81
Fiefs 46
Firangi 20
Firangis 84
Firuz Shah 16, 33
Firuz Shah, Allaudin Khalji 30
Firuz Shah Tughluq 23, 82
Folk culture 80

Forced labour 46
Foreign 26
Forts 40
Foucault 27, 28
France 70
Frank merchants 35
Franks 21
Free Thinker 203
Freethinking Masonry 94
French artillery 170
Futus -I -Salatin 23

G

G. B. Malleson 24
Gabriel 203
Garh Shankar 195
Genealogical 15
Genealogy 26, 27
Genghis khan's 43
Geography 84
Georgian 95
Germany 48
Ghakkars 53
Ghazal Mulla Shah 117
Ghazali 25, 40
Ghazi Khan Badakshi 81
Ghaznavi 45
Ghazni 19
Ghazzali 105
Ghorian 19
Ghorian institutionalisation 29
Ghor's 19
Ghur 46
Ghuride invasion 46
Ghyasuddin 46
Glory of God 40
Goa 20, 92
God Almighty 77
Goethe 87
Golconda 149, 150, 154, 155, 158, 159, 160, 192, 197
Golconda throne 159
Govind Singh's 205
Govindwal 195
Grain 23
Grammar 83
Graves 76, 89
Great Veil 127
Greece 46
Greek 80, 86, 106
Greek mythology 65
Greek sciences 83
Greeks 110
Guf Safa 68, 96
Guharara 167
Gujarat 21, 51, 54, 162, 164, 166, 192, 197
Gujarate 38, 39, 170
Gul Badan's 66
Gul-Badan 25
Gul-Badan Begam 40, 68, 76, 77
Gupta's 93
Gurkanid 50
Guru Arjan Singh 51
Guru Nanak 110, 205
Gwalior 172, 200, 202

H

Habshi 19
Habshis 47
Hadis 104
Halein Daud 200
Hamid Lahori 92
Hamlet's 194
Haram 16, 24, 49, 68
Haran Mar 47
Hariyanaka 16
Harshvardhan's rule 46
Hasanat-ul-Arifin 118, 127
Hauz Shamsi 16
Hazrat Abu Muhiyuddin Shaikh Abdul Qadir Jilani 115

Hazrat Abu Saleh Moosa 115
Hazrat Dihli 23
Heir Apparent 139
Henry Maine 45
Henry the VII's 25
Henry's case 25
Hermansen and Lawrence 126
Hindal 68, 91
Hindavi 82, 97
Hindu 69, 79, 199
Hindu (Rajput) 143
Hindu administrators 55
Hindu begams 45
Hindu jagirdars 148
Hindu Marriages 49
Hindu nobility 165
Hindu orthodox 172
Hindu priest 127
Hindu purdah 182
Hindu religion 117
Hindu temple 94, 128
Hinduism 29, 44, 97, 109
Hindus 24, 31, 47, 49, 50, 79, 110, 111, 132, 148, 153, 192
Hindus (Jizyah) 47
Hindus Rajas 149
Hindus. Conversion 50
Hindustan 17, 146, 196
History of Timur 85
Hobbesian 42
Holistic State 28
Holstein-Gottorp-Romanov 18
Holy Mecca 35
Homeric poetry 85
Horticulture 26
Host tax 48
House of Allah 114
Household 23
Hujwiri 107
Human Body 109
Humayun 18, 25, 32, 38, 50, 66, 73, 75, 76, 78, 93, 148, 195
Humayun Nama 25, 37
Humayun's 67, 91, 93, 139, 202
Hundis 52
Hyderabad 159

I

Ibadatkhana 44, 83
Ibaric tribe 50
Ibn Abi al-Dunya 70
Ibn Battuta 47, 70
Ibn El-Arabi at Aleppo 89
Ibrahim B. Adham 105
Ibrahim Khan 175
Ibrahim Lodhi (s) 36, 37
Idries Shah 85, 89
Idul Fitr 76
Iksir-i-Azam-an 118
Imam Abdu Hanifa and a Murid 117
Imam Basari 105
Immanuel Kant 87
Inayat Khan 92, 156
India 25, 84, 94, 103
Indian Musalmans and Hindus 30
Indian music 83
Indian Muslim 41
Indian Ocean 35
Indian poetry 89
Indian sadhus 156
Indian science 84
Indian State 28, 36
Indian State's 42
Indo-English 21
Indo-Muslim identity 129
Indo-Muslims 123
Indo-Persian 45, 83
Indo-Portuguese 21
Inti-khah 110
Iqta 18, 47

Iqtas 19
Iran 108
Iranian kingship 44
Iranian Monarchy 33
Iranis 50
Iraq 108
Irfan Habib 32, 46
Isami 23, 49, 83
Ishan-daulat Begam 66
Islam 44, 50, 70, 83, 84, 97, 104, 112
Islam: Neo-Platonism 42
Islamic 203
Islamic civilisation 80
Islamic identity 97
Islamic India 204
Islamic interlude 84
Islamic powers 34
Islamic revolution 80
Islamic societies 81
Islamic world 84
Islamicate 129
Islamist Arabic 89
Islam's culture 104
Ismail Hut 147
Itibar Khan 191, 193, 202
Iyaltimish 16, 19, 23, 41, 50, 81, 112, 140
Izzat Khan 148, 157, 195

J

Jadunath Sarkar 201
Jafar Khan 145, 148, 149, 157
Jagat Gosain 66
Jagir 54
jagirdars 30, 51, 155
jagirs and Mansabdari 45
Jahan-Dari 205
Jahanara 67, 93, 95, 146, 154, 157, 158, 162, 165, 172, 189, 190, 191, 192, 204
Jahangir (s)18, 20, 21, 44, 51, 55, 65, 67, 69, 71, 76, 77, 78, 80, 84, 93, 95, 110, 143, 145, 149, 150-153, 155, 176
Jahanzeb Banu 96
Jai Singh 145, 148, 163, 164, 180, 181, 198
Jains 48
Jaipur 180
Jalaluddin Muhammad Akbar Padshah Gazi 40
Jama Masjid 51, 47, 141
Jammu 181
Jamuna Canal 16
Jamuna River 16
Jani Begum 96
Jaswant Singh 145, 148, 170, 180
Jauhar 49
Jesuits 111, 205
Jewish 203
jharokas 23, 162
Jiwan Khan 197
Jodha Bai 69
Jodhpur 169, 197
John F. Richards 24
John Meanie 28
Johnson Album 68
Juddah 73
Jumla's son 170
junta 22, 93
Juyina Bahadur 43

K

K. M. Ashraf 49
Kabir 103, 205
Kabul 66, 67, 91, 93, 147
Kafi Khan 143, 178
Kaithal 199
Kalima-i-shahadat 202
Kalyani 159

Kamran 25, 78, 91, 93
Kamran's 91, 93
Kandahar 147, 148, 150, 156, 159, 165, 198
Kangra 144
Kanwar Ram Singh Kachchawa 175
Karim-un-nisa 94
Karkhanas 26, 28, 30, 49, 53
Karnal 16
Karnatik 155, 158
Kashful Mahjub 107
Kashmir 144, 199
Kaul 145
Kautilya 33
Khairaj 53
Khaitala 16
Khalilullah Khan 142, 145, 148, 149, 168, 169, 174-178, 195, 197, 200
Khalji 19
Khaljis 47
Khanaqs 108
Khanaqs 47
Khas- grass 18
Khawasapura 200
Khirzabad 202
Khokars 46
Khudkasht 53
Khurasan 108
Khurram 22, 65, 76, 78, 152
Khusrau 152, 155
Khusrau's 51
Khutba 161
Khwaja 71, 107
Khwaja Ala al-Din Attar 114
Khwaja Attar's 114
Khwaja Baqi Billah 115
Khwaja Yusuf al-Hamadani 106
King of Bijapur 167
King of Golconda 160, 168
King of Persia 161, 168
Kings of feudal England 70
Kohinoor 149
Krishna 131

L

Ladli Begum 67, 68, 150, 151
Lady Akam 66
Lady Grey 25
Lahor 66, 67, 92, 96, 144, 157, 194, 204
Lal Kalawant 70
Land holders 30
Land rights 23
Land tax 23, 53
Latin 86
Leibniz 90
Liberals 26
Lisanullah 117
Literature 84
Local satraps 31
Locke 42
Lodhi system 54
Lodis 19
Logic 83
Lord Clive 25
Lucknow 46, 52
Lyrics 89

M

Macedonian 46
Machiavellian 141
Madho Singh 92
Madina Mosque 103
Madrasas 82, 83
Madrash-i-muizzi 52
Magic 84, 97
Mahabat Khan 22, 93, 151, 148, 152, 157, 159, 167, 168, 195
Maham Begam 66, 76
Maharaja Raj Singh 180
Mahayana 103

Mahayana Buddhism 103
Mairta 197
Majma-Ul-Bahrain 90, 117, 131, 132
Makhdum Jahamiya 112
Maktabs 82
Malik Chaju 47
Malik Jiwan 200
Malik Khan 197
Mandavi Darwaza 52
Mandavis 52
Mandis 23
Mandu 166, 168
Manen 133
Mansab 18, 144
Mansabdari administration 39
Mansabdari system 19, 53, 157
Mansabdars 31, 51, 53, 54, 148, 149
Manucci 73, 94, 96, 146, 158, 159, 166, 168, 172, 175, 177, 179, 189, 190, 191, 194, 195, 196, 197, 201
Marathas during Aurangzeb's times 29
Marayam 18
Margaon 197
Market 23
Maruwwajuddin 161
Marx 15
Marxists 26
Mary of England 25, 26
Mary Queen of Scots 25, 26
Maryam Makani 68, 93
Mashariq-ul-Anwar 46
Masu I Bakk 113
Masum 194, 202
Mathematics 84, 202
Mathematics in Persian 129
Matora 193
Maulana Razi-ud- Din Hasan Saghani 46
Maulvi 153
Mauryan 18
Mauryan State 33
McClelland 87
Mecca 20, 68
Medicine 84, 97
Medieval Indian State 27
Meditation 97
Meena Bazar 95
Memoirs Jahangir 92
Merchant capital 23, 23
Metaphors 87
Mian Jiv 124
Mian Mir 124, 126
Michael Foucault 15, 27
Micro-politics 27
Mihir Shukuh 96
Mingling of The Two Oceans 72
Minhaj 81
Mir Jumla 55, 145, 154, 157, 159, 160, 167, 168, 171
Mir Qasim 169
Mira Bai's 110
Miracles 84, 97
Mirátal-asrar 126
Mirza Raja Jai Singh 195
Mocha 21
Moghuls 143, 149
Mogol-Rajput alliance 181
Mohallas 45, 51, 52
Mohammadans 148, 166
Monarchs 23
Monarchy 142, 164
Monghyr 164
Mongols 19, 47, 83, 142, 181, 194
Mongol lineage 33
Mongolia 43
Mongolian 50
Monotheistic 132
Moslem's 178, 179
Mota Raja 66

Mr. Doe 22
Mughal 23, 111, 149, 182
Mughal Army 55, 156, 165
Mughal Court (s) 36, 93
Mughal Courts 93
Mughal diplomacy 22
Mughal dynasty 142
Mughal Emperors 33, 40, 67, 78
Mughal Empire 18, 26, 29, 36, 38, 40, 54, 56, 140
Mughal family 69
Mughal girls 205
Mughal India 108
Mughal Monarchy 33
Mughal period 29, 38, 39, 130
Mughal policy 36
Mughal polity 53
Mughal power 40
Mughal Royalty 20
Mughal rule 91, 98
Mughal sea power 22
Mughal society 49
Mughal sovereignty 41
Mughal State 15, 18, 22, 26, 28, 41
Mughal system 19, 53, 83
Mughal-Rajput marriages 110
Mughals 23, 26, 50, 54, 71, 104, 110, 170, 198
Muhammad 105, 115, 192
Muhammad al-Bukhari 114
Muhammad Amin Khan 171
Muhammad Dara Shukuh 55
Muhammad Kazim 74, 143
Muhammad Parsa 114
Muhammad Salih Kamba 143
Muhammad Tughluq 82, 113
Muhibullah 72
Muinud-din-Chisti 46
Mukalima-i-Dara 117
Mukhia 17, 69, 80
Mukkaram Khan 191
Mulla Abdul Sultanpuri 85
Mulla Isami 81
Mulla Shah 74, 116, 117, 124, 125, 126, 139
Mulla Shah Badakshi 118
Multan 46, 47, 92, 112, 144, 147, 157, 165, 195
Multanis 23
Mumtaz Mahal (s) 67, 69, 92, 94, 95, 96, 139, 150, 151, 181
Mumtaz Shukuh 96
Munar 70
Murad 153, 161, 162, 167, 168, 169, 170, 192
Murad Ali Baig 179
Murad Baksh 93, 94, 122, 139, 142, 150, 157, 160, 172, 174, 192, 193
Murad's 164
Musalmans 46
Mushkin 197
Muslim 24, 25, 48, 49, 50, 110, 132, 148, 165, 169
Muslim colony in Kannauj 46
Muslim community 30
Muslim faith 202
Muslim invasion 46
Muslim mystics 46
Muslim shrines 46
Mutiny of 1857 49
Mysticism 45, 48, 85, 86, 97, 105
Mystics 77

N

Na-Haram 49
Nadira Banu Begam 69, 94, 96, 180, 198
Nahar - i Bihisht 16
Najabat Khan 157, 177

Nakir 70
Namazi 146
Naqshabandi 97, 105, 112, 115, 116, 179
Naraina 16
Narmada 161, 166, 168
Narnaul 112
Nasiral Din Tusi 81
Nasirrudin Mohammed, Timur III 161
Nasirryah 81
Nasiruddin Mahmud 113
Nathpanthis in UP 104
Nauroz 74, 76
Nausari 20
Nazare Beg 198, 200, 201, 202
Neo Platonism 107
Nepal 104
Nepal, and Bihar 104
Neptune 73
New Musalmans 33
Nicolo Conti 82
Nizami 46, 50, 80, 81, 89
Nizamiya Academy of Baghdad 107
Nizamuddin Auliya 113
Nobility 28
Non-Muslims 46
North 48, 168
North India 104
Northeast 155
Numerology 97
Nur Jahan 22, 36, 67, 68, 78, 80, 93, 95, 140, 145, 150, 151,
Nur Manzil 190

O

Odes 89
Oliver Cromwell 26, 56
Omar Shaikh Mirza 91
Omrahs 74
Oriental despotisms 17, 45
Otto I 71
Oxus 50

P

Pacific 20
Padshah 42
Padshah Begam 67
Padua 112
Paitala 16
Pak-nihad Banu Begum 96
Palam Baoli 16
Panchatantra 111, 129
Panchbhut 132
Panjab 144
Parimahal Garden in Srinagar 118
Parvez's friendship 51
Parviz 95
Parwiz 152
Patanjali's 83
Path 76
Pathans 194
Patrimonial State 15, 23, 31
Patron-client relations 28, 68
Peacock Throne 22, 92, 144, 149
Peasantry 28
Perfect One 120
Persia 151, 170, 195, 197, 198
Persian 44, 45, 83, 89, 110, 154
Persian and Central Asian 103
Persian and Indo-Persian Sufism 126
Persian dynasty 104
Persian in origin 37
Persian King 161
Persian King Abass 44
Persian Monarchy 34
Persian or Turkish 110
Persian poetry 85, 89
Persian Rubai's 89
Persian scholars 84

Persian Sufi poetry 89
Persian Sufi writes 89
Persian Sufis 126
Persian-Turkish-Indian sensibilities 32
Persians 110, 125, 142, 176, 181
Persians at Kandahar 142
Pharaohs of Egypt 70
Philosopher-Kings 43
Pir 107
Pir or Khwaja 107
Pisces 67
Plato 43, 86, 87
Popper 28
Port of Hugli 35
Port of Triconnamalee 36
Portuguese 20, 21, 22, 35, 152
Portuguese challenge 36
Portuguese sea power 22
Portuguese ships 22
Portuguese-English 21
Pre-Islamic 89
Pre-monotheism 80
Pre-Vedic 80
Prince Kam Baksh 95
Prince Khurram 55, 77, 149, 150, 151
Prince Khurram's 145
Prince Khusrau 151
Prince Salim 55
Prince Salim's 140
Prince Shahryar 152
Prince Siphir Shukuh 176
Prophet 47, 55, 66, 71, 105
Prophet Muhammad 103, 104, 106, 125, 203
Prophet Muhammad Himself 75
Proto-nationalist 44
Ptolemaic 84, 97
Ptolemy's 202, 203
Punjab 38, 94, 96, 144, 161, 192
Punjab and Kashmir 115
Punjab-Lahore 121
Purdah 49
Puritan 26

Q

Qabacha 140
Qadiri 103, 112, 122, 125, 179
Qadiri Ghazals 122
Qadiri silsila 103
Qalmaq 190
Qandahar 26, 30, 39, 44, 55, 79
Qanungo 42, 74, 79, 86, 94, 96, 141, 144, 146, 154, 157, 159, 172, 175, 192, 194, 196, 199
Qanungo calls 177
Qanungo's 156
Qasbas 45, 46
Qasim Khan 157, 169, 170
Qazi Muhammad Islam 95
Qiblah 84
Qiyat tribe 43
Quatrains 74, 89
Queen Elizabeth 24
Queen Mary 18
Queen Mother 21
Quietists 105
Quintilian 87
Qultuq Nigar Khanum 91
Quran 50, 85, 88, 108, 127, 166, 203
Qutub din Aibak's 19, 140
Qutubi Alam 112

R

Rahdari 145
RAHIMI 21
Raisina 16
Raisina Road 16
Raiyats 39
Raj Rup Singh 69, 145, 148, 157, 181, 194, 195
Raja Bhagwan Das 92

Raja Bihar Lal 92, 150
Raja Jai Singh 148, 154, 157, 163, 197
Raja Jaswant Singh 169
Raja Man Singh 92
Raja Ram Mohan Roy 130, 132, 133
Rajasthan 38
Rajput 45, 46, 70, 165, 169, 170, 178, 205
Rajput families 92
Rajput Kings 92
Rajput lineages 46
Rajput nobility 39
Rajput polity 29
Rajput queen 68
Rajputana 170, 180
Rajputs 24, 38, 44, 50, 53, 92, 104, 157, 170, 180
Rajputs to Islam 110
Raju Qattal 112
Ram and Krishna 103
Ramazan 76, 55
Ramgiri 159
Ranadil 74, 95
Rann of Kutch 196
Rao of Cutch 196
Rao Satrasal Hada 173
Rashid Pundit 47
Rathor chief 169
Rationalism 45, 90
Rationalism-Greek-Byzantine 84, 93
Raushanara 67, 122, 167, 192, 200
Rayaya 39
Raziya 19, 41, 81, 199
Red Fort 51, 141, 145
Red Forts of Agrah 32
Red Sea 20
Reformation 25
Rehman 203
Religious tax 30
Republican government 26
Reram Singh Rotella 169
Revenue collectors 31
Rhetoric 87
Rigidity 46
Risala-1-Haqnama 118
River Indus 196
Rizvi 50
Robert Clive 26
Robert Graves 75, 85, 106
Roe's 152
Romanovs 18
Romanticist 87
Romantics 87
Rose of Green 103
Roushanara 67, 93, 122
Royal 22
Royal Family 35
Royal inmates 35
Royal Navy 25
Royalty 42
Ruba'i's 103
Rudaki 89
Ruknuddin-Raziya's 140
Ruknudin Abdul Fath 112
Rule of the Company 25
Ruling Planet 73
Rumi 105
Rupar 195
Russia 19
Rustam Khan 156, 176
Rustam Khan Bahadur 173
Rustam Khan's 177
Rustan Khan Bahadur Firuz Jang 176

S

Sadat Khan 181
Sadiq Muhammad Khan 197
Sadullah Khan 144, 154, 156, 159
Sadullah Khan Market 198
Saf-Shikan Khan 196

Safavi ruler 91
Safavis 104
Safinat-ul-A'lwiya 71, 116, 124
Sagittarius 65
Sahans 23
Sakinat-ul-Auliya 117, 125
Salabat Khan 157
Salatins 67, 69
Samarkand 94
Samudra Samagam 117
Samugarh 96, 144, 145, 189, 192
Sanskrit 83, 84, 110
Sanskrit texts 44, 124
Saqi Mustad Khan 76
Sarafs 23
Sarai 18
Sarmad 127, 203
Satlej 195
Sattarri 105
Saudagars 23
Sawai Jai Singh 84
Sayyad Bahir Khan 175
Sayyid Abdur Razzaq 32
Sayyid Hidayatatullah Khan 191
Sayyid Jalaluddin 112
Sayyid Muhammad 112
Sayyids 50
Scapio 87
Scutage in England 48
Sea Trade 34
Segmentary society 44
Segmentary State 29
Sense of loyalty 97
Serfdom in 1861 19
Serwas 51
Shafi Khan 200
Shah 72
Shah Abbas II of Persia 156
Shah Buland Iqbal 142, 143, 144, 156
Shah Fatullah Khan 204
Shah Jahan 16, 20, 32, 34, 35, 55, 65, 67, 74, 77, 81, 84, 93, 94, 95, 96, 111, 122, 125, 139, 144, 145, 150, 152, 154, 155, 156, 158, 159, 161, 163, 164, 165, 167, 168, 171, 172, 176, 189, 190, 191, 192, 193, 198, 199
Shah Jahan's 16, 29, 71, 78, 92, 93, 95, 139, 140, 141, 143, 146, 148, 149, 156, 157, 158, 160, 202
Shah Mahjhan 112
Shah Muhibullah, Shah Muhammad Dilruba 127
Shah Nawaz 197
Shah Nawaz Khan 150, 180, 181, 197
Shah Shuja 77, 93, 94, 122, 139, 141, 144, 145, 150, 153, 160, 161, 162, 163, 165, 166, 180, 192, 194, 196
Shah Suri 18, 37
Shahjahanabad 16, 51, 52
Shahryar 150, 151
Shaikh Abdu Ansari 127
Shaikh Fakhruddin Ibrahim Iraqi 112
Shaikh Jalaluddin Tabrezi 112
Shaikh Mir 196
Shaikh Sadruddin Arif 112
Shaikh Shams Uddin Darayai 79
Shaikhkul Islam 112
Shaikhuni 16
Shaista Khan 144, 149, 171, 181, 193, 194, 200
Shaivites 48
Shakespeare's 162
Shakti movements 104
Shams-e Qais 119
Shamsi 19, 81
Shamsi nobility 41
Sharia 29, 40, 155
Shayista Khan 110
Shaykh Abd-al-Haqq Muhadith Dihlawi 126

Shaykh Bandgi Muhammad Ghauth 115
Shaykh Khalimullah 108
Shaykhs 50
Shaykhzadas 50
Sheikh Abdul Qadir of Jilan 117
Sher Afgan 69
Sher Shah Suri 198
Shi practice 77
Shia ladies 45
SHIA Monarch 34
Shia sect 29, 47, 104, 148
Shia Sunni 140, 178, 200
Shihabuddin 46
Shihabuddin Suhrawardi 112
Shikoh 73
Shinde 174
Ship building 53
Shiraz 84
Shivaji 168
Sidak 84
Sidhas and Yogis 104
Sikh guru 111
Sikh Guru Arjun Singh 29
Sikhism 182
Sikhs 111, 148, 155, 205
Silsila 46
Silsila of Moinuddin Chisti's 71
Silsila-igurniyya 50
Silsilas 105, 107
Simile 86
Sindh 38, 112, 161
Singhasna Bahisti 111
Siphir 180, 200, 204
Siphir Shukuh 176, 195, 196, 202
Siri-i-Akbari 117, 131
Slave 19
Social contract 42
Sophos 106
South 48
South Asians 110
Southerners 108
Sovereign 43
Sovereign King 37
Sovereign Power 28
Sovereignty 27, 36, 42
Spanish 20
Spanish Arabs 109
Spanish Armada's 20
Spanish in the Americas 25
Spanish ships 22
Spinoza 90
Sri Lanka 159
State 18, 19, 23, 78
State (treasury) 53
State and Society 29
State of India 30
State-Society 29
State/Sufis 47
Stephen P. Blake 22, 40, 53
Strait of Hormuz 36
Strait of Malacca 36
Subahs 38
Subjective genealogy 27, 106, 107, 108
Sufi 26, 72, 73, 83, 86, 89, 90, 111, 112, 203
Sufi Aphorisms 117
Sufi doctrine 109
Sufi mystics 30
Sufi or freemasonry 104
Sufi path 85
Sufi poetry 86
Sufi Rabia Basari 105
Sufi saints 85, 125, 139
Sufi variants 88
Sufi-Bhakti movements 97
Sufism 75, 81, 89, 90, 103, 104, 111
Sugar 23
Suhl-I Kul 29, 34, 44, 148, 205
Suhrawardi 46, 105, 112

Suhrawardi and Chisti 48
Suhrawardi Silsilas 55
Sulaiman Shukuh 150, 157, 162, 163, 165, 165, 168, 172, 173, 192, 204
Sulami's 106
Sultan Allauddin 112
Sultan Ghyasuddin Tughluq 113
Sultan Khurram 66
Sultan Mahmud 177
Sultan Muhammad 113, 144, 146, 150, 158, 191
Sultan Muhammad the Kotwal of Dihli 190
Sultan of Golconda's 158
Sultan Raziya 49
Sultanate 19, 41, 49, 80, 82, 104
Sultanism 22
Suniti Kumar Chatterjee 133
Sunni 153, 199
Sunni Empires 33
Sunni family 95
Sunni Hanafi Code 44
Sunni Hanafi identity 34
Sunni identity 34, 94, 141
Sunni Maulvi 97
Sunni wives 45
Sunni-Shi' 37
Sunnis 88, 104
Surat 20, 92
Suryavanshi 46
Suttee 49
Suzerainty of the Crown 25
Syria 108
Syrian named Abu Hashim al-Sufi 106

T

Taj Mahal 32, 92, 141, 149, 151, 190
Tantrism 104
Taqurrak Khan 200
Tara Chand 103
Tariqat-Ul-Haqiqat 71
Tarkovsky 70
Tartar 190
Tavernier 198
Temples 155
Temples of the Hindus 205
The Compass of Truth 109
The divine light 42
The East India 18
The East India Company 18
The External Wisdom 110
The Mingling of the Two Oceans 116
Theology 80, 90
Thomas Aquinas 72
Tibet 46
Timur/Turkish 33
Timuride 43
Timurids of Iran 83
Tota Maina 111
Translations 80
Translations in Sindhi, Gujarati and Punjabi 123
Transoxiana 34, 108, 115, 141
Treaty relations 22
Tudor 20, 26
Tughluqs 19, 54, 112
Turanis 50
Turkey and Transoxiana 143
Turkic 89
Turkish 19, 44
Turkish danda in India 48
Turkish nobility 41
Turkish rule 50
Turkish wife 178
Turks 47, 176

U

Uchch 196
Udaipur 180
Udepuri 95

Ujjen 164
Ulamas 30, 40, 47, 75, 112
Ulema 40, 47, 155
Ummayyids 48
Upanishadic concepts 107
Upanishads 94, 129, 132, 203
Urdu translations 123
Urdu/Hindustani 82
Uzbek 95, 190
Uzbeks 176, 179

V

Vaishnavism 103
Vaishnavite 48
Vedic ages 80
Vedic logic 84
Velodra 20
Victorian England 25
Villages 45
Vistara 73

W

Wahadut-ul-wajud 111, 113
Waldemar Hansen 142, 143, 152, 171, 179, 180, 192, 196
Wali of Allah 115
Waqianavis 54
Warren Hastings 26
Waseem 79
Wazir-Azam 159
Weber 15, 22
West or the East 106
Western coast 20
White cloth 103
Witfoegel 17

Y

Yoga philosophy 83
Yoga Sutra 83
Yoga-Vasistha 117, 118, 131
Yogi 111, 156
Yogic practices 131
YoginiPura 16
Yulduz Khan 43
Yunani 82

Z

Zafarnama 205
Zakariyya 112
Zakat 84
Zamani 18
Zamin Dawar 34, 142, 147, 156
Zamindars 31, 53, 55
Zikhr 125
Zikr 105
Zikr or Dhikr 108